# SCHOOL'S OUT

## Challenges and Solutions for School-Age Programs

**Tracy Galuski, PhD**
**Arlene Rider, PhD**

ExtendED Notes
Extending Learning Beyond the Classroom

# Copyright

## Bulk Purchase

Gryphon House books are available for special premiums and sales promotions, as well as for fund-raising use. Special editions or book excerpts also can be created to specifications. For details, call 800.638.0928.

## Disclaimer

Gryphon House, Inc., cannot be held responsible for damage, mishap, or injury incurred during the use of or because of activities in this book. Appropriate and reasonable caution and adult supervision of children involved in activities and corresponding to the age and capability of each child involved are recommended at all times. Do not leave children unattended at any time. Observe safety and caution at all times.

# Dedication

## Tracy Galuski

This book is dedicated to my children, Genevieve and Erik, who are the most amazing school-agers I know. Each chapter was written with them in mind, as I thought about what type of program would meet their unique, funny, and very individual needs. It is also dedicated to my husband, Larry, who kept them busy on more than one occasion so I could write. I'd like to recognize my children's 4-H leaders, who provided such great examples of the type of activities that children enjoy in out-of-school environments. Through making sushi and baking apple pies, sewing and crafts, and building rockets, lamps, and birdhouses, these leaders generously shared their time and talent with me and my kids. Lastly, I'd like to thank Arlene for being such a supportive and engaged partner in this project. I continue to enjoy our regular meetings to discuss the book content and share stories about work and life in general.

## Arlene Rider

This book is dedicated to many special people in my life. Without my husband, Donald's, support and encouragement, this entire process would not have been accomplished. I also dedicate this book to my children, Tony, Gina, Amanda, and Scott, and my grandchildren, Lola, J. J., Anthony, Matthew, Lucas, Lydia, Cameron, Audrey, Logan, and Liam, who all supported my journey and creatively vied for computer time, babysitting time, or time with their "Mima." In addition, this book is dedicated to my sister, Sandy, niece Becky, and aunt Marisa, who provided the emotional support, and to Tracy, whose dedication and perseverance made my longtime dream of writing this book a reality.

Together, we especially dedicate this book to all the professionals working with children in before- and after-school care, summer camps, and youth programs. They are generous with their time with children and steadfast in their commitment to provide quality programming. We recognize all the technical-assistance agency professionals, directors, mentors, and school-age credential instructors and advisors who encourage and inspire. All these professionals are wonderful gifts to our nation's children, and they work very hard to honor the precious gift they have been given: time to get to know some really amazing kids.

# Acknowledgements

*School's Out: Challenges and Solutions for School-Age Programs* was written to be a resource to those working in the field of before- and after-school care, summer camps, and other youth services. The book is organized into twelve chapters that address topics of interests in working with children, families, and colleagues and in providing quality programming.

Several individuals contributed to the development of this book. Erin Broderick, capacity-building director, New York State Network for Youth Success, recognized the importance of providing a resource that includes challenges and solutions for those working in the field. Erin reviewed and gave extensive feedback that enriched the content in several chapters. Darla Fulmer, school-age child care registrar and professional development coordinator for the Child Care Council of Dutchess and Putnam Counties, New York, provided regulation information and national recommendations for the health and safety portion of our book.

Acknowledgement must be given to all the New York State school-age credential candidates whom Arlene advised over the past eighteen years. They taught her so much, including but not limited to how programs on a budget encourage children to make wonderful art from recyclable items and how small programs with only one staff member learn to optimally supervise children while allowing freedom within structure. They all shared the struggles they endured as they worked toward offering quality programming. Learning about these challenges and experiences helped Arlene to understand how professionals working in this field work tirelessly—and often with few available materials or resources—to nurture and support children's development, to encourage children to fully explore their interests, and to build confidence and competence in all children.

We wish to thank all the men and women working with children in this field who continue to share their experiences, challenges, solutions, and love of working with children so others in the field may grow. Thank you, Candace Thompson and Sara Rickan from the Child Care Resource Network in Buffalo, New York. This book is our hope and vision that those working in the field will gain knowledge and will develop new skills and ideas that will allow them to continue to provide quality programming.

> Be generous with your time and your resources and with giving credit and, especially, with your words. It's so much easier to be a critic than a celebrator. Always remember there is a human being on the other end of every exchange and behind every cultural artifact being critiqued. To understand and be understood, those are among life's greatest gifts, and every interaction is an opportunity to exchange them.
>
> —Maria Popova, writer and literary critic

# Table of Contents

# Introduction

There are a multitude of programs for school-age children across the country that serve various needs in each community, from offering affordable care for working families to building and supporting academic success, health, and fitness to providing recreational activities and enrichment opportunities that nurture all the development of children. Each program is staffed by a wide variety of professionals, including the mom of three who is returning to work after her children have grown and the retiree who is hoping to give back to the community by working with youth.

This book is designed for practitioners who serve children in licensed school-age child-care programs. However, it's important to note that school-age care is a segment of a much larger field that includes before- and after-school programs, summer programming, as well as development and enrichment programs for youth from ages five to eighteen and for children with special needs up to age twenty-one.

Each chapter begins with a scenario that outlines a challenge often experienced by practitioners from a wide variety of programs. We will offer tips, suggestions, and solutions through practical examples and professional recommendations. We particularly want to provide guidance for those who will be starting a school-age care program. The book is divided into three major sections.

- In the first section, we define high-quality school-age care, including the role of the administrator, and explore how to develop safe, high-quality school-age programming and curricula based on the interests, skills, and needs of the individual children.
- In the second section, we review the developmental characteristics of children, including physical development, social and emotional learning, and cognitive development, and how these characteristics affect a program.
- The final section highlights opportunities for creating a comprehensive program, including building behavior skills, developing family partnerships, and providing summer camps.

While our goal is to provide an overview of school-age care and the challenging aspects of caring for children, this book is not intended as a complete resource guide and cannot cover every situation that practitioners are likely to face. Practitioners will need additional hands-on training, support, and resources to succeed.

Welcome to the rewarding field of school-age care!

# Building the Groundwork

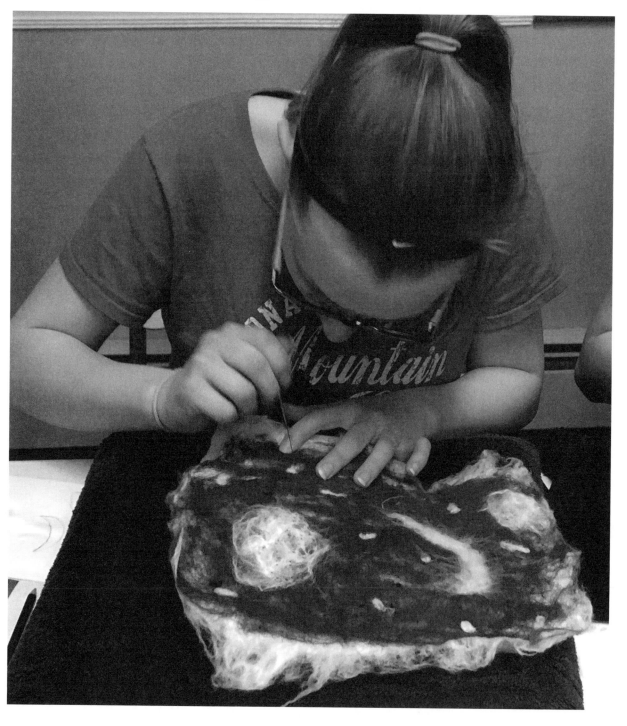

# chapter 1 | Defining High-Quality School-Age Care

**M**arisa will be the director of a new after-school program at a public elementary school. She has limited experience gained from working in school-age programs and summer camps while earning her degree in child development. How can she be sure she has enough knowledge to create a successful, high-quality program?

High-quality programs for children don't just happen. They are the result of careful planning, staff training, and creative programming efforts on the part of those who care about children. In this chapter, we will discuss the important components of high-quality programs for school-age children, different styles of care available, state regulations and standards, and the roles of the teachers and staff, including professionalism, ethics, and confidentiality.

What does a high-quality school-age program look like? High-quality programs:

- are tailored to the developmental characteristics and needs of the children they serve.
- provide resourceful, responsive, and caring staff who have knowledge about predictable child growth and development.
- recognize the importance of peers to school-age children and facilitate the development of peer relationships and social skills.
- offer a variety of activity choices and schedules that allow flexibility for children.
- foster positive self-concept and independence.
- encourage children to think, reason, question, and discover.
- encourage leadership opportunities for children.
- promote awareness and involvement in community activities.

There is a wide array of programs for school-age children, and these programs—also known as out-of-school-time programs—are designed to provide fun and safe environments for children when they are not in a school. Both educational and recreational, these programs are open before and/or after school, during school holidays and breaks, and in some cases, for extended days during the summer. They care for kindergarten through sixth-grade children ages five to twelve; although, in some states, there is a growing need for after-school programs in middle schools, extending care to the age of fourteen. Some communities may offer specialized enrichment programs that include youth up until age eighteen, and in some cases, children with special needs up to age twenty-one. In most cases, school-age child-care programs fill a need for working families so they know their children are safe and well cared for during work hours. These programs also fill the important needs of children to feel safe, to be with friends and caring adults, and to unwind from a day at school. The programs typically offer a curriculum with a wide variety of activities, but some may offer an academically focused program, such as science, music, religious education, or language arts.

# A BRIEF HISTORY OF AFTER-SCHOOL CARE

With the rise of single-parent families and dual-income families in the 1970s, by 1985, seven million of our nation's youth between the ages of six and thirteen had been identified as so-called "latchkey kids"—children who regularly come home from school to empty houses and self-care (Donald, 1985).

Growing widespread interest in what to do for these children led to increased funding for child care, crime-prevention initiatives in after-school care to prevent juvenile crime and keep children safe, and school reform that drew attention to children's out-of-school time.

Since the 1990s, school-age care has evolved from drop-in informal settings to more formal, comprehensive programs with expectations to meet measurable outcomes. New research demonstrates what practitioners have known for years: more consistent time spent in after-school activities during the elementary school years is linked to better outcomes in school, including narrowing the gap in math achievement among low-, middle-, and high-income families (Warner and Neugebauer, 2016).

Demand is growing steadily. According to Warner and Neugebauer, in 2014, 10.2 million children participated in after-school programs, an increase from 6.5 million in 2004. In addition, for every child in an after-school program, approximately two children would be enrolled if a program were available to them (Warner and Neugebauer, 2016). Yet, in 2017, it was still estimated that more than 40 percent of all school-age children are still latchkey children (American Academy of Child and Adolescent Psychiatry, 2017). As the number of dual-income and single-parent households has grown, so have the problems that surround providing adequate supervision of school-age children at a reasonable cost. Many people and agencies are committed to helping solve these issues.

# Types of Programs for School-Age Children

School-age care takes place in a wide range of programs and facilities. Some programs are housed in school buildings, and children simply need to walk to a different space in the building, such as the library, multipurpose room, or cafeteria, at dismissal time. These programs might be run by the school or by an agency that is contracted by the school. Many programs take place off-site, and children are bused to a separate location. Examples include licensed family child-care homes that serve small multiage groups of children in a home setting and licensed child-care centers that reserve classroom space for a school-age program. Additionally, local elementary schools, churches, or community programs such as the YMCA or a Jewish community center offer a variety of activity, sports, and enrichment programs. In the summer, a myriad of community-based camps are offered.

# Staff Qualifications, Training, and Credentialing

The quality of programs came under close scrutiny as challenges in staffing and professional development became evident. In the late 1990s, many states enacted regulations and quality standards. In most states, programs are legally expected to adhere to a set of minimum licensing standards, so if opening a program is your goal, researching your state's requirements is the first step. Some programs, such as those located in churches with limited hours of operation, might be exempt. You can begin your search at www.ChildCare.gov to find the link to your state's resources, such as licensing information, regulations, and requirements for background checks.

Regulations generally include guidelines for staff qualifications, the ratio of staff to children, program expectations, and health and safety requirements. Many licensing agencies also have built-in resource and referral programs, which help parents find appropriate local care for their children, provide support and training to staff, and report data regarding child-care needs to local and state agencies.

School-age programs use many different titles to refer to the people who care for children in these programs, including *teacher, practitioner, program staff, counselor, child-care worker, aide, recreational supervisor, caregiver, administrator,* and *director.* While different people have different roles and responsibilities in a program, for the purposes of this book, professionals will be referred to as *program staff.*

High-quality programs have staff who understand the basics of child growth and development and the unique characteristics of school-age children; they use this knowledge to aid in the creation of a developmentally appropriate after-school activities. Directors and administrators evaluate their staff to be sure they have the aptitude for working with school-age children and develop a set of individual competencies that will allow staff to succeed. This could take shape in the form of additional training in a specific area, such as guiding children's behavior or curriculum, or, more broadly, staff may earn a child development associate (CDA) or school-age credential.

Many community colleges and universities offer at least some coursework that will prepare school-age and child-care directors to hire and supervise staff, develop and oversee a budget, and create developmentally appropriate programming, as well as other administrative training. Often, these courses help staff meet the licensing requirements for education. It is important for staff to have a current understanding of their state's licensing laws and the best-practice recommendations of professional school-age organizations, so they can ensure legal compliance and high-quality out-of-school time.

High-quality programs offer orientation and review of policies and procedures for new staff. They have a library containing current materials, books, and journals on a variety of school-age-care subjects, either on the premises or at a central or home-office location. High-quality programs provide support to directors and staff to attend courses, conferences, and trainings by offering release time and reimbursing travel, training, and conference costs. Many states require minimum training hours, either annually or within a licensing period. Professional development is relevant for directors and staff so they understand the shared body of knowledge that includes theory and practice in school-age care.

Regulations in most states consider the adult-to-child ratio. The ratios are designated as considerations for minimum standards for safety and supervision, but they can vary dramatically, and each state has different guidelines for the age groupings, maximum group size, and qualifications for staff. For example, Massachusetts requires two educators—one of them must be a group leader—in a mixed group of kindergarten and school-age children. The maximum group size is twenty-six, for a ratio of one adult to thirteen children (606 CMR 7.00 *Regulations for Family, Group and School-Age Child Care Programs*, 2010). In New York, the ratio for children six to ten years old is one adult per ten children, with a maximum group size of twenty (NYS Office of Children and Family Services, 2017). If one child is younger than six years of age, the ratio is one adult to every nine children. When caring for children five years of age and older in Florida, the staff-to-child ratio must be at least one adult for every twenty-five children (Florida Department of Children and Families, 2019). It should be noted that in most cases, state regulations are bare-bones minimum health, safety, and program standards that include minimum staff requirements for the operation of a school-age program. The regulations do not refer to staff turnover rates, hourly wages, benefits, or best practice in school-age curriculum. Programs that meet minimum standards may keep children busy, but there is nothing special in the program to inspire, engage, and challenge children. Through training and credentialing of program directors and staff, programs can move from the minimum standards to high quality.

Let's first look at where we stand as a nation in quality standards. To better understand the landscape of quality systems that exists in the school-age care field, according to Building Quality in After-School at American Institutes for Research (2017), currently six of our fifty US states do not have quality standards in place for after-school care. An additional seven states are in the process of adopting quality standards and guidelines. While many states, including Oregon, New Mexico, Wyoming, Utah, Arkansas, and much of the eastern half of the country, have school-age credentialing systems in place to educate program staff in quality standards and best practice, twenty-one states still do not.

To increase the quality of your program, administrators can encourage or require staff to work toward a credential. Credentials offer individuals an opportunity to examine and improve their practices through training and education. The Child and Youth Care Certification through the Child and Youth Care

Certification Board (CYCCB) is one example of a process designed to support individuals' professional growth. The CYCCB provides assessment and certification to child- and youth-care practitioners who demonstrate a commitment to high standards of care and ongoing competence development.

New York State Network for Youth Success (the Network) is another example. It developed a school-age child-care credential in June 2000, modeling it after the US Army School-Age Credential. The Network is the official state affiliate of the National AfterSchool Association (NAA) and serves as a nonprofit membership association for after-school professionals in New York. Through an extensive network of intermediaries, training organizations, and child-care resource and referral agencies (CCR&Rs), the Network provides information, training, credentialing, and support to professionals to build high-quality, sustainable after-school programs that meet the needs of children, youth, and their families (*Network for Youth Success Credential Manual*, 2017–2018). The credential provides competency standards in fourteen skill areas, including professionalism; child development; health and safety; guidance; out-of-school environments; families; operational program management; and areas of development such as cognitive, physical, and social. To obtain this credential, the individual school-age program staff member must complete coursework and a resource file and portfolio and must be observed three times by a trained advisor. Then the staff member must demonstrate an applied understanding of the content of the course in an observation by a final endorser and must complete an interview.

Of the states that offer a credentialing program, they have the following in common:

- Half the states that offer a credentialing program offer it through a college for credit or through a CCR&R agency.
- Entry requirements are minimal.
- Staff may obtain a waiver for any regulation education requirement to allow them to continue to work while obtaining the credential.
- Many states offer a state-funded educational incentive program to offset costs.

Individuals do the work to earn a credential, and they can take the credential with them if they choose to work in a different program. Individual credentialing can raise the bar toward high quality. The school-age credential is a hallmark of excellence for an individual, and program evaluation and accreditation is a hallmark of excellence of a program as a whole.

# Environmental Assessment Tools and Accreditation

Many credentials and quality standard programs use the *School-Age Care Environment Rating Scale* (SACERS) developed by Thelma Harms, Ellen Jacobs, and Donna White (Harms, Jacobs, and White, 2000). The SACERS, a nationally recognized environmental rating scale, is designed to assess group-care programs for children of school age, typically ages five to twelve. The scale consists of forty-nine items, including six supplementary items for programs enrolling children with disabilities. The items are organized into seven subscales:

- Space and Furnishings
- Health and Safety
- Activities
- Interactions
- Program Structure
- Staff Development
- Special Needs

A trained observer assesses each subscale and its component categories.

The SACERS can be used to discover areas where the classroom or program is strong and where staff need more training and support. An assessor, trained administrator, or quality-improvement specialist observes in the classroom environment for two to four hours, interviews staff to assess anything that was missed, then calculates a score based on the observation. Armed with the results, staff can make changes, add materials, attend specialized training, and develop the environment further to raise their scores. Any program staff wanting to increase the quality of their school-age program may find this rating scale to be a useful tool as they assess the program environment, set goals, and work toward higher standards of care.

While environment assessment tools look at the quality of the learning environment, national accreditation looks at school-age programs as a whole within the context of national standards. The NAA is a national organization with a mission to promote development, provide education, and encourage advocacy for the out-of-school-time community to further the after-school profession (NAA, 2018). NAA has thirty-two state affiliates across the United States aligned with the mission to inspire, connect, and equip after-school professionals. Affiliates promote quality after-school programs and professional development in their states.

Other professional organizations, such as the Afterschool Alliance, bring together experts and fellow practitioners to provide information about the latest trends in after school, including program funding, research and analysis, and practical guides and webinars.

The Council on Accreditation provides standards for child and youth development that are designed to promote a program's capacity to provide quality experiences that help children and youth thrive. Their standards apply to after school, expanded/extended learning time, and out-of-school-time programs. As programs develop and work on quality issues, it's worthwhile to look into accreditation as the highest standard of care. The accreditation process is an in-depth review of the program services, administration, and management functions and usually takes nine months to a year to complete. Once accredited, the program renewal takes place every four years. For more information about accreditation, visit the Council on Accreditation (http://coanet.org). Several states have their own accreditation model; this can be a complex but rewarding process that highlights the programs that meet the highest voluntary standards in the state. In New York, for example, the Network offers the New York State Afterschool Program Accreditation. According to the Network (2018), "Program accreditation is the ultimate indication of program quality. It also provides afterschool professionals with performance indicators [and] benchmarks of quality—to guide program planning, implementation and evaluation. Accreditation also serves to guide families in making more informed choices about afterschool care for their children. Moreover, the accreditation process supports a team approach to program improvement and fosters a competent, caring and qualified staff."

All programs serving school-age children in New York are eligible to apply for New York State accreditation, which is valid for four years. The process consists of a self-study tool that aligns with the New York State Afterschool Quality Self-Assessment (QSA), the SACERS, and the Youth Program Quality Assessment (YPQA). Programs self-assess with assistance from an accreditation coach who provides feedback and recommendations for program improvement. Then an endorser visits the program to obtain additional evidence of program quality and review program documentation and self-study materials. Finally, all paperwork is submitted to the Network for accreditation.

## What Does It Mean to Be Professional?

Professionalism in school-age care means committing to developing a knowledge base in the field and completing some type of training. People who choose to work with school-age children should really enjoy working with, and appreciate the nuances of, this age group. Program staff should be willing to share their own interests and abilities, such as knitting, music, or outdoor hikes, with the children. Staff should be good role models by maintaining a strong work ethic; being honest, dependable, and reliable in performing duties; and having good attendance and job performance. Staff should model good communication skills and enjoy learning about and working with youth. Professionalism is more than having the knowledge and skills necessary to work with children. It also includes how staff apply their knowledge and skills daily as they work with the children, their families, and their colleagues and participate in the community. It means doing the job to the best of one's ability. Professionals are committed to doing what is best for the program and for all children in their care.

Many states have educational requirements for program staff and directors, with continuing training-hour expectations per licensing periods. Training and professional development are important for many reasons: it enhances the work climate, boosts morale, enhances programming, helps with risk management, and improves interactions with children and their families. Program staff must learn about and adhere to state licensing and best practices as they set a high standard in their work with children.

The program staff should have some knowledge of child development so they can understand the behaviors, actions, and feelings of the children in their care. Program staff should be able to foster all aspects of children's development—cognitive, physical, and social-emotional—and they should know how to apply that knowledge to guidance and discipline as they encourage children to become independent and confident. The staff should have a repertoire of positive guidance techniques and problem-solving skills. Staff bring their unique personal styles to their programs; some are calm, while others have lots of energy. Both styles are valuable and can positively affect their interactions with the children in the program.

Program staff can use their knowledge to create a quality program that encompasses children's interests. While it's important to have time and space for children to relax after a busy day at school, they will need activities to promote growth and development throughout the program day. All of these important skills will be discussed in depth in future chapters.

Professionalism means behaving ethically toward children and families, as well as coworkers, demonstrating care for all children, and respecting the privacy of children and families. Lastly, professionalism means growing through continuing professional development training, obtaining a credential, supporting program accreditation, joining professional organizations, reading their publications, and networking with colleagues.

Consider the following scenarios, and think about how you would handle each situation. We will offer possible solutions at the end of this chapter.

## ❓ CHALLENGE

Michelle works at an after-school program in which she is one of three staff. She is late to work most days, arriving after the children arrive, leaving the two other staff to set up the program before the children arrive. She often calls in sick, dresses inappropriately, and does not do her assigned duties. She rushes out the door when the last child is picked up, leaving the two remaining staff to do any last-minute cleanup, a final premises check, and closing duties. If you were Michelle's site director, what would you do?

## ❓ CHALLENGE

Ping, the executive director of a three-site after-school program, needs to hire a director for the site across town. After reviewing applications and interviewing a number of people, the best candidate has a child development associate (CDA) certification in infant-toddler care and has worked with infants in a day-care center for five years. She has no additional education or experience. Does this person qualify? What do you think should Ping do?

## ❓ CHALLENGE

Moira is an administrator of a school-age program that has six sites in elementary schools that span three school districts. Moira holds staff meetings once a month to discuss programming and any issues the sites may have, and most staff do attend. However, when Moira arranges for professional-development opportunities, most staff have excuses as to why they cannot attend, and therefore, most staff are not meeting training-hour requirements set forth by state regulations. What can Moira do?

# Ethics in After-School Care

Many professional fields have codes of ethics to guide members in performing their jobs. These codes offer guidelines for responsible behavior and set forth a common basis for resolving any ethical dilemmas that arise. The NAA developed a code of ethical conduct that outlines personal and professional excellence and encourages the professional development of those working in the after-school field (NAA, 2009). In addition, the NAA *Code of Ethics* defines the principles and practices that guide ethical decision making to ensure safe, nurturing environments and positive relationships with children. There are four sections of the *Code of Ethics* that include ethical responsibilities to children and youth, families, colleagues, and community and society. Ethical dilemmas appear on a daily basis, and the code can serve as a starting place for discussion and possible solutions.

An important part of professionalism is confidentiality, which means ensuring that information is accessible only to those authorized to have access. All information contained in a child's records, such as medical conditions, family information, and behavioral issues, should remain strictly confidential. Furthermore, other parents or children should not be in a position to overhear discussions regarding behavior, family situations, or other sensitive matters.

> As a director of a school-age program, Arjeta recalls a time when she was just beginning her new role. She struggled at first with knowing what was confidential and what was not. A new family disclosed to Arjeta that their adopted twins were HIV positive. Once the children were enrolled in the program, Arjeta shared that information with her program staff at their staff meeting because she thought it was important for them to know. This was a violation of the children's rights, because she had an ethical responsibility to keep that medical information confidential.

The NAA *Code of Ethics* states that "the afterschool professional should respect and protect the confidentiality of the child, families, colleagues, program and partner organizations and agencies." Further, many states have confidentiality laws. New York, for example, has a specific HIV confidentiality law. NYS Public Health Law article 27-F requires that information about AIDS and HIV be kept confidential (NYS Department of Health, 2002). Parents of children who are HIV positive do not have to disclose this to schools; and teachers or program staff who are HIV positive also do not have to disclose this information. If proper health and safety precautions are consistently followed, this does not become an issue.

While she thought she was doing the right thing and did not hold any bias, Arjeta breached confidentiality, the NAA *Code of Ethics*, and her state law when she told the program staff about the twins' medical condition. Instead, Arjeta could have broadly addressed the issue by having a refresher training on health and safety, reminding staff to use universal precautions for every child all the time.

Program staff might overlook the importance of confidentiality as it applies to social media. Reputations and safety can be harmed by posting personal and inappropriate information or photographs about individuals, colleagues, or the children and families online. Professionalism means demonstrating the highest standard of individual conduct, personal accountability, trustworthiness, fairness, and the consideration of the rights of others, and means holding to the highest principles of good business practices and relationships (National AfterSchool Association, 2009).

Ethical dilemmas happen regularly, and serious situations will present themselves from time to time. It is important to understand it is our professional responsibility to work with those involved to find the most ethical action to take in every situation that is presented.

## Conclusion

School-age programs in the United States are growing, but despite a nationwide attempt to raise quality in after-school programming, issues continue to exist today. In this chapter we reviewed factors that support high-quality programing for school-age children, including state regulations that set the baseline for care, and we offered suggestions for how staff can develop a knowledge base that is essential for high-quality programming through training, credentials, use of environmental rating scales, and support of professional organizations. Once professionalism, ethics, and confidentiality have been established, a high-quality, nurturing, child-centered after-school program is a manageable goal.

# SOLUTIONS

## Marisa Needs Additional Training

In our opening vignette, Marisa has been hired as the director of an after-school program in a public school, and she is wondering if she knows enough to provide quality care. Marisa could look into local credentialing agencies and professional organizations in school-age care for some information. They could help her find the state and local regulations for school-age care so she can understand the licensing requirements. She might find some local training in after-school programming and credentialing offered by the licensing agency, which would help her get started. More importantly, she could find a director's workshop or organization that would offer her insight and support. Lastly, she should read professional journals and magazines, as well as school-age care websites such as ExtendEd Notes to increase her knowledge of current practices and other information related to providing high-quality care for children. After reviewing all of this information and taking some training, Marisa would be armed with knowledge to guide her practice.

## Michelle's Behavior Is Unprofessional

Ethics are principles and guidelines that direct acceptable behavior; professionals should follow the ethics of their profession. Professionals are honest, dependable, and reliable in performing duties. They model a good work ethic by maintaining regular attendance, dressing appropriately, and performing assigned duties on schedule. Michelle, as you recall, is often late to work, frequently leaves early, calls in sick, dresses inappropriately, and does not do her assigned duties. She provides less than the minimum standard of care; Michelle's behavior has been unprofessional. The site director should review the staff handbook with Michelle and discuss the expectations of the job, reviewing any sections that need reinforcement. In addition, the director should review with her the NAA *Code of Ethics*. This meeting should be documented for Michelle's next performance evaluation. The site director should check in with Michelle at the end of one week and then again in a few weeks, to see if her actions and behavior are more professional. At that point, the site director can evaluate whether or not more training in professionalism is required or can determine if perhaps this is not the right career for Michelle.

## Ping Needs to Hire a New Staff Member

Ping needs to hire a director for one of her sites across town, but the best candidate for the job has infant-toddler experience and no school-age experience. Ping should consult her state's licensing requirements for minimum qualifications for after-school program directors. States differ in minimum qualifications, but they typically include education and experience requirements, such as an associate degree with additional experience in a supervisory capacity. Professional practices would dictate that the candidate have some experience working with school-age children, to ensure her ability to provide developmentally appropriate practice for this age group. Because this candidate meets the minimum qualifications but is lacking in direct experience with school-age care, if Ping wants to hire her, she should offer training and connect the candidate with local resources.

## Moira's Team Needs Professional Development

As school-age professionals, staff should take advantage of opportunities to learn more about children's development and school-age programming and to develop and improve their skills. In this way they can assess their work and can be open to fresh ideas and new perspectives. Trained staff ensure program quality. Because there is good attendance at staff meetings, Moira could offer an hour-long training after each monthly staff meeting and include a light dinner, such as salad and pizza for her staff, to show her appreciation. To keep a record of attendance, Moira could have staff sign in on a sheet that includes the date, title of the training, and the instructor's name. Recommended practices dictate that Moira pay staff for their time in required meetings and training and respect their time by being prompt and ensuring that training topics are meaningful to their work.

# THINK. ACT. REFLECT.

## Think.

Ethical dilemmas are rarely easy to solve, and the best course of action is not always obvious. It is the program staff's professional responsibility to work with those involved to find the most ethical action to take. Let's look at an ethical dilemma.

> Scott is a director of an after-school program located in a very small, close-knit community. His staff share much information about program families with other community families in general conversation. Further, his staff have been taking pictures and posting them on the program's Facebook page and in personal social media, sharing what the children are doing or saying in program. They are also sharing sensitive family issues. Scott has confidentiality concerns, as well as ethical concerns. What should he do?

## Act.

Develop a list with many possible solutions. Then, using the NAA *Code of Ethics* (found at http://naaweb.org/images/NAA-Code-of-Ethics-for-AferSchool-Professionals.pdf), highlight the points you think Scott can use to discuss his concerns regarding confidentiality, professionalism, and ethical practice with his staff. List all of the principles that seem to relate. Then review your list of possible solutions, select the strongest option, and back up your choice with one of the principles that relates.

## Reflect.

Based on the solution you recommended, reflect on your role as a professional. What might you do differently as a result?

# chapter 2 | Understanding the Roles of the Administrator and Staff

**A**nthony is an administrator of an after-school program that oversees seven sites. Until now, he has had a hands-off approach with the directors of the sites as long as there were no major issues. Recently, he was told that one site does not offer many activities other than gym time, and another location has staff coming and going at leisure, so the program is out of ratio much of the time. Further, when Anthony arranges for a staff meeting, most staff have excuses. Consequently, he has not held a staff meeting in more than six months. What can Anthony do to reorganize this program and get things heading back in the right direction?

Staff provide direct supervision and care for children, but many also handle administrative tasks to keep the program running efficiently. Some school-age programs have administrators who oversee the organizational management of the program, leaving directors of individual sites to handle the curriculum and day-to-day operations. In this chapter we will explore the different roles and the tasks involved in planning and implementing a high-quality program. In addition to program administration, these tasks include human resources and relations and aspects of personnel management, such as the staff handbook, staff meetings, and professional development that set the standard for each program. As programs build their foundation and work toward excellence, administrators are also responsible for the program assessment that can go a long way in helping them review the skills and knowledge base of staff and evaluate the environment, the program as a whole, or their personal skills.

## Role of the School-Age Program Administrator

School-age program administrators have primary responsibility for planning, implementing, and evaluating the school-age program. The administrators set policies, procedures, and standards in conjunction with state licensing and best practices. Staff follow these policies and procedures, and the administrator assists the staff in working toward those standards. The administrator may oversee the activities of staff and children and ensure that lesson planning and implementation is completed. The administrator hires qualified people to staff the program and ensures that they are trained. Administrators are also responsible for communication among the program, staff, and families of children enrolled. They intervene in problems that may arise between staff, children, and families and try to resolve the issues ethically and in the best interest of all parties involved. Typically, the administrator does not work in the classroom on a daily basis but plans and implements the daily operation of the program from an office. Administrators handle record keeping, are often responsible for purchasing equipment and materials, and may be responsible for accounts payable. That said, the administrator may on occasion fill in for staff to meet mandatory staff-child ratios. School-age program administrators are typically competent organizers, planners, record-keepers, and communicators and are cooperative coworkers (NYS Network for Youth Success, 2018). They use all available resources to ensure an effective operation. While programs may have different hierarchal structures, every program should have clear job descriptions to ensure efficiency and productivity and provide a means for evaluating and providing meaningful feedback to staff.

# Administration Levels

Many school-age programs have a hierarchy of responsibility, and each level has a different set of educational qualifications that vary by state.

- **Program administrator:** The program administrator typically has after-school-management experience, some education in fields related to child development and programming, and has made professional contributions such as leadership in a professional organization, presenting at professional conferences and advocacy events, and publishing articles in the field of school-age child care. Program administrators may oversee many sites in various locations. They develop and maintain all the policies and procedures outlined in the staff handbook and parent handbook. In some cases, they develop the program's mission, philosophy, and goals. They may be responsible for the budgeting and fiscal management of the larger organization and hire, train, and develop human-resource support.
- **Site or location director:** While administrators set policy and procedure, a site or location director oversees the daily operations and concerns of the program, such as supervising staff and children, maintaining attendance and medical records, filing fire and shelter-in-place drill reports, ordering supplies and snack items, handling program planning and activities, and communicating with families. In some cases, they train new staff and evaluate all staff. Directors typically follow the direction of the administrator's goals and motivate staff to meet those goals.
- **Lead teacher:** This person, also referred to as a group leader, group teacher, or head teacher, typically has the most qualifications for overseeing a group of children. The lead teacher is responsible for duties including supervision and guidance of the assigned group of children, conducting child assessment, and providing additional program planning and activities within the group. The lead teacher also might have some mentoring or supervisory responsibilities for other staff, such as supervising assistants and aides.
- **Assistant teacher:** An assistant teacher, also referred to as a *teacher aide*, generally works with a group of children under the direct supervision of the lead teacher and assists with tasks such as snack duty, setting up the environment, or organizing and leading one of several groups of children in the program. Depending on the size of the program, there may be more than one person designated as an assistant teacher.

Unlike early childhood programs in which administrative and teaching duties are usually separate, the integrated nature of school-age program administration means that administrative functions take place at both the local program site and at a centralized office that may oversee many program sites. For this reason, general program-administration duties may be divided among a few different people. Despite shared responsibilities, all members of the program staff must understand the program vision, mission, philosophy, and goals, as well as strategic planning and program priorities. A benefit of this knowledge is a greater opportunity for shared decision making, in which both program staff and management contribute to developing policy and finding solutions to administrative challenges (Bumgarner, 2017). A systematic and responsive approach to program management, through which the program staff can anticipate and respond to the needs of the program, children, and families, ensures an effective operation (NYS Network for Youth Success Credential Manual, 2018).

# Human Resources and Personnel Management

Administrators are responsible for implementing effective methods for staff recruitment, background checks, personnel development, management, and evaluation. Program administrators create and maintain a staff handbook that includes all pertinent program information and provides a framework for orientation and training. Staff handbooks may vary in style, but generally they address the following:

- Program vision and mission
- Job descriptions and expectations
- Expectations of regular staff meetings and training
- Information about performance evaluations and expectation for staff-development plans
- Relevant information from human resources, such as benefits, holiday pay, and sick days
- Program details, including hours of operation
- Any relevant state regulations
- Individual program policies and procedures, such as the discipline policy and emergency procedures
- Standards of behavior and ethical conduct

New staff should understand whether there is a probationary period and how often they can expect feedback on their performance. Additionally, the staff handbook should include a disclaimer to reinforce to staff that the contents are simply policies and guidelines. While staff are typically required to sign a form stating that they have reviewed the contents of the handbook and agree to them, the form is not a contract or an implied contract with the program owners or employers.

Substitute program staff also need to be aware of the program's mission, philosophy, goals, and policies and should be provided a staff handbook and be included in staff meetings to ensure they are receiving all current information about the program.

## Orientation

To support new staff, high-quality school-age programs offer orientations. All new staff have to start somewhere, and someone who is joining the staff of a school-age program is bound to require a period of adjustment. Administrators cannot expect new staff to show up on their first day and dive into the work, immediately providing the results that administrators want and expect. New staff cannot be expected to know everything about best practices for school-age children, but with guidance from the administrator and/or site director, a thorough staff handbook, and opportunities for professional

development in best practices, staff can grow and develop. Administrators support this growth with a plan to supervise and guide marginal employees and have a written plan of action for employees who need to be terminated. It's recommended that administrators work with staff during orientation to review all the components of the handbook over several days or the first few weeks and then continue to review the components with staff on a regular basis.

Establishing clear standards through an initial orientation helps reduce the risk of disputes and disagreements. New staff should have the opportunity to observe the program they will be assigned to and meet children and other staff members. Making new staff feel welcome and comfortable will establish a successful and productive working environment. New staff should have the opportunity to offer feedback about the orientation process in order to provide information that can be used to improve the orientation process for future employees (Talan and Bloom, 2011).

## Staff Evaluation

Administrators and/or site directors should work with staff to ensure program excellence by conducting periodic observations of staff members. Using this information, the administrator should conduct a performance evaluation and appraisal for each staff member. Performance evaluations and appraisals identify both areas of strengths and areas of growth opportunities. To be effective, appraisals should be conducted in a cooperative, constructive, dialogue approach. This approach puts both the administrator and staff member on the same side and working toward the same goal of a high-quality program, so staff performance can only get better. The administrator should determine how often program appraisals occur, but ideally they should occur within the first several months of employment and then yearly, and written goals should relate to improvement in practice.

## ❓ CHALLENGE

Eleanor has been working in an after-school program for nine years. When she first came on board, she attended a brief orientation that included a review of the program's goals and mission, a tour of the program, and a discussion regarding benefits. Since then, she has not received any training or a performance appraisal; she functions in the program as she has for the past nine years. Things seem to be going well, but she is bored with her job and often wonders what else she could be doing. What do you think her administrator should do?

# Professional Development

Staff development is another responsibility of the program administrator. Staff should be required to have a certain number of hours of training each year, most commonly fifteen hours per year—something that is usually determined by state regulations. In some cases, the administrator, site director, or experienced staff can provide the training, but local agencies also offer training and conferences in many communities and may offer sessions that are well worth the time and cost. Opportunities to obtain training online are growing, as well, with many licensing agencies and professional organizations responding to the needs of working adults who cannot always attend in-person training. The administrator should be familiar with sources of public funding, scholarships, and wage-enhancement initiatives for professional-development opportunities and workshops (Talan and Bloom, 2011). Several states offer professional-development incentive funds that reimburse staff or programs for the money spent on training opportunities and, in some cases, on college courses related to child development and programming.

Training topics can vary widely, but it makes sense for staff to attend training that is meaningful and relevant to their work, such as maintaining health and safety, nutrition and food service, curriculum and environments, child development, or working with families. The staff handbook should include information on the professional-development policy, such as the following:

- How many training hours are required
- The training categories, if specific topics are required (such as child abuse and mistreatment)
- Whether the trainings will be provided on-site or off-site
- Whether the program will pay for the professional development, or options for funding if it will  not
- The process for keeping track of staff training hours, usually a log or folder with training certificates for each staff member

## Staff Meetings

Regular staff meetings ensure that all staff, especially new hires, understand the program expectations and receive training and support. Through regular staff meetings, the team can review the day-to-day operations, look for areas that need improvement, or start planning curriculum as a team. The discussions may include issues and challenges, as well as brainstorming sessions that value the opinions of all staff. Programs should have a written policy regarding handling staff disputes and should provide training for staff on conflict resolution. These meetings can also be used to review the staff handbook, the parent handbook, and all program policies and procedures at least once or twice a year. Of course, meetings should be documented with meeting minutes so important discussions are recorded and someone is responsible for following up if action needs to be taken.

# Record Keeping, Budgeting, Fiscal Management, and Marketing

Administrators often prepare operating budgets, tracking all money that comes into the program from tuition. They keep accurate records of what is spent to maintain operations, including staff salaries and benefits, training, marketing, maintaining the facility, and other expenses. To do this, administrators typically have access to the program's current operating budget, which includes detailed line-item breakdowns of revenue and expenses. Programs are expected to be on time with payroll, taxes, and insurance.

An important expense is liability insurance. While it can be expensive, the cost is well worth the security, and insurance policies (called umbrella policies) can cover an entire organization. There are also policies that specifically cover injuries to staff or children, lawsuits, use of motor vehicles, special events, or any other particular needs you may have. Check with your state's CCR&R agency or child-care licensing agency to find out whether your state requires you to have a certain type or amount of liability insurance in order to operate a program. You may wish to consult with an insurance agent or broker to determine what kind of insurance is best for your situation. Talk to other leaders of programs and organizations to find out what types of policies they have. When speaking with insurance providers, explain your program and your needs, and ask about options and premiums.

For many programs, there are larger administrative offices that develop the overall budget. Then site directors are assigned a smaller budget specific to their sites, and they are responsible for monitoring the income and expenses based on the budget. This smaller budget usually covers disposable items such as food, paper products, art materials, and games for use on-site. Frequently, site directors are required to purchase small items, save receipts, and maintain accurate records and then request reimbursement. If you do not receive a budget from your administrative office, you may want to create one.

# Conducting a Needs Assessment

To create a budget that meets the needs of the program, the administration must know the fixed costs of expensive items such as taxes, insurance, utilities, and building maintenance and must evaluate the expenses related to day-to-day operations, which may vary depending on the type of program you are developing. Consider the following questions about the building, staff, and daily costs as you develop your budget.

- If the program owns the program site, what maintenance is expected annually?
- If the program owns the program site, what are the annual costs for anticipated equipment replacement?
- Who is responsible for maintaining or replacing large shared playground equipment?
- Are there at least six paid sick/personal days a year, in addition to vacation time?
- Will you provide a retirement plan?
- Do you want to purchase health insurance for program staff?
- Will you provide raises or step increases?
- Will you provide healthy snacks and/or meals, or will you receive assistance for them?
- How much money will you set aside for toys and materials that are necessary to meet the programs goals and objectives?

Most administrators will benefit from professional advice regarding the answers to these questions because there are so many factors involved. Consider your options as you begin to prioritize the budget items for your program.

# Marketing

Successful programs market their program to the public. There are many public-relations tools that can promote a school-age program. Consistent branding on stationery and business cards, as well as advertisements that are neat and grammatically correct, are effective ways to market your program. Consider having a brochure, vibrant signage, newsletters, a website, a social-media presence, and promotional items, such as T-shirts, stickers, mugs, and caps, to help promote the program. For programs located in elementary schools, a booth in the lobby for the first parent open house in September would let families know who you are and what you offer. Staff uniforms, such as matching collared shirts with an embroidered logo, can also make a good impression and increase brand recognition when the staff are out in the community. Word of mouth from satisfied families is always the best form of marketing, and maintaining an excellent program results in a great reputation.

# Administrators as Community Leaders

Community involvement is a wonderful way to make connections and build awareness of your program. Administrators may take a leadership role in the community by being involved in a director's network, being a member of an after-school organization such as NAA, or getting involved with local community organizations. There are also ways to volunteer in the community, such as joining the local chamber of commerce or attending events at the local library, which can help the program build respect and a network of support. For programs located in a school facility, it may be helpful for members of the staff to occasionally attend events at the school, join the parent teacher organization, or periodically attend school-board meetings to find out more about strengths and challenges within the school district. For programs run by larger nonprofit agencies, there may be opportunities to volunteer, get involved, and build relationships with other nonprofit agencies.

In one community, Jamir, the director of a large school-age program, volunteered as a board member of the local United Way. His involvement enabled him to learn more about other nonprofit organizations in his community. He made connections with a group that was collecting toys for needy families, a group that collected books for a literacy program, and another that filled backpacks with food for children to take home in the summer. In addition to learning more about the services that were available to the families in his program, he discovered ways for the children in his program to give back to the community by making cards for a veterans' group on Veterans Day and making homemade dog treats for an animal-rescue organization. Building relationships across the community can be very powerful and can promote leadership and volunteerism in children.

# Maintaining Ethics and Professional Standards

As reviewed in chapter 1, it is the responsibility of all staff to act ethically, but it is the responsibility of the administrator to introduce ethics and guide staff as they make decisions on behalf of children and families. Administrators need to be able to model and articulate professionalism and ethical standards, including confidentiality, in all aspects of their work. They should be familiar with the NAA's *Code of Ethics of Afterschool Professionals*. Ethical decision making requires judgment and interpretation, and the administrator should be familiar with the *Code of Ethics* to be able to apply those values to situations occurring in the program. Working through some sample ethical dilemmas during staff meetings is a great way to initiate a dialog and build ethical responsibility and professionalism among staff as they work together to develop solutions.

## ? CHALLENGE

Lucas, a new site director, is heading inside the school building of the after-school program. As he passes the playing field, he sees Ricky, a staff member, supervising the children's soccer game while smoking a cigarette. This is in violation of both the program's policy and the school's policy. Lucas wants to be an effective leader, but he struggles to enforce policy because he wants to be liked by staff. What do you think Lucas should do?

# Addressing the Needs of Children, Parents, and Families

Exceptional administrators engage parents and families each year in developing the program. The administrator's role is to establish communication with families about the program as a whole, to be sure the program is meeting the needs of both children and families in the community. In an effort to include families and to build relationships, administrators could invite families and extended-family members to visit the children in the program, could ask if they would consider offering enrichment activities, and could ask if they are willing to volunteer to do routine activities in the program or help organize a monthly newsletter.

High-quality school-age programs also involve families by including their input derived from parent and/or family surveys and open-ended questionnaires that collect information about children's interests and can be used as feedback to evaluate the program. Remember to offer these questionnaires or surveys in languages other than English as needed for program families. Establishing effective partnerships early on will ensure success because they give administrators an opportunity to check in regularly and gather feedback. That feedback then guides programmatic decisions, such as how the parents feel about offering a later snack, extending hours, closing on an upcoming holiday, or changing the daily activities.

Consider establishing a parent advisory board to aid in the direction of the program and help keep the program current. Another way to encourage parent involvement is to survey parents and families for information about children's interests. This information can aid staff in developing engaging activities that the children will enjoy. It is unfair to assume that children in this year's program will like the same things as the children in last year's program.

We will share more ideas for including family members in the development of the program in chapter 10.

# Assessing the Program and the Role of the Administrator

Administrators should take time to assess their program and themselves, identifying areas of strength and those needing improvement. They should then use this information to craft a professional-development plan to address the areas that need improvement. To begin this process, administrators should take a look at the information gathered from parent and family surveys, to gather firsthand information and feedback about the program. Next, they should survey staff and talk with colleagues to gain valuable input on program issues, current areas of strengths, and areas that may need improvement. They should also survey program staff on their interests and hobbies; appreciating these strengths can lay the foundation for new interest opportunities for children in planning the program.

Next, administrators can look to the many resources that can aid administrators in assessing their program and their own performance. There are a number of assessment tools that can pinpoint both strengths and areas of opportunity for a classroom environment or the program as a whole. These tools provide a context for gathering information, seeking feedback, and collecting recommendations from program staff, parents, and families.

The SACERS, introduced in the previous chapter, is useful for finding ways to improve the program environment. As areas for improvement are indicated, administrators can develop a plan of action to address deficiencies in the environment. Another option is the *Program Administration Scale* (PAS), which can support self-improvement within the structure of the program. The PAS, developed by Teri N. Talan and Paula Jorde Bloom, includes items that measure both the leadership and management functions of child-care programs: human-resource development, personnel cost and allocation, center operations, fiscal management, family partnerships, and marketing and public relations. The scale is useful in highlighting organizational strengths; pinpointing areas in need of improvement; and guiding administrators to make incremental changes that benefit staff, parents, and children (Talan and Bloom, 2011). While some components are specific to centers that care for infants through preschoolers, many items are broad and can be used for evaluation and improvement of the leadership and management of school-age programs.

The Quality Self-Assessment (QSA) tool (available at http://networkforyouthsuccess.org/wp-content/uploads/2019/09/QSAGUIDE2018.pdf) provides an opportunity for programs to identify strengths and weaknesses free from the pressures of external monitoring and evaluation. The QSA tool is meant to be used in concert with other formal and informal evaluation methods, such as youth, parent, and staff meetings; youth and parent focus groups; as well as external monitoring and evaluation. Each of these methods can help identify program strengths and areas in need of improvement (New York State Network for Youth Success, 2017).

Administrators looking for professional development can pursue an administrator credential, such as the national director credential, which focuses on the core leadership and management competencies that early childhood and school-age leaders need. Training topics include program operations, business strategy, planning indoor and outdoor environments, and partnerships with families. Some states have their own version of the credential, so be sure to research your state agencies and state or local organizations for opportunities and resources that support high-quality school-age programming.

## Advocating for Staff, Children, and Families

One important role of the administrator is serving as a liaison among all program stakeholders and advocating for what is best for children and families. Advocacy begins with informed practice and building relationships that enable leaders to see multiple sides of an issue. As an advocate, sometimes administrators are negotiating with the larger organization on behalf of the staff, such as for an increased budget to purchase materials for the science area or more fresh fruit for snack. Sometimes advocacy means working with a school-building principal for use of the gym or resolving an issue with a cafeteria space that is too restrictive. Often, administrators serve as liaisons between parents and a host agency to solve disputes related to policy or procedures that don't seem to be working. Advocacy includes serving on local boards or professional organizations to advocate for changes with local, state, or national issues that support high-quality programming. Advocates are active, engaged, and informed about issues that are important to the children, families, and staff in their program.

Gina is a new director of an after-school program. The principal of the elementary school where her program is held offered the small cafeteria as a space to hold the program. Gina quickly realized she needed additional space and asked to use the gym and outdoor playground for an hour or so each day. The principal offered the playground but not the gym, leaving the children with little room for physical activity on inclement-weather days. A month into the school year, Gina realized she would be sharing the cafeteria with a Girl Scout troop on Wednesdays and the school chorus on alternating Fridays and would be evicted into the school hall on days the cafeteria is needed for other after-school activities or preparation for evening events. Gina is frustrated, as she cannot develop a quality program with so many distractions and uncertainties about whether she will be able to use her space on a given day. What can Gina do?

## Conclusion

In this chapter, we learned about the role of the administrator, including program administration, human resources and relations, and personnel management. We learned about good practices that build a strong foundation, such as a staff handbook, orientation, and regular opportunities for professional development. If you are new to school-age programs, take some time to assess your personal skills and knowledge, and set some goals. For those of you who have been working in school-age programs for some time, consider one of the other tools to help you see your program through a different lens and set some goals for the program as a whole.

## SOLUTIONS

### Anthony Needs to Reorganize His Program

In our opening vignette, we met Anthony, who needs to reorganize his program and get all his program directors on the same page. One recommendation would be for Anthony to schedule a mandatory staff meeting. In this meeting, all staff would be given the mission and philosophy of the program and a copy of state regulations. Anthony would review the expectations he has for his directors and program staff as they relate to the mission. Anthony should consider holding weekly, or at the very least monthly, staff meetings to discuss new information and any issues that may arise.

If there is a staff handbook, he would review each item with the staff to be sure they understand the expectations. If the staff handbook is outdated, or if there is no staff handbook, Anthony could ask a few directors to help him create or update one. He would certainly take suggestions and recommendations from all the directors, but in the end, the handbook should reflect sound principles and best practices of quality school-age programming and should reflect the mission and goals of the program.

In Anthony's efforts to organize the program, he should look into some type of leadership training. For example, he could enroll online for the national director's credential offered by the McCormick Center for Early Childhood Leadership at National Louis University. The program is eligible for college credit, supports National Association for the Education of Young Children (NAEYC) program accreditation, and aligns with state professional-development credentials (McCormick Center for Early Childhood Leadership, 2019). He could also consider earning a specialized credential in school-age care administration, if one is available in his state. Training in leadership and administration would give Anthony a better understanding of what it takes to run an effective after-school program.

### Eleanor Is Feeling Unchallenged

We met Eleanor, who has not had a performance appraisal in a very long time and is feeling bored and unchallenged in her work. After some discussion with Eleanor about her goals for herself and her work, her administrator might find that she is interested in taking up additional duties within the organization. It's very likely the entire staff would benefit from an opportunity to meet regularly as a group and to attend additional training to motivate them with some fresh ideas. For example, each year, Eleanor's administrator could formally observe her for an hour and then provide suggestions on how she can continue to improve her after-school program practices. Her administrator may notice, for instance, that Eleanor does a wonderful job with engaging activity selection but does not provide opportunities for the children to be leaders. With collaborative discussion, they may determine that the children can, for example, plan and implement a fundraiser for a worthy cause.

## Ricky's Behavior Is in Violation of Staff Conduct Standards

Lucas, who noticed an employee smoking while supervising children outdoors on school grounds, should immediately walk over to the soccer game and signal Ricky to step away for a minute. When they are out of the children's hearing, Lucas should remind Ricky about the program's policy and ask him to put out the cigarette. In some cases, a gentle reminder or just getting caught smoking is enough, and the behavior will not happen again.

If Ricky gives Lucas a hard time and the smoking continues, Lucas needs to report the incident to his supervisor, if there is one. But as the program director, he needs to enforce the policy. Many states prohibit tobacco use in school buildings and on school grounds. Besides being in violation of the program and school policy, children likely look up to Ricky; his modeling of cigarette smoking may influence some children to smoke. Lucas or the administration must get involved to prevent Ricky's smoking during program hours on the grounds. There should be a plan of action in place, likely in the staff handbook, that spells out which program violations merit warnings and which violations are cause for immediate removal from the program. In either case, Lucan should place written documentation of the issue in Ricky's personnel folder, should there be future instances.

## Gina's Program Needs More Space

It is clear that Gina needs to negotiate to have the cafeteria as a single-use space or to advocate for an alternate space for her program. She needs to do this systematically and respectfully to achieve better outcomes at the bargaining table. First, Gina needs to manage her emotions so she can succinctly and calmly present the needs of her program. She should review any state regulations regarding space usage and be prepared to discuss this information. If possible, she should ask for the support of the licensing agency or program administration. Successful negotiation includes persuasive tactics and the input of the right players: the licensing agency, program administrator or staff, and school principal. Together, they can address the issues and develop a draft of a resolution that will benefit all parties. Administrators and program staff should not attempt to get into major dispute with the principal, as this would hinder any positive outcomes. Simply making the needs of the program known to the principal may create a framework for success.

# THINK. ACT. REFLECT.

## Think.

School-age programs use staff handbooks to provide a consistent set of policies and procedures. They also use staff handbooks to describe working conditions, workplace behavior, attendance, sick-time policies, information on severe-weather closings, and contributions they expect from their staff. Based on everything you have learned about school-age care and administration, what do you see as the strengths of your staff handbook? What do you see as weaknesses or opportunities for improvement in your staff handbook?

## Act.

Give your program's staff handbook a serious look. When you discover gaps in information, review them and think about ways you can fill those gaps, then schedule a meeting for staff and administration to go through the staff handbook together to be sure it is current and relevant to the program.

If your program does not have a staff handbook, create a committee or approach the board of directors of the program to begin surveying staff and creating one.

## Reflect.

Revisit the weaknesses or opportunities for improvement. Have you addressed these areas? Does the staff handbook align with new-staff orientation material?

# chapter 3 | Maintaining Safety and Health

**S**herry arrived at her after-school program with ten minutes to spare so she would be ready for the children as soon as the bus dropped them off. She opened the storage cupboards, laid out a couple of planned activities, and started preparing the snack. As the children began to stream in through the front door, she realized that the juice was almost gone, so she ran downstairs to the storage room to get a fresh container. On her way upstairs, she heard a loud thud and entered the classroom seconds later to see one child holding his head while blood gushed from the nose of another.

This chapter lays the groundwork for a program that is safe and healthy for children and youth. We begin with a broad discussion of building requirements and regulations and then move into looking at policies and procedures that help staff maintain a safe and healthy program. *Safe* typically refers to an environment that is designed and organized to prevent and reduce accidents and injuries through risk management. *Healthy* practices encompass not only the medical and dental practices handled by families but also the nutrition, exercise, and social-emotional supports that programs offer. Together, safe and healthy practices serve as the foundation for school-age programs.

At the time of publication of this book, the COVID-19 pandemic is ongoing and fluid, and we're learning more and more about this disease and how to respond in group settings. In this chapter, we will explore the use of universal precautions, which require us to follow best practices, such as handwashing and regular sanitation, to reduce the spread of disease and illness.

In the case of an outbreak of an infectious disease, please follow the directions of your local health department, state requirements, and recommendations from the Centers for Disease Control and Prevention (CDC). Make sure that all staff are trained in the most up-to-date recommendations and requirements, and work with families to be sure all children remain safe and healthy.

Starting with the facility, programs that are located in schools, places of worship, commercial buildings, or community centers need to have a certificate of occupancy that requires zoning approval, water-supply testing, accessibility, radon-test results, heating-system inspection, proof of fire alarm/detection system inspection compliance, and a fire-suppression system inspection, such as fire extinguishers, a sprinkler system, and hood. Building safety is monitored and enforced by local professionals, such as building inspectors and fire inspectors, assigned to make sure the facility is safe for occupancy.

# Regulations

Depending on the rules in your state, before- and after-school care programs may or may not be required to be licensed. Licensing does not guarantee quality; however, it sets minimum standards for health and safety and ensures that programs are monitored for compliance with these standards. For those that are required to be licensed and follow state licensing requirements, the program will need to ensure that at least the minimum licensing standards are met. These standards, also known as regulations, are monitored and enforced by state licensors. There are considerations for heating, ventilation, and lighting equipment, to ensure that all areas utilized by children are well lit, well ventilated, and maintain a temperature of 68 degrees F. The building should be free of toxic paint or finishes and peeling or damaged paint or plaster, and cement floors should be covered. Clean toileting and handwashing facilities should be located in the best place to meet the developmental needs of the children, with access to running water or an acceptable alternative for regular handwashing (American Academy of Pediatrics, American Public Health Association, and National Resource Center for Health and Safety in Child Care and Early Education, 2019). Some states have square-footage requirements; for example, in New York, children must be accommodated in rooms having a minimum of 35 square feet for each child (Office of Children and Family Services, 2017), as well as requirements for outdoor spaces, such as access to a playground and/or green space for play. (For more information and recommendations on national professional standards that represent best practice, visit Caring for Our Children at https://nrckids.org/CFOC) Program staff should familiarize themselves with the minimum building requirements and regulations, if required, to be sure that all local, state, and national standards are met.

While licensing standards vary greatly from state to state, they typically cover a wide array of requirements related to nutrition and food service and other aspects of programming that help maintain safe and healthy programs. Staff are responsible for maintaining these licensing standards and should expect regular visits by enforcement.

# Policies and Procedures

Administrators develop individual program policies based on the program setting. Procedures define a consistent set of practices to be performed on a regular basis; policies and procedures go hand in hand. The policy sets the rules, and the procedures define the steps that staff follow to enforce those rules. All policies and procedures should be clearly stated in the staff handbook. Staff are expected to perform procedures before the children arrive, such as cleaning up anything from the previous day; checking bathrooms for cleanliness; refilling toilet paper, paper towels, and hand sanitizer; setting up daily activities; meal or snack preparation; sanitizing tables; and in some cases, attendance and bookkeeping.

Rules for a specific program should be based on regulations

and professional practices. For example, every program should have a policy regarding pickup and drop-off times, what to do in case children become ill during program hours, and how to determine when they are healthy enough to return. Each program should have a parent handbook that aligns with the staff handbook and clearly defines program policies for families.

As an example, staff should complete a daily health check to informally assess each child both visually and verbally. This health check should be conducted as soon as possible after the child enters the program and whenever a change in the child's behavior or appearance is noted while that child is in care (American Academy of Pediatrics, American Public Health Association, and National Resource Center for Health and Safety in Child Care and Early Education, 2019).

Some programs might have access to a nurse or health professional, but in most cases, procedures include separating the sick child and arranging for prompt pickup by a family member. As indicated earlier, in the case of an epidemic, programs should follow current professional recommendations. This includes having a current plan in place that describes how to respond to a reported case of a particularly contagious disease or suspected exposure to a contagious disease.

Policies tend to evolve over time, can be adjusted based on changing needs, and should be informed by staff and parental input. For example, a program may have a generous policy about the snacks the children can bring from home, but if a child who has food allergies or food restrictions is enrolled, the program may need to re-evaluate the policy. The management, in consultation with staff and families, may decide to provide a list of acceptable snacks, request all snacks come to the program in original packaging so staff can check for allergens, or provide snacks for everyone to eliminate any potential problems. The most successful plans are those created with the participation of stakeholders. Whatever is decided, the keys are to develop standard policies, explain them clearly for families, provide training for staff so they are enforced consistently, and meet regularly to resolve any conflicts.

# Safety

The key to developing a safe program is risk management. When planning a school-age program, it's important to start with the basic building requirements, then create policies and procedures that ensure a safe and healthy environment. Something as simple as a CD player can become dangerous if it is sitting on a high shelf with a cord that dangles down to the outlet. Older children may know better than to play with electrical cords, but what if the cord accidentally gets caught up in a broom handle, which causes the CD player to get yanked off the shelf and onto a child sweeping the floor below? Each member of the staff needs to be trained in basic safety requirements, regulations, policies, and procedures so they can adequately set up the environment and supervise the children in an effort to reduce risk. Program staff should adhere to all safety requirements and make it a habit to scan the room throughout the day for potential issues.

Someone needs to be responsible for checking the environment daily, both indoors and outdoors, before children arrive. This includes looking for any hazards, removing broken or unsafe items, and ensuring that play equipment is free from rough edges and sharp corners. It's recommended that every program develop a safety checklist based on their space for daily and monthly review. Here are some examples of items you would expect to see on a daily safety checklist:

- All equipment is in good repair.
- All electrical cords, cleaning supplies, and anything that appears unsafe are secured.
- Room is organized to ensure all children are visible at all times.
- Proper child-to-adult ratio is maintained.
- Bathroom is clean and adequately stocked.
- Refrigerator is at the correct temperature.
- Clear pathways to all exits (both inside and outside) are maintained.

Certain tasks should be completed monthly, such as evacuation drills, fire drills, shelter-in-place drills, and inspection of the premises to observe possible fire and safety hazards. Here are some additional examples of items you would expect to see on a monthly safety checklist:

- Shelves are no higher than chest height for the average size of the children in attendance; any shelves higher than that are affixed to a wall.
- Only light items are stored on the highest shelves.
- First-aid kit is stocked and available.
- Smoke detectors are working properly.
- Staff know the location of all fire extinguishers and how to use them.

 CHALLENGE

An after-school program is located in a large room in one wing of a community center. The community center is being renovated. For the last week, the children have been walking into the program on torn-up floors and entering their wing through a doorway at the head of the corridor that is covered by plastic. Haruka, the director, contacts the community center's board of directors to inquire about the situation. The board chair assures her that the facility is safe for the children. What should Haruka do, if anything?

In addition to a safety checklist, it's the responsibility of the staff to prepare the environment before the children arrive. The space should look ready and inviting to the children: all the chairs should be taken down and arranged, and the tables should be in position and sanitized. Staff should have some activities planned, and materials should be laid out and available before the children arrive, to help them transition quickly.

Supervision is a key component of safety, and staff should stay actively involved throughout program hours to ensure that everyone is engaged in activities. All children should be visible to one or more adults at all times, and staff should stand in different parts of the room during the day and continually scan the room. They should discreetly listen to conversations, observe body language, and move around the room accordingly. Expectations may differ, based on the type of program and developmental needs of the children, but direct supervision requires staff to ensure all children are monitored, even as they head to the bathrooms or to the fountain for a drink of water. For example, a large program might determine that children under age seven must always be visible to staff and escorted from one space to another. Children ages eight to twelve can sign out and go to another area (such as the computer room or outside) as long as there is a staff member stationed near the door at both locations to monitor hallways. Walkie-talkies work well in this instance, so staff at the gym know three children are heading their way around the corner from the main program room. Of course, supervision of all spaces will vary depending on the activity taking place. Staff should position themselves close to children in areas that include physical activity or cooking; on the other hand, the game tables and arts and crafts can be observed from a distance. Staff should walk around the space, observing and scanning the activities, and maintain a balance of supervision and engagement. Staff should plan to get involved in activities, as long as they remember to keep scanning the room and remain alert to whatever else might be happening.

On a daily basis, staff need to be aware of how each child arrives and leaves the program and must ensure safe means for their transport. Some children may walk or arrive by the public-school buses, but others may be dropped off and picked up by parents or caregivers. Some programs might have a private bus or van that is operated by a trained staff member and staffed with an aide to ensure that no child is left unsupervised. Whatever form of transportation is used, someone from the program should be outside waiting for the bus or close to the door to ensure that each child arrives and departs safely. During operating hours, doors should be monitored and secured, and staff should be alert and count heads regularly to be sure someone isn't dawdling in the bathroom or hiding out on the playground.

In communities where children live close to the program or are allowed to walk home after program hours with parental permission, it is especially important to monitor a child until he or she has left the program and then document the time the child left. There have been reports of children being inadvertently locked in a building after programs have closed, because staff assumed they left the premises and walked home. Others have reported finding some children exploring school science labs and custodial supplies that could cause injury, severe burns, and other mishaps.

Children should be checked in on arrival and out on departure promptly and properly so the program has an accurate attendance count. Staff should create a plan for days when a child is not planning to attend the program on a regularly scheduled day and a plan for what staff should do if a child does not arrive as expected. Each program should have a detailed policy regarding who can pick up a child and what parents need to do to notify the program if there are changes. This is especially important in cases in which family-court orders are in place.

Communication is an important component of safety. In programs with many staff members completing different tasks, such as preparing food, assisting in bathrooms, and answering the phone, staff need to communicate with each other and check in regularly to be sure someone is responsible for supervising children at all times. If staff or children are shifted to accommodate ratios, that should be clearly communicated so everyone remains accounted for.

When staff are alert, engaged, and communicating with each other, they are ready to act in the event of an emergency. Staff should have CPR and first-aid training (which is required in some states). First-aid and safety supplies should be readily available, even when the children are outside, and staff should have up-to-date emergency contacts for each child. Emergency numbers such as police, fire, ambulance, and poison control should be posted, and staff should know when it's appropriate to contact emergency services. As mentioned earlier, larger programs might use walkie-talkies as effective means of communication among staff, especially in the event of an emergency. Despite well-designed programs and close supervision, accidents do happen. Programs should have procedures in place for reporting and documenting any incidents and injuries and notify families accordingly. Afterward, staff can debrief to think about what happened and discuss ways to prevent it from happening again.

Don't forget to check the playground before the children arrive each day. Depending on the community, there may be a wide variety of hazards. In one program, local teenagers began using the large ship climbing structure for an evening hangout. Teachers began finding beer bottles and trash tucked inside. In another program, an animal began raiding the trash cans for lunch leftovers in the playground area at night, and teachers had to pick up shredded trash until the school was able to obtain cans with secure lids. No matter where your program is located, it's wise to take a few minutes to check the playground for safety every morning and afternoon. Check the area for trash, animals, drug paraphernalia, and broken glass. Then check the equipment for rough edges or any pieces that may have been damaged the previous day. Bring out any additional equipment that you plan to use.

Help children develop safe habits. It takes a lifetime to develop safe habits, and we learn about new hazards all the time. As you check the room or playground for safety, involve the children. Show them safety concerns, and elicit their help to make the environment safe. (Of course, you would not ask children to handle any unsafe materials. Instead, they can help by alerting you to anything that might be a hazard.) Explain rules for games every time, encourage children to report things that are unsafe, and be sure to respond promptly when they are observed playing in an unsafe manner.

In summary, good programs inspect grounds, facilities, and equipment frequently for potential hazards, and those hazards are immediately dealt with. High-quality programs ensure that all children and staff know the safety rules and explain these rules to parents. These programs ask parents to monitor children so that dangerous objects are not brought to the facility.

# Health

The classroom environment should be clean, organized, and well maintained. Similar to safety considerations, there are many common health policies and procedures that programs can develop and enforce. Most medical and dental practices are the responsibility of the family and developed at home, but staff can support and promote good hygiene in any program. Staff serve as role models and should be healthy and model healthy behaviors. Many states require staff and volunteers to submit medical statements along with the results of a Mantoux test or other federally approved tuberculin test performed within the twelve months preceding the date of the application for employment. Smoking and vaping indoors or in outdoor areas used by children or near school grounds should be prohibited.

Programs should outline a health-care plan, with rules for administering medication to children, along with training and certification for staff administration of medications that aligns with professional standards and regulations. In these cases, a health-care professional, such as a nurse or consultant, should be consulted regularly to be sure the health-care plan and medication administration rules are reasonably followed.

Preventing the spread of illness is a key factor in risk management. While staff are not nurses, their job is to ensure that children are healthy while in attendance. Staff should model and enforce good practices. Teach children to cover their noses and mouths with a tissue when they cough or sneeze, to discard the tissue appropriately, and to wash their hands immediately afterward. If a tissue is not available, they can sneeze or cough into their upper sleeve (CDC, 2016).

Infection control is paramount; therefore, program staff must thoroughly wash their hands with soap and running water at the beginning of each day, before and after the administration of medications, when their hands are dirty, after toileting, before and after handling or eating food, after handling pets or other animals, after contact with any bodily secretion or fluid, and after coming in from outdoors. Children should wash their hands just as frequently. Yes, it may seem like the handwashing is nonstop, but most childhood illnesses are contagious several days before symptoms appear. By the time the child appears ill enough to be sent home, she may have played with a number of children, helped prepare a snack, and touched all the door handles.

# PROPER HANDWASHING PROCEDURE

1.   Check to be sure a clean, disposable paper (or single-use cloth) towel is available.

2.   Turn on clean, running water to a comfortable temperature.

3.   Moisten hands with water, and apply liquid or powder soap to hands. Do not use antibacterial soap or bar soaps.

4.   Holding the hands out of the water stream, rub hands together vigorously until a soapy lather appears. Rub areas between fingers, around nail beds, under fingernails and jewelry, and on back of hands. Continue for at least twenty seconds. (Sing "Happy Birthday to You" twice.)

5.   Rinse hands under clean, running water until they are free of soap and dirt. Leave the water running while drying hands.

6.   Dry hands with the clean, disposable paper or single-use cloth towel.

7.   If faucets do not shut off automatically, turn faucets off with a disposable paper or single-use cloth towel.

8.   Throw disposable paper towels into a lined trash container; place single-use cloth towels in the laundry hamper.

(National Resource Center for Health and Safety in Child Care and Early Education, 2020)

All rooms, equipment, surfaces, supplies, and furnishings accessible to children must be cleaned and then sanitized or disinfected. Follow universal precautions, handwashing, cleaning and disinfecting, and using gloves for contact with any bodily fluids as if they are known to be infectious for HIV, HBV, and other blood-borne pathogens (CDC, 2007). In other words, staff should treat all potentially infectious materials with appropriate precautions. At the time of publication of this book, recommendations still vary in the use of masks to reduce the spread of respiratory illness. Please follow the guidelines outlined by local health officials, and be sure that both staff and children have whatever equipment is required to follow the recommendations appropriately.

All programs should have policies in place for when parents should keep their children home, how teachers should handle illness or injury, and how teachers will keep the school-age care facility clean. The policies should be strictly enforced. Staff should also stay home when they are ill and follow the same guidelines for illness that the children and families are expected to follow.

Another aspect of maintaining a healthy program is through daily health checks. Staff should informally check each child daily for general health and well-being. Record anything that seems unusual or out of the ordinary, and follow program policy if a child appears ill.

Lastly, staff should check that health supplies are available. Are paper towels, tissues, soap, and hand sanitizer stocked, filled, and within reach? Is the first-aid kit stocked and accessible? This task should be completed before the children arrive, and supplies should be checked regularly during program hours.

# Nutrition and Food Safety

Any food that is served should be nutritious, prepared using proper food-handling procedures, and served to the children in a relaxed manner that reinforces healthy practices. While cost and simplicity are always important considerations, staff should be very thoughtful that they are offering the best options for growing children. Rather than inexpensive snacks that are high in carbohydrates, such as crackers, pretzels, and animal crackers, look for opportunities to serve fresh fruit with cheese, yogurt with a few raspberries on top, celery with peanut butter, and hummus with carrots. Children should always have access to water, juice, and/or milk with snacks, based on the nutritional guidelines followed by the program. It takes a little longer to prepare fresh snacks, but the health benefits are worth the time, and school-age children are able to help prepare these snacks with supervision.

## FOOD SAFETY

- Anyone who will handle food should wash their hands thoroughly ahead of time.

- Clean and sanitize all food-storage and food-preparation areas before introducing food.

- Wash and sanitize cutting boards and utensils before using and after each use.

- Use separate cutting boards and utensils for meats than the ones you use for fruits, vegetables, and other foods.

- Wash and sanitize can openers after each use.

- Purchase only inspected meats.

- Select pasteurized milk and 100 percent juices.

- Do not purchase or use food in cans that are bulging or leaking.

- Put away frozen or cold foods promptly after purchase. Keep the refrigerator temperature at 32–40 degrees F. Keep the freezer temperature at 0 degrees F or lower.

- Thaw frozen foods in the refrigerator.

- Wash fruits and vegetables before use—even those that are labeled prewashed.

- Cover up or wrap foods and refrigerate them until needed.

- Never use the same spoon for tasting and serving.

- Keep children's foods brought from home refrigerated until use.

- Serve children food on individual plates, napkins, or bowls. Do not serve food directly on a tabletop.

- Throw away leftover foods. Discard foods in a covered garbage can with a liner, and empty the garbage can at the end of the day or when full.

(Childcare Extension, 2019)

The Child and Adult Care Food Program (CACFP) provides aid to child- and adult-care institutions and family or group day-care homes for the provision of nutritious foods that contribute to the wellness, healthy growth, and development of young children, and the health and wellness of older adults and chronically impaired disabled persons. Some programs that serve at-risk populations may be eligible.

The CACFP nutrition standards for meals and snacks served in the CACFP are based on the *2015–2020 Dietary Guidelines for Americans*, 8th edition; science-based recommendations from the National Academy of Medicine; cost and practical considerations; and stakeholders' input. These guidelines (available at https://fns-prod.azureedge.net/sites/default/files/cacfp/CACFP_childmealpattern.pdf) define required components for meals and snacks and the average portion sizes for children. For example, for children ages six to twelve, a healthy breakfast should include 8 ounces of milk, ½ cup of fruit, and 1 slice of whole-grain bread or 1 cup of cereal. It's hard to make sure that children are getting the correct portions, especially when picky eaters claim to eat nothing all day, then request a third bowl of cereal. Serving directly from measuring cups will help staff get a better feel for a real serving size and how 1 cup of cereal looks in the bowls provided by the program. This same information can be shared with families. In a trend to prevent obesity, many states have required that programs share information on healthy food and beverage choices and information regarding the prevention of obesity with parents and families. It's worth a little effort to find healthy recipes that the children will enjoy, make them with the children, then share the recipes with families.

When serving water to the children, the staff should follow the same general protocol, and they should model healthy habits by drinking water too. School-age children are very observant, and they will notice if a staff member is drinking soda or an energy drink. Staff should be expected to drink water when the children drink water and to save their personal favorite beverages for break time, out of the children's view.

Plan all food items in advance, so preparation does not take time away from the children, but school-age children are capable of helping with the snack and meal preparation. In fact, many of them are likely responsible for chores at home. By the time a child is eight years old, she can learn how to safely use a stove, oven, and other appliances, and she can cut fruit and make fruit salad with some careful supervision.

For programs that do not have access to a kitchen, there are many healthy snacks that do not require cooking that children can help prepare. Trail mix, granola, veggie dip, or fruit-and-cheese kabobs are just a few examples of simple snacks that children can prepare on their own, even without a kitchen, as long as some of the prep work has been done in advance.

In small programs, encourage the children to sit down together to eat family style. Set the tables, put the food in large serving bowls, have the group sit down together, and pass the food around like you might see at a family dinner. This allows program staff to sit with the children and eat and drink with them to support socialization, manners, and good eating habits in a relaxed atmosphere. In larger programs, expecting a large group to sit together can create a lot of wait time. It may be easier to set out the snack in a buffet format for a brief window of time (30–45 minutes), so children can serve themselves and sit down in small groups. In this case, staff should try to mingle and sit with children during snack as well. Sufficient time, based on age and individual needs, should be allowed for them to eat their snacks so that children will not be hurried.

Some programs, such as those that do not have direct access to a kitchen, may have decided not to offer meals or snacks. Instead, they may require that families send a brown-bag lunch or healthy snack option with their children. While this approach is well-meaning, staff need to understand that different families have different definitions of what constitutes an appropriate breakfast, lunch, or snack. One child may arrive with a bottle of diet soda and ten-pack of doughnut holes from the local fast-food establishment. Another child may arrive with an apple, homemade granola, and a water bottle. If the parents are asked to send in snacks, staff need to be respectful of their choices and support their role, rather than judge and evaluate the items sent in. This can also pose a problem when programs ask families to provide snacks from a selected list. However, if staff observe a lot of junk food being sent in and it is becoming an issue, they can share ideas, brainstorm possible solutions, and develop a plan that supports children and families.

In one program, a couple of families regularly dropped off their children with a fast-food breakfast from the restaurant down the street. As the scent of egg sandwiches and hash-brown patties filled the room each morning, the other children asked questions, begged to share, and complained about their own snacks. Using the NAA *Code of Ethics*, the program decided that they would begin to offer a snack to everyone and level the playing field a little. The additional cost of some healthy options, such as a bag of apples, English muffins, butter, and some sliced cheese, was well within their budget, and they knew that this was a fair and healthier option for the children than the fast food.

While most programs will plan to offer daily meals or snacks, each program will have a different set of challenges to manage as they determine the best plan. It's rare for a program to have the perfect combination of kitchen space, ample room where children can sit around tables, and a sink nearby where children and adults can wash hands. Instead, programs have to find ways to make it work when the refrigerator is down the hall, the children arrive at different times, or the program is too large to have one set snack time. Despite these challenges, meals and snacks should provide a relaxing opportunity for children to sit down with peers and staff, talk about their day, and relax. Here are some examples of programs that have found ways to enjoy snack time with the children.

# Early Morning Programs

Since families need care for their children both before and after school, the typical day may begin as early as 6:00 a.m. or 6:30 a.m. The children are typically dropped off by a family member on the way to work; although, a handful of programs may have transportation to pick up children. In these programs, it's important to define expectations and determine whether the program will offer a morning snack or a more substantial breakfast. Early morning programs tend to offer flexible snack/mealtimes, because not all children are ready to eat when they first awaken in the morning and their arrival times will vary. Additionally, programs need to balance what may or may not be available at the school; many schools offer breakfast options, and some serve an early dinner before children go home.

Popular snack or meal solutions include a simple buffet that remains open from 7:00 a.m. to 8:00 a.m. Some food options might include a few types of cereal with milk, fruit, yogurt, and a selection of cereal or granola bars. In programs with access to a kitchen, the children might receive a more substantial breakfast, such as pancakes with fruit or egg muffin sandwiches. Early morning programs typically offer a more flexible atmosphere with a few limited activities for the children, and the snack buffet can be a viable option.

# After-School Programs

An after-school program starts at a specific time: directly after the school day, if it is held in a school facility, or as soon as the bus drops off a group of children for a program held off-site. For many programs, it makes sense to have all children place their bags in their cubbies, lockers, or designated space, wash their hands, and eat a snack when they first arrive. That way, staff can have everything out and available, so there is no need to leave the space to retrieve refrigerated food items from the kitchen. Since the teachers have a little time to prepare before the children arrive, they can cut up cheese and fruit, measure out servings of peanut butter to serve with rice cakes, or bake a pan of fresh zucchini bread. School-age children are able to serve themselves family style if the food is divided up into separate bowls and left on each table. Or children can self-select their items from a buffet and find a seat, which is more likely what they are used to in a school cafeteria. Water should always be available. When they finish eating, children can clean up their areas and move into planned learning centers or activity zones.

# Community-Based Programs

In some community-based programs, children may arrive by bus from several different schools, which means different arrival times. When that is the case, offering the snack to small groups is preferable to scheduling a time for everyone to eat together. Some programs find it very helpful to assign specific tables for snack—usually those closest to the kitchen or serving area. They post signs to indicate serving size, such as "Take 3 Please," and let the children help themselves. However, the program space may dictate the snack time if the children are expected to eat in a special place, such as a shared cafeteria. Whatever the case, try to find ways to help them minimize wait time, in case they arrive hungry and cannot wait until other groups arrive. As an additional service, many programs that serve low-income communities and receive additional funding collaborate with nonprofit agencies or raise funds so they can provide both a snack and dinner to children and, in some cases, their families. These meals can be generous dinners, such as a chicken breast, mashed potatoes, gravy, a salad, fruit, a dinner roll, and water, juice, or milk. Many of these community-based programs also offer a food pantry for community and program families in need.

# Crisis Management

It's important to establish a plan for managing various crisis situations, such as fires, floods, storms, earthquakes, power failures, and injuries. Staff will need proper training so they know the specific procedures for emergency situations, including an established method for contacting families. Much of this is required by state regulations, but programs should continue to revisit their plans regularly and practice the plans when appropriate. The staff should discuss these plans and be prepared to respond in an emergency to ensure that damage is minimized in the event of a crisis.

As an example, in many communities, snowstorms are an issue during the winter. Staff should revisit their plan every fall and make sure parents know what to do if schools are closed or dismiss early. When the schools close early, delay starting, or cancel the day due to the weather, how will the local programs respond? Will they close, or will they keep the doors open for parents who are still required to work? Parents will need to know what to do and whom to contact if there are questions.

More programs are scheduling drills for shelter-in-place scenarios and thinking about lockdown procedures, as many states are adding these requirements to the regulations. While this is always a difficult discussion, it's best for staff to discuss and practice a number of crisis scenarios. Regulations in many states require schools and school-age programs to take appropriate measures to keep users of a site safe, so it may be helpful to start with the local school district. Find out more about their lockdown plan and follow a similar plan.

Although most people use the term *lockdown* to refer to getting everyone into a safe place and sealing the exits, it can also include moving everyone to a space that can't be seen from windows or outside the building. Examples of incidents that could require a lockdown may be a dangerous animal, an intruder, an angry or intoxicated parent on the grounds, or a nearby civil disturbance in the area that could affect the program. Ideally, a lockdown area should have no windows or doors to the outside and should have a door that locks from the inside. In the staff handbook, include the policy and procedures to implement in the event of an active shooter or other intruder on the premises.

Practice lockdown drills or talk through the process so your team will be prepared in the event there is ever an intruder in the building. Also practice shelter-in-place drills for incidents in which you do not want the children in the hallways or outside, such as an ambulance taking a child or teacher to the hospital, as this event may upset the children. No drill involving children should include fake weapons, costumed actors, fake gunfire or other loud noises, or other scare tactics. In a calm environment, reinforce the steps to take. Organizations such as the Institute for Childhood Preparedness (https://www.childhoodpreparedness.org) offer resources to help educational professionals create policies and prepare for emergencies.

# Child Abuse and Maltreatment

Certain professionals, such as social workers, teachers, child-care providers, physicians, nurses, and other health-care workers, are recognized as holding the important role of mandated reporter of child abuse or maltreatment. These professionals can be held liable by both the civil and criminal legal systems for intentionally failing to make a report. Anyone serving as staff in a school-age program is considered a mandated reporter, which means staff are required by law to report instances of child abuse or maltreatment when they are presented with reasonable cause to suspect child abuse or maltreatment in their professional roles (Child Welfare Information Gateway, 2016). It's important to note that reporting is required when a caregiver or other mandated reporter suspects abuse or neglect. Proof of abuse or neglect is not required to make a report.

All staff should obtain specialized initial and ongoing training in child abuse and maltreatment to fully understand how to prevent, recognize, and respond to suspected child abuse and neglect. They must know how to document and follow state mandated reporter policy if there are signs that indicate reasonable cause to suspect abuse or neglect. Integrate these responsibilities into program policies and procedures, so staff know exactly what to do. (For more information on individual state statutes, see *Mandatory Reporters of Child Abuse and Neglect*, available at https://www.childwelfare.gov/pubPDFs/manda.pdf)

 **CHALLENGE**

Sara and Tammy have worked in an after-school program for six months and have become good friends. One day out on the playground, Tammy sees a child running toward her from the other side of the playground, with Sara chasing her. Sara catches up, grabs the child by the arms, and shakes her furiously while shouting at her. The child breaks free and runs to Tammy, crying. Tammy can clearly see the child's upper arms and face are very red. What should Tammy do, and why?

# Conclusion

There is a lot of work involved in setting up a safe and healthy program. In this chapter we reviewed building requirements and regulations and shared a number of examples of policies and procedures that help staff maintain a safe and healthy program. Much of this preparatory work is required by officials, which means someone needs to keep track of it all. Therefore, staff are responsible for having a system in place to collect and maintain records of aspects of program safety, health, and nutrition. Evidence that staff have completed daily health checks, fire drills, evacuation or shelter-in-place drills and offer approved menus are just a few examples of the documents your local officials may expect to see during a visit. Use a binder to keep all the required information in one place. Laying the groundwork for health, safety, and nutrition takes time, but in a safety-conscious environment, children will learn to protect themselves and look out for others.

 SOLUTIONS

## Sherry and the Accident

Let's review the scenario about Sherry, who was getting some juice out of the storage room as the children arrived, and missed an accident. While it's important to set up some activities to prepare for the day, Sherry forgot to make sure her supplies were fully stocked. She didn't have enough time to gather any additional materials she might need. She also ran out of time before she was able to check the room to see if anything was damaged, broken, or out of place. Ideally, at least one staff member needs to arrive at the program well before children are expected to arrive, to check every aspect of the program for health and safety and to plan for the day. In the future, it would be helpful if Sherry arrived earlier and had a safety checklist that she could follow each day. Fortunately for her, one child had just bumped the nose of another child while putting away backpacks, and she was able to handle the situation swiftly. (It's amazing how much a nose can bleed!) If Sherry had been a little better prepared, she would have witnessed the bump and been quicker with emergency supplies. With a safety checklist in place and an earlier scheduled start time, Sherry can avoid this situation in the future.

## Dealing with Construction

Haruka is correct in expressing concern for the safety of the children as they walk through a construction zone each day in the community center where her program is located. If hers is a licensed program, she should contact the licensing agency to make sure the program is complying with regulations by remaining open during renovations. Professional recommendations indicate that "alterations of structures during child-care operations should be isolated from areas where children are present and done in a manner that will prevent hazards or unsafe conditions (such as fumes, dust, safety, and fire hazards)" (Caring for Our Children, 2019). If the only way to get to the program space is across torn-up floors, then Haruka may need to work with her licensing agency to come up with a plan, such as using an alternative space or planning arrival through a secondary door, until the construction is complete. Another option is to work with the community center to set some clear limits with the construction staff. Could the floor be replaced on the weekend or the ceiling patched after hours so the plastic could be taken down during her hours of operation? In the future, she knows that she has to be more involved in the planning process so that she is aware of any construction project that may affect her program. Although it's too late to postpone construction now, she should be able to develop a safe temporary alternative so she will not need to shut down her program.

## Concerns about Abuse

As a mandated reporter, Tammy needs to remember it is her job to protect all children from harm. She witnessed a child being restrained and shaken, and she can see the red marks on the child's arms. It is not Tammy's job to investigate what happened or determine whether Sara's actions were a momentary lack of judgment, poor guidance practice, or abuse. However, based on what she observed, Tammy is mandated to file a report of suspected child abuse. Her program should have a policy in place with a clear protocol, including how to make a report and contacting program administration about the staff member. She should discreetly notify the family about the situation and, depending on the program structure, whom the parent can contact with additional questions. Whether or not they have outlined the protocol for her, she should call her state's mandated reporting center. Best practice dictates that reporting procedures and policies should be clearly stated, including where to report and the telephone number for reporting suspected child abuse or maltreatment.

# THINK. ACT. REFLECT.

## Think.

Jonathan, the school custodian, is loved by all the children and helps the staff to clean up the school-age program that is housed in the cafeteria at the end of day. During program hours, Jonathan rolls his cart, where he keeps many cleaning supplies and materials, along the hallway as he cleans bathrooms and classrooms. One day, three boys from the program happen to pass the cart on their way to the bathroom. They swipe some cleaning supplies as they pass and secretly make a mixture in a toilet. The chemicals react and create toxic fumes that cause the boys to faint. When a staff member comes to check on them, she finds them lying on the bathroom floor. Think about the health and safety issues involved in this scenario.

## Act.

Many states have regulations requiring such materials to be kept in a place inaccessible to children. The supplies also must be kept out of reach of children when they are being used. Research your state's regulations. What do they say regarding cleaning materials? What do regulations in your state say about supervision to and from toilet areas? Is your program in compliance?

## Reflect.

What can Jonathan and the program staff do to prevent this from happening in the future? What recommendations would you make?

# chapter 4 | Creating Child-Friendly Spaces

Shanelle is the new director of a school-based program that operates in the school cafeteria. She heard from the school administrator that she'd have plenty of space, but the lunch tables need to be left in place. She also heard that last year the children spent most afternoons playing games at the large tables. Although this seemed adequate, program enrollment was low, and some of the children complained that the program was boring. She has been asked to develop a more inviting learning space, but with the restriction against moving the lunch tables, Shanelle isn't sure what to do.

Now that you have program space and have set the foundation with health and safety guidelines, it's time to develop the environment into a warm and welcoming space. Research on children's views of school-age care generally emphasize the critical importance of space to play, do activities, and connect with friends. In an Australian study by Simoncini, Cartmel, and Young (2015), researchers found that "Children regarded [school-age care] SAC as a time and place for playing, making friends and doing activities. Their responses show SAC as a context for development where they were building skills and competencies." This also highlights the importance that children place on spatial aspects of school-age environments, preferring more space and fewer rigid rules.

This chapter will describe the daily schedule and furnishings and equipment typically found in comprehensive programs and will highlight opportunities that support positive relationships. Topics will include examples of typical learning centers both indoors and outdoors and some solutions for common challenges created by space.

# Defining the Daily Schedule

Each program needs a schedule and routine that reflects its unique circumstances and supports the needs of the children. It is also important to allow for flexibility—a planned art activity may have to be postponed if the children want to play in the first snowfall. Children gain a sense of security with a consistent routine and knowing that on most days events at the program take place in the same order and at the same time. It is, however, important to plan a schedule that provides many opportunities for children to make choices, since they have spent the entire day in a structured school setting. The program should allow children the choice of what to do, where to do it, with whom, and with which materials.

As the schedule begins to take shape, think about how it might feel to have a long, structured day. Let's pretend you are required to arrive at your office at a specific time and complete a series of tasks with short scheduled breaks. If you are lucky, you might enjoy some of the tasks assigned to you, but others are rigid or you experience constant interruptions. You have to push through a boring meeting after lunch, even as you are feeling an afternoon slump. As the clock ticks on, you are more than ready to check out for the day. What's on your mind as you head out of the office? Some people might enjoy some time alone in the car ride home to decompress as they listen to music. Others might prefer a trip to the gym to clear their heads, while others are eager to get home and start dinner.

School is very much like an office job for children. They may like some classes and may struggle in others, but the whole day has been structured for them. They are told where to go and what to do and are frequently interrupted as they complete their work throughout the day. Even their lunch is scheduled (sometimes as early as 10:30!). They may arrive at your program exhausted, hungry, or excited to share something with their friends. Try to organize a schedule that offers a balance of activities based on these different needs at the end of a school day. Some children may need to start with a drink and some snacks. Others might need to run out to the playground and expend some energy. Still others may just need to be alone in a comfortable, cozy area for a little while. Find out how they like to unwind, and ask them to help you develop a schedule. Try to have realistic expectations and develop an environment that meets their needs.

Charlie is an active third grader who is involved in Cub Scouts, plays basketball, and takes religious-education classes at his church. His schedule is packed full, so his parents have asked the staff at his after-school program to go through any homework assignments with him before they arrive to get him for activities. Unfortunately, the staff have not had a lot of success. He arrives tired and wants to start with a snack, and then he doesn't seem to have enough time or energy to complete his work. His parents are getting increasingly upset, as his teacher continues to send home schoolwork that has not been completed.

# Examining the Environment

Building a program space that is interesting and engaging for children takes time. Out-of-school-time programs are housed in a wide variety of facilities, each with unique challenges to setting up a workable environment, space, and furnishings. In terms of space, there are two major categories: programs that utilize a classroom solely for the purpose of school-age care, such as a church basement that only runs school-age care out of that space, and programs that share space, such as a child-care center that has a half-day preschool program in the morning, followed by school-age care in the same space in the afternoon. Developing a program within space that is utilized for only one purpose is easier than sharing space, which requires staff to set up and clean up each day. But school-age professionals are skilled and resourceful and can develop wonderful opportunities within any space that is provided. For the purpose of this chapter, we will share general recommendations, but staff should work together to plan an environment that meets the needs of the children in their care within the space available to their individual program.

Developing program space begins with an overview of the environment. Think about the following questions as you survey your program space. Once you have answered these questions, staff can develop a plan for room arrangement.

- Where is the home base that will be used for the majority of the program each day?
- Will the program remain in that space, or will the children have access to different areas, such as the library, gymnasium, computer room, community room, or cafeteria?
- Is there shared access to the playground or outdoor play space?
- Where are the permanent areas, such as the exits, bathrooms, windows, and large equipment, located?

Areas with a linoleum or tile floor that can be easily cleaned are well suited for meals and snacks, sand and water play, cooking, art activities, or anything messy. Carpeted areas are well suited for just about everything else, including quiet relaxing spaces, board games, and floor activities. Blocks and building also fit well into a carpeted area but should be placed far from the quiet activities to reduce disruptions. Try to envision the flow. Where are children likely to congregate and spend their time?

Each program space has a unique set of challenges, so it may be helpful to move some furniture around and try to envision how it might be used by the children. Large rooms, such as a gym space or cafeteria, can be broken up into smaller areas and activity centers. This can be accomplished by moving tables or using shelves to create separate spaces. In one program based in a large cafeteria, the children seemed to use the long open space between tables as a runway. They were frequently running back and forth, which caused many issues as they bumped into peers and interrupted games. The staff discovered that by turning one table across the runway area, they were able to break up the space a little more and resolve the issue. This shift in space, coupled with a little more time to run outside, solved the problem almost immediately.

## Typical Furnishings

An ideal school-age program would have a warm, inviting feel with appropriately sized furniture. Typical space and furnishings vary greatly depending on the space available to the program but should take into account the age and interests of the children. Whether your program is housed in a shared space, such as a multipurpose room, cafeteria, recreation center, or gymnasium, or in a single-purpose space, the following equipment and furnishings are essential:

- Tables for games, homework, snacks, and projects
- Chairs for sitting and holding backpacks and personal belongings
- Shelves or closets to store snacks, supplies, games, and manipulatives
- Roll carts to transport materials from storage spaces to the room
- Storage bins for materials for interest areas and for transporting materials to the room
- Area rugs to create softness and warmth

# Defining the Program Space

In a program with dedicated space, it may be easy to see which parts of the room belong to the program, as activity centers are set up and labeled. In large shared spaces such as a cafeteria, gym, or multipurpose room, staff need to find ways to clearly define which parts of the space are utilized by the school-age program and for what purpose by labeling the areas with signs each day. Something as simple as printed trifold signs or card-stock paper tents help define a space and provide some direction. You can also use furniture, tape, or floor coverings to define interest-area boundaries. Here are some additional tips to help you get started:

- **Define storage space.** Find a convenient location for materials that are used daily, including food and cold storage. Create a systematic, labeled storage plan, and include sufficient time for setup and cleanup. Use portable items such as baskets and carts to arrange materials in shared spaces.
- **Include a soft and cozy area.** Arrange a space with books and age- and interest-appropriate magazines, and include supplies for children who want to go there to decompress after a long day at school. This might be a carpet, some blankets, pillows, stuffed animals, or cushions.
- **Provide access to water.** Handwashing should be completed in the bathrooms, but you will need quick access to water for cleaning, and the children will need access to water such as a drinking fountain, water bottles, or a pitcher of water and cups. Messy projects should be stationed as close as possible to sinks. Provide hand sanitizer in stations throughout the space.
- **Add plants and natural lighting.** Create a warm atmosphere by adding some plants near a window and a table lamp in a reading area. Programs in shared space may not be able to control these aspects, but staff should consider what they can do to make the space look home-like and comfortable.
- **Include children in planning discussions.** Ask the children how the space feels. What are the most popular activities and how can you provide those regularly in the space? Seek the children's ideas and suggestions for arranging the environment, and include them in transition activities such as setting up for snack, collecting the trash, or washing off the paintbrushes.
- **When appropriate, hang decorations.** Oversized items such as a large scarf, tapestry, or a wall decoration help define the activity areas and can soften the program space with a pop of color. One creative program strung up some long, woven grapevines for a natural look in one corner, and the children hung lights and seasonal decorations from them. Be cautious with ceiling drops, however, and follow any local guidelines or state fire-department codes regarding hanging or flammable objects that may become fire hazards. A large potted or silk plant with twinkle lights may serve the same purpose.
- **Involve the children in setting up and dismantling in shared spaces.** While some activities should be planned and ready to go, many children like the routine of setting up and closing down the program.

# Learning Centers

Setting up a variety of learning centers, also known as activity centers or interest areas, allows children to control their activities. Examples of common learning centers include arts and crafts, music and movement, blocks and construction, dramatic play and theater, math and reasoning activities, reading in a relaxing cozy area, and science and nature activities. Based on the number of children in the program and their ages and developmental abilities, these learning centers can provide interesting activities that encourage learning through play without rigid rules and expectations. While it's ideal to have many of these centers available each day, smaller programs may offer fewer interest areas but rotate them to reflect changing skills and interests. If a program is located in an area where there is not enough room for many children to participate in a favorite activity at the same time, staff can be sure to provide enough materials and let the children rotate through the area and activity in a limited number at a time. Some programs may find it useful to include a timer so all children can play with popular activities, but this can disrupt children who are not finished and lead to hard feelings. Instead, for popular activities such as Legos, staff can try to provide additional supplies or try to rotate something else in as an alternative.

## Arts and Crafts

The art center is always a popular one in programs for children and youth. Look for ideas that are open ended, which means the children can work and explore their own ideas without too much structure that dictates the final project. The *School-Age Care Environment Rating Scale* (SACERS) (Harms, Thelma, Jacobs, and White, 2014) defines four categories of materials that should be available:

- Drawing materials, such as paper, markers, chalk, and colored pencils
- Painting materials, such as easels, tempera or watercolor paints, paintbrushes, and paper
- Collage materials, such as glue, scrap paper, pompoms, felt scraps, and ice-pop sticks
- Sculpture materials, such as clay, playdough, cardboard boxes (large and small), wood scraps, carpentry tools, and pipe cleaners
- Crafts such as weaving, origami, jewelry making, or embroidery

Using these categories as a guide, staff can build an art center with a wide variety of materials that are always accessible for the children to self-select and use. As a bonus, the materials may come in handy as children complete homework projects.

When it comes to art, open-ended projects that encourage individual expression are always encouraged. They allow children to explore materials and express themselves in different ways. In comparison, crafts offer more structure and require the children to learn a new skill or technique. Many older children are ready for more structured activities with multiple steps, and they like to learn new skills as part of the art-making process. They may enjoy learning how to make a specific item, such as a clay vase, stationery, a beaded necklace or bracelet, or an origami crane. As long as they control the creative process and make the creative decisions, they will likely enjoy the process. This doesn't mean that someone has to come up with an exact project with a model and show them what to do; it means that someone can teach them new skills, show them examples of the process, then let them explore their own ideas with time to practice those skills. One example is origami. Staff can help the children get started by showing them how to follow the instructions to make a paper crane, then set out the origami paper with an instruction booklet that provides different examples of origami for the children to choose from. In another example, some children will enjoy learning skills such as knitting, hand-sewing, weaving, or crochet; many children find this work calming and relaxing after a busy school day. Staff can bring out a large bin of sewing materials and show the children some simple hand-sewing techniques. Then staff can help the children develop

some ideas about what they would like to make. It's important to let the children choose whether they wish to participate. Art should be fun and creative, not an extension of the school day.

## Music and Movement

As children grow, their taste in music changes, but it is still helpful to offer a wide variety of musical experiences. Provide an old CD/tape player with an assortment of tapes or CDs from varied genres, such as classical and popular music, as well as examples of music from other cultures. There are many ways to stream music online, but staff should be cautious and select options that allow them to filter age-appropriate selections. Headphones are also a good idea to have available so some children can listen while others focus on other things. Musical instruments can be a good addition to the program. If you do not have any available, staff can work with children to create some.

Dancing is great exercise and a lot of fun. Encourage the children to dance to music, and give them props such as scarves to use as they dance. The SACERS indicates that music or movement instruction should be offered weekly as either an individual or group activity. You might consider singing and dancing during group time, offering guitar instruction as an option, arranging karaoke or a chorus, or planning a special activity such as a talent show the children plan and develop. In some programs, staff may work with the children as they develop the program, as well as participate in the show.

## Blocks and Construction

Large programs with permanent space can provide a large selection of wooden building blocks. But all programs can develop a block and construction center with different kinds of interlocking building blocks such as Lego or K'nex or Roylco straws and connectors. Encourage the children to work on their projects for as long as needed, and provide a safe place to store their works in progress. For programs that want to take these activities to the next level, age-appropriate carpentry tools and soft wood or simple kits for birdhouses, feeders, and picture frames are fun and interesting construction projects.

## Dramatic Play/Theater

The foundation of dramatic play is a housekeeping area or a home office. Some children ages five through seven will continue to enjoy these activities, along with a wide variety of props. Include dress-up materials and costumes that support many different roles. Include materials, such as puppets, that support language development. Children are more likely to use items that are hanging on a rack or in an organized display than they are to dig through a bin full of clothing. Display the clothing and prop options in an inviting way, and keep the items clean and in good repair. Rotate the materials and replace worn or damaged items over time. Add new props based on the current topics. Consider providing dolls, army figurines, and wrestling and other action figures. Older children will show a declining interest in playing house, but they will enjoy opportunities to put on drama or theater productions. Staff can work with them to provide support and help bring their ideas to life.

## Math/Reasoning Activities

For younger children, a math area might include pegboards, tangrams, or dominoes. Programs can support the school curriculum by offering scales with items for weighing and measuring, rulers, and unifix cubes, which may be useful as children work on math homework. There are many enjoyable board games that integrate deeper mathematical thinking into the game play. Games such as Qwirkle, Ice Cool, and Robot Turtles help students develop skills such as multistep problem solving, spatial reasoning, and pattern recognition. Card games such as Crazy Eights or Euchre can be fun to play. Offer math activities that enhance children's curiosity and support vocabulary associated with math, such as *estimation*, *values*, *measurement*, *formula*, *probability*, and *variable*.

## Science/Nature Activities

This learning center can include a wide variety of science materials and natural items. Consider rotating collections of natural items, such as leaves, pinecones, a variety of rocks and minerals, and seashells, along with magnifying glasses and tweezers. Provide living things such as plants or a classroom pet. Other ideas include magnets, scales, puzzles, or items for sorting. This center can include materials and activities that combine the fields of science, technology, engineering, and math (also known as STEM). Staff can support youth by providing activities such as science experiments, catapult competitions, building simple machines, robotics, or coding. In school-age programs, STEM activities are about children exploring materials, doing the activity or experiment, and discovering the results, not the staff performing the experiment while the children watch. Frequently, art is integrated as STEAM activities.

Many skills make up scientific inquiry. They include children's ability to:

- raise questions about objects and events around them.
- explore objects, materials, and events by acting upon them and noticing what happens.
- make careful observations of objects, organisms, and events using all their senses.
- describe, compare, sort, classify, and order in terms of observable characteristics and properties.
- use a variety of simple tools, such as hand lenses, measuring tools, eyedroppers, and a balance, to extend their observations.
- engage in simple investigations including making predictions, gathering and interpreting data, recognizing simple patterns, and drawing conclusions.
- record observations, explanations, and ideas through multiple forms of representation including drawings, simple graphs, writing, and movement.
- work collaboratively with others.
- share and discuss ideas and listen to new perspectives.

Planned science activities that include hands-on experimentation are always popular. Using the scientific method, the staff might initiate an experiment by asking a question, then help the children move through the steps, documenting their work.

## THE SCIENTIFIC METHOD

- Ask a question.

- Do background research.

- Construct a hypothesis.

- Test the hypothesis by doing an experiment.

- Analyze the results and draw a conclusion.

- Communicate your results.

Consider including some research activities, such as the following:

- How can we make an egg float?
- What happens when you mix baking soda and vinegar? Why?
- What might happen when we combine a soda, such as Diet Coke, with a candy, such as Mentos? (We advise doing this one outside!)
- How can we make a ping-pong ball float in midair?
- How can we build a paper bridge between the tables that will hold weight?

Cooking is a fantastic activity to do with children that integrates math, science, and literacy. Some programs may be lucky to have a kitchenette in their program space or in a nearby location. If not, you can find many simple recipes online for snacks that do not require cooking.

## Gross-Motor Activities

Some programs have the benefit of the use of a gymnasium, multipurpose room, or a section of the classroom that can be reserved for active play. Programs should have some use of outdoor or large indoor space for physical play. While a playground is ideal, green space such as a grassy area behind the building or access to a blacktop area that can be used for gross-motor activities will work too. Gross-motor play is not an opportunity for staff to sit and chat; rather, they should engage the children in games and actively supervise the group.

## Writing Area

Younger school-agers are still exploring basic writing skills and introductory cursive, while older children and youth can explore calligraphy and fancy writing. Plenty of pencils, a pencil sharpener, erasers, glitter pens, clipboards, a word wall, letter charts, graph paper, and fresh paper will encourage them to write. This could be integrated as part of the homework area or with the arts and crafts. There are many websites available that provide practice sheets for fancy alphabets. Offer encouragement to get the children writing, such as journals and letters.

## Sensory Table

Children need sensory activities after a busy or stressful day in school. In programs that offer them, the sensory table is frequently the most popular area. Tactile materials feel so good when you run your hands through them. Prepare the materials, such as playdough, goop, sand, birdseed (without capsaicin), used and dried coffee grounds, or shaving cream, in advance and put them out. Consider letting the children make their own playdough, slime, or goop from recipes and materials provided for them. This area can also be used to extend science experiments, such as adding plastic tubing and pails to a water table so children can observe the flow of water. When the children are finished exploring birdseed, you can put it out in feeders for the local birds.

Many programs find it challenging to offer sensory activities because the materials can get messy. Yes, that is the point! It can be messy—that's why children like it. But, for example, if the staff use an inexpensive disposable tablecloth and have the children use shaving cream on it, staff can just pick up the tablecloth when they're finished, folding it inward to keep the mess in the center, and dispose of the whole mess easily. We cannot stress enough the value of this area. Children love this area because it relieves stress and is just plain fun.

## Cozy Corner/Reading Area

Children need access to a quiet area where they can read and relax. For programs that do not have carpeted space, blankets and pillows, stuffed animals, or gymnastic mats can be laid out to define relaxing spaces. One program used plastic PVC pipes to create an easily assembled frame. The staff could set it up and throw a blanket or sheet over it to create a privacy wall that was easily taken down at the end of the day.

## Board Games, Manipulatives, and Table Toys

In a school-age program, this area should include a wide variety of age-appropriate board games. Common favorites include Chutes and Ladders, Trouble, Uno, Stratego, chess, checkers, dominoes, Battleship, and playing cards. Even Twister is a popular favorite for times when the children need to move. It's important that the games be in good condition and have all the pieces. Manipulatives include items such as lacing beads, lacing cards, small blocks, and jewelry-making kits. Favorite table toys might include Legos or puzzles. Provide a wide variety, take time to be sure the children understand the rules for each game, and observe to see how they use the materials. Be sure to consider their ages, and select items that are age appropriate. While young children may enjoy Chutes and Ladders, older school-age children might prefer something more complex, such as Stratego or chess. Use the ages recommended on the boxes as a guide. When children seem to lose interest, remove a game and replace it with something new. You'll notice that any of these games support math and reasoning as well.

## Homework Area

While this may not need to be a specific activity center, programs should plan and organize a good space where children can complete their homework, if desired. Ample table space in a quiet area with access to school supplies and staff support will help children complete their work.

Space for Clubs

As school-age children begin to develop interests, clubs may emerge. Encourage these clubs as an opportunity for children to explore their interests in a healthy, inclusive way. In one program that was housed in the cafeteria, children began setting up space under the cafeteria tables. The space was awkward and unfriendly, and boys seemed to gather under one table, while girls gathered under another. These "clubs" didn't have much of a focus except to antagonize each other. Repeatedly, the staff tried to lure them out with other activities, but day after day the groups continued to gather under the tables. The staff brought in round carpets and pillows and helped the children set up a better space to facilitate clubs, with the goal to channel the children's enthusiasm into something more productive.

Then they all sat down as a group to develop a better plan together. The children created a long list of club options, including Harry Potter Book Club, Pokémon Club, Chess Club, and Sports Club. Finally, they voted and agreed on three clubs. Everyone who wished to join found a space. Together, they developed rules and made signs, and the children began to gather in their club space a couple of days a week.

Time is an important aspect of all these activities. During the school year, the children are in out-of-school-time care for limited amounts of time. Plan activities that can be easily started and completed, or plan for ways children can save and complete activities the following day. As an example, one group of children loved large puzzles. They would start the puzzle, work on it as hard as they could for about twenty minutes, and then inevitably the staff would call for cleanup time to move them to a snack. Day after day the children started a puzzle without the accomplishment of completing it. The staff decided to offer some options: the children could complete the puzzle on a table that was set aside so they could return to finish it the next day, or the staff could obtain a puzzle mat (a nonslip, felt mat), where the children could work on the puzzle. If they needed to stop, they could roll the mat up (with the puzzle inside) and store it for the next day.

# Creating Special Spaces

School-age children need to have ownership in the program and program space. There are many ways staff can support their involvement. First, observe the space and the children to see how the program flows, where they congregate. Ask them about the space. Then allow them to create spaces of their own. Think about your bedroom as a child. How did you make it special? What did you do to make it your own? Some children like to hang pictures they have made. Other children like to paint with wild colors or put up posters with inspirational messages or a favorite musical group. Children like to have some say in their personal spaces and to be surrounded by things they like. They also need space for long-term, more complex activities such as a detailed puzzle, Lego creations, or a game they'd like to finish the next day. Finding space for these items shows respect for them as individuals.

Margaret has a group of older children who are about to age out of her program. Some of the parents have expressed an interest in keeping their children enrolled through the summer and coming school year. She enjoys working with the group, and she really likes the idea of extending her program, so she is working with her licensing agent for permission to extend the age of children in her care. She knows that older children have different needs, and although they still need supervision, they are getting bored of her daily activities and are ready for more autonomy and a shift in programming. What does she need to consider as she prepares to extend her program to middle school?

## Consider These Budget-Friendly Ideas

It's common for school-age programs to have limited materials, and requesting an infusion of money to restock the game shelf may be out of the question. However, there are many simple ideas to add a new flavor to the classroom materials.

- **Gather natural items:** Children enjoy using natural materials to create. Next time you take a walk, look around to see what you can find to bring into the classroom. On a recent walk, the children in one program found pinecones in a variety of sizes, seed pods that had fallen off a tree, acorns, and large chunks of bark. Their teacher laid the materials out on newspaper to dry overnight, and the next day she placed them in the art center along with some modeling clay. The children paired the natural items with beads, pompoms, and ice-pop sticks to make a wide variety of sculptures.
- **Make old games new again:** Every program has a handful of games with missing pieces. Instead of throwing them away, why not collect all the loose parts and challenge the children to make up their own game? Re-cover the board with plain paper, and encourage them to draw out something new, then develop a concept and game rules.
- **Provide loose parts:** Gather loose parts such as tiles, wood pieces, nuts and bolts, rocks, pebbles, grasses, seeds, paper tubes, boxes, and plastic bottle caps. Place the materials in bins around the space. It may be helpful to think of loose parts as something that will help inspire the children's imagination and creativity on their own terms and in their own unique way. Ask parents to donate recyclable materials, such as paper-towel rolls, egg cartons, milk and gelatin cartons, and scrap paper. These materials offer a lot of options beyond what the program's budget can provide. One program placed old radios and clocks on large cafeteria trays and gave the children some basic tools so they could take them apart to see how they work.

- **Seek community resources:** Every community has a wealth of small businesses that have access to a wide variety of materials; the key is finding them. The local newspaper office may have end rolls of paper that they can donate or sell at a discount. The home-furnishing store might be able to donate fabric scraps, carpet squares, or discontinued wallpaper books. Local construction crews may have piles of small blocks of wood left over from projects. Who do you know in your community?

## Outdoor Spaces

Programming doesn't just happen inside; it happens outside too! Programs need some access to an outdoor play space that includes age-appropriate gross-motor equipment. Children need time to run and play outdoors. Typically, this is required as part of licensing regulations, but it's also just good practice. The play space should be accented with portable materials, such as bikes and wheeled toys with helmets, balls, jump ropes, large plastic hoops, and sporting goods, depending on the ages of the children in the program. These materials need to be accessible and available—which requires the staff to have some items out and ready before the children arrive. Let the children choose and bring out additional materials. Support outdoor play with new materials, such as logs, wooden planks, boxes, sidewalk chalk, or ropes, that can serve different purposes and encourage the children to think and create.

Additionally, as the seasons change and the weather warms, everyone will enjoy some added time outside. Are there other aspects of the program that can be brought outside to extend the program to the outdoors? Consider bringing learning-center activities to the playground, such as art, blocks and building materials, or books and games on a blanket.

# Negotiating for Space

Negotiating for adequate program space, including storage space, is important. Programs located in a gym may want to utilize the cafeteria or access the kitchen for special cooking projects. Programs located in a small, carpeted multipurpose room may need a little extra time in the gym or on the playground. Each program has to advocate for appropriate space based on the program structure and what is best suited for the children and a wide range of activities. Advocating for space generally means coming up with a proposal and working with administration, such as the school principal, center director, or regional manager, to obtain access to the needed space.

One program started the day in the large open gym, but despite plenty of gym space the children needed tables for activities. The staff obtained permission to arrive early to roll over four lunch tables from the lunchroom across the hall. They used these to form a large square to be utilized as the program home base. On a main table, the director set up a trifold display board with the program license, safety information, and notes for families, to draw attention to the space. On the remaining tables, she set up different activities each day.

Several programs run by the same agency in a different school building wanted to obtain access to bulletin boards or wall space to hang program materials and artwork. The schools in the district had strict guidelines for wall decorations, so they struggled to personalize the programs. At a program meeting, the staff brainstormed a number of possible solutions, and each individual program came up with a different proposal based on what they observed from staff in the school buildings. One program offered to purchase a bulletin board to be hung in the hallway outside the program space. Another program asked if they could use a trophy case in the hallway that was almost always empty. A third program determined that hallway space would not work, so they purchased some trifold boards that the children could decorate for regular displays. They put the displays up and took them down each day. Instead of bulletin-board space, they requested a little extra space in the storage closet to keep the trifold boards safe. Each program successfully advocated for a different solution to their problem.

Another program was located in a cafeteria where they had all the tables they needed, but the children really needed some open space for active games. They had access to the playground area, but during inclement weather the children had limited options. Over time, they worked with school administration to obtain access to an indoor commons area that was typically set aside for the special-education teachers and therapists during the school day. They just had to agree to follow specific rules for that space, bring in their own toys so the children were not drawn to the equipment used for therapy, and sweep the area at the end of the day.

Program staff need to work with their administrators and school administrators to find appropriate space. As noted in the examples above, there is a give and take to shared program space. Imagine how school administrators would respond if teachers reported that special equipment had been used or broken while used by the school-age program? Most likely the school-age program would lose the privilege. Both staff and children need to be respectful of the shared space, which includes using only program materials and cleaning up after themselves. Together, program staff and building administrators should discuss expectations, set clear boundaries, and work toward shared success.

# Considering Diversity

How an adult regards play, facilitates it, plans for it, sets up the environment, and interacts with children are all influenced by the adult's culture. Therefore, cultural conflicts can arise between adults regarding differing perspectives on learning through play. Maintaining open communication with and respect for staff and families and understanding and acquiring skills to work through differences in ways that honor diversity result in equitable decisions in programming.

Staff tend to provide materials and activities that are familiar to them, which is a great place to start, but every program has a diverse group of children with different skills, interests, and abilities. A wide selection of materials paired with the freedom to make choices provide diverse opportunities for children. Looking for trends in the community and following conversations between children may offer some clues to the types of materials children would be interested in. In one district, badminton became a favorite pastime at one school, soccer was taking off at another school, while another program was seeing a lot of interest in origami. These ideas didn't come from the staff; they came from the diverse interests of the children and were tied to their cultural backgrounds. Parents can also offer examples of favorite games that may differ from those you might find at the average store. For example, families from Nigeria may enjoy playing mancala; families from China may enjoy mah-jongg.

# Culture

Directors and staff can support diversity by selecting materials and planning the environment in a way that supports and enhances understanding of the children's cultures, as well as those of the wider community. By stressing similarities in children and honoring their differences, you can develop a program that respects diversity. Focus on areas such as food or language, to demonstrate children's common bonds, but show how interesting different people's languages or food can be. Children love to explore new foods, and it provides a great way to share their experiences together. Visit the international section of your local grocery store for some ideas.

One diverse program invited parents who spoke a language other than English at home to come into the program and teach the children that language. But rather than learn a few common phrases, such as "Hello" or "How are you?" or counting to twenty, the program had the parents spend time with the children in the various learning centers. Together, they played games, speaking nothing but the second language. The children were able to pick up enough nonverbal cues to understand, and eventually they were able to reply in and learn some of the second language. The program incorporated picture books using the second language and included books about the culture of the country where the language is spoken. They even found some bilingual books in both English and the second language. Staff labeled classroom items in multiple languages, and all children were enriched by this opportunity.

In addition, program materials should include dolls, puzzles, books, and games that represent children and families with different ethnicities and with different abilities. Art materials should include paper, pencils, markers, and paint in a variety of colors that can be used to represent skin tones. Staff can introduce examples of art through books and invite the children to participate in art activities from other cultures, such as creating ceramics, mandalas, and fiber arts. Outdoor time can include games from other cultures. For example, *kabaddi*, played in India, South Africa, Southeast Asia, Japan, and Iran, is a game similar to rugby. It can be played by tagging, rather than tackling, opponents. *Kongki noli* is a Korean game similar to jacks, using five small stones. Instructions for playing these games can easily be found online.

Dance is a great way to honor many ethnicities and cultures. Programs can invite staff, family members, or volunteers (or watch YouTube videos) to show children a wide variety of dances, such as tap dancing, ballet, break dancing, square dancing, the electric slide, and hip-hop. Children will love learning *palmas*, which is hand clapping, and *golpes*, which is foot stomping, that are in salsa, a Latin dance from Cuba.

Children can learn the hula from Hawaii, the flamenco from southern Spain, the tango from Argentina, Irish step dancing, and the conga, which is a fun line dance from Cuba. Bollywood, the southern Indian film industry, features dancing styles from all around the world mixed with Indian dancing. One after-school program taught children African drumming and a West African dance called *sinte* from Guinea.

## Diverse Needs

In considering your program space, look through the lens of universal design. Just as staff are expected to treat all children with the same universal precautions to minimize potential illness, staff should ensure the room is designed in such a way that all children can be successful. The Americans with Disabilities Act (ADA) sets certain standards and recommendations for physical environments to be accessible and appropriate for children with special needs. For example, even just a few stairs can be a barrier for some children. Including ramps makes places easily accessible to children with mobility limitations. Signs and rules, no matter how well placed and written, do no good for a child with a visual impairment, unless the signs are in predictable places and are in large print or can be read by touch. Consider training on thoughtful planning and creating a supportive environment to ensure the space is appropriate for all children served by the program. Planning for wide aisles and clear pathways and eliminating potential barriers supports all children.

# US LAWS PROTECTING PEOPLE WHO HAVE DISABILITIES

The ADA is legislation that extended civil rights protection prohibiting discrimination against persons with disabilities in employment, transportation, public access, local government, and telecommunications.

The Education for All Handicapped Children Act (Public Law 94-142) requires states to provide a free and appropriate public education for every child between the ages of three and twenty-one years, regardless of how or how seriously the child may be handicapped. The Individuals with Disabilities Education Act (IDEA) amended Public Law 94-142 to focus on the individual child, rather than the disability. Broadly, IDEA specifies that a child who qualifies for services must have a team made up of teachers, service personnel, and the child's parents who all work together to provide the child with a free and appropriate public education in the least restrictive environment (Woolfolk, 2019).

One program had a child enrolled who had some limited gross-motor function. He struggled to keep up with the other children on the playground, and on days the staff planned an organized game such as dodgeball or kickball, this particular child opted to sit out. Over time he began to sit out more and more often with a book. Noticing there was a problem, the staff worked with his parents to find some outdoor games that he could confidently play. The parents suggested parachute play and a few cooperative games that he had enjoyed previously, so the staff added these games into the rotation. On other days they planned more choices, so there was always an option that appealed to everyone. The child began joining in more often, and all the children were able to participate in favorite games.

In general, if the basic ideas presented in this chapter are carried out and the individual needs of every child in the program are considered in the planning spaces, schedules, and activities, the intent of ADA is likely being met. It is recommended, however, that staff review and become knowledgeable about the ADA standards.

## Conclusion

School-age programs take place in a variety of settings, including school buildings, places of worship, and community buildings. To meet the needs of the children they serve, school-age programs should be appealing, nurturing, and responsive and should offer a wide variety of interesting activities that allow children the opportunity to explore, discover, be challenged, or just have fun. This chapter describes the daily schedule, typical furnishings, and examples of learning centers both indoors and outdoors. It offers some solutions for common challenges created by space and ideas for diversity in programming. With these examples in mind, take a fresh look at your program environment. Is it child friendly?

 SOLUTIONS

### Shanelle Organizes Her Program Space

In our opening vignette, Shanelle has some concerns about her new program space. Every program has different challenges, so her first step was to visit the program and view the cafeteria area assigned to her program. The tables were fine but very large and stationary, and they took up most of the space. She decided to make up trifold signs so she could label each table with different activity centers, such as arts and crafts, board games, sensory, and so forth, keeping quiet activities on one side and noisy activities on the other side. She consulted the SACERS to be sure she was adhering to best practices in school-age programming and made lists of materials and supplies as recommended, to be purchased over the year as her budget allowed. She arranged a meeting with the building principal so she could share some of the comments made the previous year and share her desire to better utilize the space. The principal was open to her new ideas and agreed to ask the custodian to fold up two tables each day. She was pleased to discover that this simple adjustment left enough space for her to lay out some blankets and create a cozy book nook each day, improving the space and creating a warmer environment. With a variety of learning centers in place, she felt confident that she had addressed the concerns from previous years and was excited to start the new year.

## Charlie and the Homework Dilemma

Homework is always a challenge for programs that run after school. It's not uncommon for parents to request that staff make sure their child completes homework before doing anything else. The solution is not simple, but each program should work with families to develop an adequate compromise. The fact is that children have just spent most of their day in restrictive, mostly sedentary activities. Children need a chance to rest and renew after a long day at school, and staff should respect that they need a mental break from academic work. Staff should make it clear that when a child enters the program they will meet a child's physiological needs first: snack, toileting, and physical activity. No child whose body is aching for physical activity should be forced to remain inside for an arbitrary amount of time doing homework before going outside to play. The reverse is also true. Too many children are required to spend time outside in a playground that holds no interest for them when they would prefer to go inside and work on crafts, read, or complete their homework. Children should be able to make choices. In most cases, once a child has had a chance to rest and revitalize, a selection of activities—homework included—can be offered. As a compromise, perhaps the child can use the toilet, have a snack, and play for an agreed-upon amount of time, then work on homework for a while and save some homework for home. While it is great for parents if all the homework is done in after-school programs, parents also need to help or at the very least review children's homework so they know what the assignments are and what concepts are covered and can follow up with teachers as needed. Some programs have tutors come in to help children, especially older children or young readers. This is fine but not at the expense of the child not being able to engage in any activities because of the time it takes to do homework or work with a tutor. Certainly, some homework time can be set aside, and a tutor service is admirable, but children also need to run and play after a long day of sitting in school learning.

## Margaret Responds to Needs of Older Children

Developing school-age programs for middle schoolers is challenging because the interests of this age group differ from those of younger children. In addition, there is a widespread perception that these children do not need care in the hours before or after school; although, thankfully the trend is growing that includes this age group in programs. Research supports the need for community-linked programs for older children, as these can reduce teen involvement in drugs, alcohol, violence, and crime (Goldschmidt, Huang, and Chinen, 2007, as cited by American Institutes for Research, 2008). Successful school-age programs help this age group develop a new skill or advance to the next skill level, give a feeling of personal satisfaction and accomplishment, and link program participants to their community in some way. As children grow older, it's increasingly important for programs to incorporate children in program planning and activity evaluation. It's clear that Margaret's program is needed in the community, but she will need to offer more challenging activities for this group of children as they mature. First, Margaret should survey the children for their interests and work with them to build an expanded curriculum. She should provide some leadership opportunities for the older children and encourage them to develop and lead activities within their skill sets. Some programs train students as junior leaders and assign responsibilities. For example, twelve-year-old Finn is excited to show other children about robotics and would love to lead an activity for anyone who shows interest. Thirteen-year-old Molly is learning to crochet and is eager to share her

hobby. Margaret should also help this age group feel part of the larger community by giving children the opportunity, for example, to be involved in making cookies and walking as a supervised group across the street to an assisted-living facility to share some treats with their elderly friends.

# THINK. ACT. REFLECT.

## Think.

Several parents approached Debbie, the director of a large after-school program, with a petition to stop the program from including Spanish-speaking activities and teaching Spanish to the children. Twenty percent of the program population speaks Spanish at home. The parents who signed the petition feel that all children should learn English, even immigrant children, and that including even the smallest amounts of Spanish in the program will hinder all children from learning English. How should Debbie respond?

## Act.

Develop a list with many possible solutions. Don't put too much thought into which ones will work until you have generated your list. Next, consult the NAA *Code of Ethics*, found in English and Spanish at https://naaweb.org/resources/code-of-ethics.

> Above all we will bring NO harm to any child. We will participate in practices that respect and do not discriminate against any child by denying benefits, giving special advantages or excluding from program activities on the basis of his or her race, ethnicity, religion, gender, sexual orientation, national origin, language, ability or their status, behavior or family beliefs.

## Reflect.

Reflect on the ethical dilemma just described and your list of possible solutions. Using the NAA *Code of Ethics* to support your response, which possible solution has the most potential? How do you think Debbie should handle it?

# chapter 5 | Planning the Curriculum

enisha runs a small after-school program in a suburban community. Her program is only open a few hours in the afternoon, so the children start with a snack together, then they work on homework or read books, then she plans a craft or game. It was fun for a while, but after about three months she overhears two children complain that they're bored. Over time, they begin to resist doing homework and start to complain about the activities. She wonders what else she could be doing to keep the children engaged.

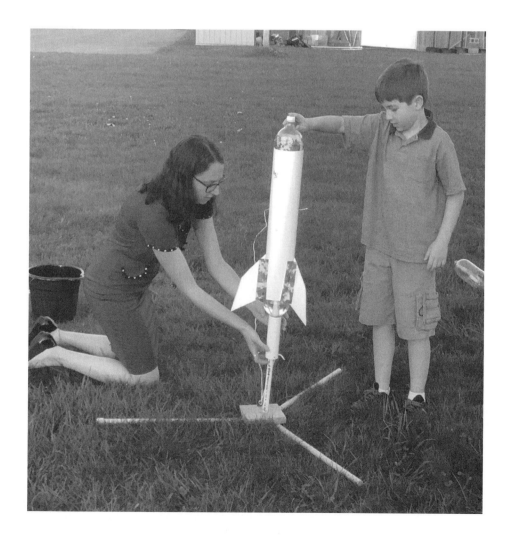

Once the environment is organized, the next step in developing a high-quality program is to develop learning activities and games that become the program curriculum. The curriculum is a written plan of the materials and activities that the staff plan to provide, including the following:

- Goals for children's development and learning
- Experiences through which they will achieve these goals
- What staff can do to help children reach the goals
- Materials needed to support the implementation of the curriculum

Based on the principles of child development and developmentally appropriate practice, the goal of a good curriculum is to improve children's school success by enhancing their early skills and knowledge. In this chapter, readers will develop expertise in project-based, youth-centered learning that supports learning standards. Topics include the planning cycle for developing curriculum: developing topics, writing outcomes, planning activities, and assessing learning.

Developmentally appropriate practice means creating programs with curriculum that matches what we know about how children learn and how they develop. This practice requires meeting children where they are developmentally and supporting them so they can reach goals that are both challenging and achievable. This approach to curriculum respects both the age and the individual needs of the child.

NAEYC's framework for developmentally appropriate practice serves as the primary context in which to develop curriculum for children from birth through age eight. Age appropriateness and individualization are essential to understanding effective practices in early childhood. As children continue to grow, practices that support individualization are important, especially for children who spend so much of their day in controlled classroom situations. Having the freedom to explore their interests and relax after the structured day is very important. Careful observation of children's interests and areas of popular engagement help provide learning outcomes that are best suited to a group of children with a wide age range.

# The Planning Cycle

The typical instructional cycle includes ongoing observation and assessment to find out where students are in their skills development and understanding of concepts. Based on this information, staff can plan and set curriculum goals and adapt instruction to help students meet those goals. The cycle begins as staff observe and have conversations with children to understand more about their learning and development. This information helps staff determine what the children and youth can do and what they are ready to learn next. Once individual learning goals are identified, staff can develop both individual and group activities to support the individual and group goals. During this phase, staff collect information to inform the next planning phase and to write new individual and group goals. Let's break down these steps with some practical examples that apply to school-age programs.

# Observation, Assessment, and Individualizing

School-age children are formally assessed by their teachers as they turn in homework, take tests, and complete activities in the classroom setting. In contrast, assessment in school-age programs is fairly informal. The best way to learn about the needs of the children in your program is through periodic observations. For example, this might happen as the children play. An anecdotal record (or anecdote) is one of the most popular forms of record keeping because these bits of information are quick and relatively short. They can be used to detail a specific behavior or a conversation between children. Anecdotal records can be shared with staff at the end of the day to solve problems and to plan new activities for the children. Take a look at the following examples, which illustrate ways to use assessment, planning and curriculum goals, and implementation to adapt program activities.

Shantel was overheard telling her friends about a cupcake competition she saw on a television show. The staff had observed that baking was a special interest for Shantel, so they arranged for someone to come into the program to show the children how to decorate cupcakes with frosting flowers. They distributed the cupcakes to their schoolteachers on Teacher Appreciation Day.

As the spring baseball season got underway, staff noticed that several boys were talking about their teams. They didn't have space outside for a real game, but staff found some softballs in the storage shed, and they encouraged the players to bring their mitts to the program. Several parents located additional mitts to donate so everyone who was interested could play catch outside. Staff played with the children, helped reinforce rules for playing, and encouraged more experienced players to share strategies and tips with newer players.

Jonathan, who was very shy, excelled at his music lessons and enjoyed practicing his clarinet. The staff found a space for him to play toward the end of the day when it wouldn't be too disruptive and made an effort to sit and listen to him, encouraging others to do the same. Although they lacked the background to help him with his music, they did provide time and space for him to practice his skills. When he was selected to play a solo at the school concert, one staff member planned to attend to support his efforts.

Notice that in all of these situations, the instructional cycle of informal assessment, planning and setting curriculum goals, and implementing activities supported children's individual interests. Individualizing does not mean that someone has to provide different materials or plan a different activity for everyone. Instead, staff should think about what they have observed and what new materials can be added to reflect different interests and abilities. Not everyone may want to play a game of baseball, but program staff can provide new materials and help some children get started while still providing different options for the other children.

To gain an accurate assessment of children's knowledge and skills, the staff might observe small groups of children and take anecdotal notes about what is happening, record interactions with children, reflect on group time, and review children's work. For example, a staff member notices that a kindergartner is struggling with fine-motor activities such as tying his shoes and pulling apart linking blocks. With this information, program staff can set a goal to integrate more fine- motor activities to support this child's development. Another staff member might notice that a fourth-grade girl seems to have some difficulty making friends and often plays or reads by herself. Staff might talk with her to find out more about her interests and use that information to develop activities that might help her engage socially. For example, if they find her reading the Warriors book series about cats, and they know that other children are reading it as well, they might encourage her to develop a Warriors book club and work with her to set up some activities for the children related to this common interest.

## Developing Curriculum and Creating Learning Outcome Statements

You may be familiar with curriculum models such as Montessori, the Creative Curriculum, or High Scope. These models provide a framework for how staff should think about the planning process. There are few curriculum models that are specifically designed for out-of-school environments, but in addition to planning based on assessing individual needs, staff can plan activities based on what's happening in the local school or district.

Classroom teachers in educational settings are required to plan lessons and activities based on the learning standards that have been adopted by their respective state and/or district. These standards typically describe educational objectives based on what students should learn by the end of a course, grade level, or grade span. Based on national, state, or local standards, elementary and middle school teachers develop the classroom curriculum to help children meet these standards.

Let's take a look at an example of a learning standard and then look at how different teachers might implement that standard. For example, the Common Core/Next Generation Learning Standards ask students to read stories and literature, as well as more complex texts that provide facts and background knowledge in areas such as science and social studies. In assessments and classwork, students will be challenged and asked questions that push them to refer to what they've read. This approach stresses critical-thinking, problem-solving, and analytical skills that are required for success in college, career, and life (www.commoncore.org, http://www.nysed.gov/next-generation-learning-standards). Standards vary, so take some time to locate the learning standards that have been adopted by your state or school district.

All teachers within a district need to follow the standards, but individual classroom teachers select some of the texts the children will read and determine the activities they will organize to challenge the children and encourage critical thinking. The standards typically do not describe any particular teaching practice, curriculum, or assessment method. The curriculum in a school setting is fairly controlled, and teachers are required to plan every lesson or activity based on the educational objectives that tie back to the standards.

Out-of-school-time programs are typically not required to follow any learning standards, so staff have a tremendous amount of flexibility in the environment and activities. However, it's always useful for the program staff to familiarize themselves with learning standards for the children and youth in their care as a way to support and enhance that learning. As an example, fractions are a typical part of the second-grade curriculum. While an after-school program would not need to teach the children fractions, as staff notice the children completing homework with fractions, they could add in math games and cooking activities to give the children additional experiences with the topic. The same goes for skills such as telling time or counting money, which are fairly easy to integrate and reinforce through games and activities in the program.

Consider the skills and concepts you want the children learn, and begin to formulate activities with learning outcomes in mind. Learning outcomes are specific statements of children's performance that can be demonstrated at the end of an activity or lesson. Outcome statements set the expectation for what students will be able to do and how they will apply that knowledge or skill. Take a look at the following examples:

As a result of this activity, the children will be able to:
- interpret a chart.
- count money and calculate change.
- compare and contrast the wants and needs of individuals.

Look carefully at the verbs in the examples above. Notice that they are statements of anticipated skills the children will demonstrate, rather than mere lists of activities. They describe what the children will be able to do or think as a result of instruction, and these outcomes can be measured in some manner. The following are not learning outcomes. Do you see why?

· The students will paint a picture with fall colors.
· The students will listen to a reading of a book.
· The students will keep journals about birds.
· The students will sing songs about the weather.

These activities might fill the blocks of a planning chart, and they explain what the children will do, but they do not describe what children will be able to do as a result of the activity. In the first example, no evaluation is possible, other than looking at the artwork to be sure everyone painted a picture. The second example is too vague: the children may listen to someone read a book, but for what purpose?

Learning outcomes should be stated in terms of **s**pecific, **m**easurable, **a**ction-oriented, **r**ealistic and **t**ime-bound (SMART) goals. For example, see the following description of a fund-raiser the children will hold to raise money for a local hospital.

As a result of organizing the lemonade stand and bake sale to raise money for the children's hospital, the children will be able to:

· bake cookies following written step-by-step directions.
· count money and make proper change at the lemonade stand.

See how these are SMART outcomes? They are specific; the children should be able to do these things, and if they cannot, someone can work with them until they master the task. They are measurable and action oriented; you know exactly how to assess the learning—just ask the children! They are realistic goals for the ages of the children who will be participating. They are time bound, as this goal can be met after the fund-raiser takes place (Galuski and Rider, 2017).

It is important to remember that while these rules for writing learning outcomes are helpful in describing what children will demonstrate, including all of the possibilities for a lesson is not very practical. Ideally, you should draft learning outcomes in terms that are specific enough to inform teaching and assessment but flexible enough that they do not limit the teacher's ability to modify the lesson as needed. According to Gunter, Estes, and Schwab (1995), "One must not take statements of objectives to such extreme specificity as to lose sight of the learners. Many times, the opportunity to teach an important lesson is unexpected and unintended." Consider someone who has created a lesson about cooking. Is the outcome following the recipe? Is it doing the math required in doubling the recipe? Is it understanding the chemistry involved in the process? Is it charting children's likes and dislikes as they sample the final product? Stating outcomes for learning allows teachers and children to focus on what is important in a learning experience. In addition, this approach helps the teacher clearly identify the type of instruction, materials, and facilitation that are needed to achieve the stated objective(s) and to evaluate the success of the instruction.

During snack time, a conversation emerged about different kinds of bread. Kai, the lead staff member, loves to bake, so she decided to use the children's interest in bread as an opportunity to explore food from different cultures. After making several kinds of bread, such as pita, challah, pretzels, naan, and Italian bread, with the children over time and learning about the areas of the world where the recipes originated, the students met the following learning outcomes:

- Demonstrate awareness of and appreciation for different cultures.

- Explore three simple chemical reactions, such as mixing baking soda and water and observing yeast dough rising, with teacher assistance.

- Describe three of the foods related to the student's own culture.

These outcomes are SMART because they are stated in terms that are specific, measurable, action oriented, realistic, and time bound. Through this learning experience, Kai could talk with the students as they were baking or ask them which kinds of bread they have eaten at the snack table, which are simple ways to assess whether or not the learning goals had been met.

## Using Bloom's Taxonomy to Develop Outcomes

Bloom's taxonomy offers a helpful framework for generating a list of verbs to create learning outcomes. In 1956, Dr. Benjamin Bloom led a team of experts in educational evaluation. They created what was coined Bloom's taxonomy to promote higher forms of thinking in education, such as analyzing and evaluating concepts, rather than having students merely remember and recite facts (in other words, rote learning). Bloom and his colleagues developed a taxonomy, or classification system, of educational objectives—clear and unambiguous descriptions of educational intentions for students.

Bloom's objectives were divided into three domains: cognitive (knowledge), affective (growth in feelings or emotional areas), and psychomotor (physical skills usually assessed with a checklist). In real life, of course, behaviors from these three domains occur simultaneously. While students are writing (psychomotor), they are also remembering or reasoning (cognitive), and they are likely to have some emotional response to the task as well (affective) (Woolfolk, 2010). Bloom's taxonomy has guided educators for more than fifty years.

Here, we will focus on the cognitive domain, which involves knowledge and the development of intellectual skills (Bloom, 1956). According to Woolfolk (2010), there are six basic objectives listed in the revised Bloom's taxonomy of the thinking or cognitive domain:

- Remember (Knowledge): Recognizing something with or without understanding it
- Understand (Comprehension): Grasping material without relating it to anything
- Apply (Application): Using a general concept to solve a particular problem
- Analyze (Analysis): Breaking a concept down into its parts
- Evaluate (Evaluation): Judging the value of methods as they might be applied in a particular situation
- Create (Synthesis): Creating something new by combining different ideas

It is common in education to consider these objectives as a hierarchy, with each skill building on those preceding it. The lower-level objectives (remember, understand, and apply) and the higher-level objectives (analyze, evaluate, and create) help us to think about objectives and plan assessments (Woolfolk, 2010).

When working with children, we often find comfort in using only the lower levels of Bloom's taxonomy. During group time, for example, we may have children recite multiplication facts or name state capitals. These are lower-level knowledge and comprehension activities. While some memorization serves as a building block for future learning, activities that allow children to analyze, evaluate, and create are higher-level objectives that expand their cognitive knowledge.

Instead of asking children to recite information, such as shapes, colors, or numbers, by rote to show that they remember them, we can ask them to, for example, compare and contrast the characteristics of different buttons (which is analyzing). The children can sort the buttons by shape, color, or number of thread holes. In analyzing, the children will also be demonstrating their understanding and knowledge of the specific characteristics.

Bloom's taxonomy offers action verbs in each of the six domains that you can use to create objectives that explain what learners will know or be able to do in specific, measurable terms.

# BLOOM'S TAXONOMY PYRAMID

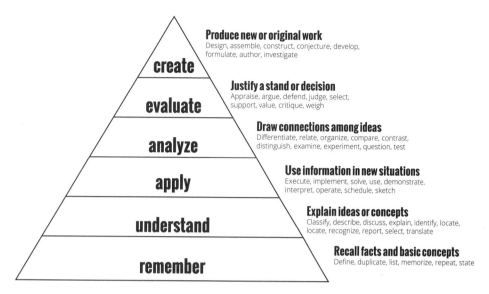

**create** — **Produce new or original work**
Design, assemble, construct, conjecture, develop, formulate, author, investigate

**evaluate** — **Justify a stand or decision**
Appraise, argue, defend, judge, select, support, value, critique, weigh

**analyze** — **Draw connections among ideas**
Differentiate, relate, organize, compare, contrast, distinguish, examine, experiment, question, test

**apply** — **Use information in new situations**
Execute, implement, solve, use, demonstrate, interpret, operate, schedule, sketch

**understand** — **Explain ideas or concepts**
Classify, describe, discuss, explain, identify, locate, locate, recognize, report, select, translate

**remember** — **Recall facts and basic concepts**
Define, duplicate, list, memorize, repeat, state

Source: Vanderbilt University Center for Teaching (https://cft.vanderbilt.edu/guides-sub-pages/blooms-taxonomy/).

Bloom's taxonomy can also be used to balance assessment and evaluative questions in program activities to ensure that the children are exercising all orders of thinking in their learning.

## Applying Outcome Statements to Activities

In daily activities we can observe children based on specific learning outcomes:

- Do the children use the new vocabulary during play?
- Are they able to rhyme along as the class sings songs and reads rhyming books together?

While it's not expected that every activity in a school-age program will have specific learning outcomes, this approach provides a framework and ensures that staff are thinking about curriculum that supports the learning needs of the children in the program.

Start with topics the children are interested in. Younger children enjoy everyday topics such as farming or pets; older children might prefer something that is relevant to their lives, such as an interesting theatrical play, music, the local sports team, or planning a fun fair for charity. Take some time to brainstorm potential topics on your own based on the children's interests and the resources available to the program, then share your ideas with the students to see what topics seem to generate excitement. Be sure to consider options that are interesting to both you and the children, so you can get excited about it together. Once you have selected the topic, the students will enjoy brainstorming potential activities with staff, who can then further develop the ideas along with learning outcomes to be sure activities serve a purpose.

In one program, the sibling of a child had a serious illness. The staff could see that the children wanted to do something to help their friend, so they researched local charities and learned about the Make-A-Wish Foundation. Over the next month, the children planned a bake sale to raise money to donate to the foundation. They sent a letter to the administration asking for permission, set up a budget, wrote a grocery list, baked the cookies within program hours, made flyers, and advertised the bake sale. They worked on the project over an extended period of time and were engaged in solving real-world problems. They ultimately demonstrated their knowledge by running the bake sale, a task that incorporates higher-level thinking skills, and collecting money and making change for a real audience—the children and families who attended the program and purchased the baked goods.

In another program, the staff developed a theme around money. The children made their own version of pretend money, set up a bank, and filled out job applications to be bankers who collected deposits and calculated bank interest. They learned about writing checks, earning interest, and various skills related to budgeting. Over the course of the theme, they earned pretend money for "jobs" such as organizing the art closet, raking leaves, making good grades, and exhibiting good behavior. They were fined for things such as leaving their coats on the floor or leaving trash at the snack table. The staff and students developed a successful token economy that was a lot of fun for everyone. At the end of the month, all the students had earned some money that they used in a classroom auction of donated used items. The learning outcomes in this experience supported math in many different ways.

## Using Project-Based Learning to Develop Outcomes

Some of the examples we've explored lend themselves to an approach called project-based learning, which is a teaching method by which students gain knowledge and skills by working for an extended period of time to investigate and respond to an authentic, engaging, and complex question, problem, or challenge. You for Youth (https://y4y.ed.gov/) offers free professional development, along with technical assistance for 21st Century Community Learning Centers, a federally funded initiative dedicated exclusively to after-school programs. The You for Youth website includes information about project-based learning and describes the benefits of authentic projects and engaging students in a process of inquiry. You can view their free online resources for more information about how to how to design hands-on projects and move from a driving question to a culminating event to a reflection on learning.

While developing curriculum, it may be helpful to note that older children, especially youth, need expanding opportunities for long-term activities. This can be challenging in programs where the children only attend for a brief period of time each day. Long-term activities can take many forms. For example, it might be a weaving project that children work on a little each day until it is complete. Or it might be an activity that has multiple steps, so the students continue to work through the steps and build on it day after day.

A challenge for many school-age programs is finding an appropriate space to save works in progress so they are available for prolonged periods of time. Staff can work through these challenges with the help of the children doing the work. For children who are working on small crafts, placing their materials in a labeled shoe box or bin might be enough so the projects can be safely stacked in a cupboard for another day. For something like a building-block project, it might be possible for children to build on a lunchroom tray or cookie sheet, which can be placed on a cabinet or tucked away in a closet. In programs that have permanent space, placing activities, such as a large puzzle or a game of Risk that takes several hours to complete, on a table that can be set aside or marked with a sign might be a possible solution.

# Finding New and Different Ideas

If you are new to the planning process, finding a fresh topic and coming up with a variety of activities can be challenging. There are many resources available online to help you get started, but keep in mind that not all resources are professional, and the ideas provided may be out of date or not particularly relevant for your program and the interests of your students. It's easy to find activities to copy and worksheets and games to print out online, but staff need to carefully evaluate these materials to ensure they are age appropriate and offer quality experiences. As a starting place, look for activities shared in free publications by the National AfterSchool Association and other professional websites. The following is a list of other websites that offer examples of activities to challenge school-age children:

- Steve Spangler Science (https://www.stevespanglerscience.com/)
- PBS Learning Media (https://pbslearningmedia.org/)
- Science Kids (https://www.sciencekids.co.nz/)
- Funbrain (https://www.funbrain.com/)
- Multiplication.com (https://www.multiplication.com/)
- Math Game Time (http://www.mathgametime.com/)
- iCivics (https://www.icivics.org/)
- Stanford History Education Group (https://sheg.stanford.edu/)
- Historical Thinking Matters (http://historicalthinkingmatters.org/)

Terrance has worked really hard at safely integrating woodworking and other challenging activities into his program. One vocal parent disagrees with the program's use of a woodworking center, as well as the take-apart center that includes radios, clocks, keyboards, and so forth. She feels that despite the careful supervision and mandatory safety goggles in these two centers, it's unsafe for school-age children to use real tools. Terrance has explained that these hands-on activities contribute to children's eye-hand coordination, small-muscle development, cognitive development, and curiosity, but the parent has threatened to report the program to the licensing agency. How would you handle this situation?

One program was focused on the topic of animals, so when someone brought in a bag of dried catnip, the children were inspired to sew tiny pillows stuffed with polyester fiberfill and catnip for their pets. The staff developed the curriculum by offering a series of activities around the topic of pets. In this specific example, the instruction occurred as someone had previously taught a small group the skill of sewing, which supported state instructional standards for art. The staff then conducted informal assessment by simply observing which children chose to sew the catnip pillows and were growing comfortable with their new sewing skills. Not everything has to be directly related to the topic, and the children could have chosen just about anything to sew, but in this case the ideas flowed naturally as the children discovered animal-print fabric in the bin and the staff were able to support their ideas.

Dakota is a director of a site with about twenty children, and she has two staff members. In the arts and crafts area, children were using collage materials and glue to create different types of projects, but the staff insisted that the children's creations have something to do with the theme of the week: dinosaurs. One boy, JJ, felt particularly inspired by the dinosaur theme and decided to create his very own species of dinosaur. As he was making his paper-plate dino, he asked for scissors to cut some yarn into short pieces to make a mane. One of the staff members told him that they were not going to take out scissors today and that dinosaurs do not have manes. JJ grew frustrated with this limitation on his creativity. He stood up to leave the area, but the staff member reminded him that it wasn't time to switch areas, gestured toward the stopwatch, and asked him to wait five more minutes before he changed activities.

# Evaluating Activities

The typical instructional cycle is one of ongoing assessment, planning and setting curriculum goals, and implementation. We've gone full circle, starting with assessing children's needs, interests, and skills, moving to developing a topic, defining the learning outcomes, and planning the instructional activities. Now we are ready to loop back around to assessment. For the purpose of school-age programs, informal assessment is typically the most appropriate way to determine what learning has occurred. Let's see what this might look like in practice.

## Daily Planning and Evaluation

Justin's program is small, as he works with only about six to eight children on a daily basis. Because he is the only staff person, he is very flexible with the curriculum and can move from one topic to another fairly quickly. The children move through many activities as a group, but he offers choices and lets them decide what they'd like to do and tries to be flexible based on their needs. Every day he checks in with them to see what they are doing and talks with them about what he can add to enhance their activities the following day.

One Monday a child brought in a catapult kit that he had received as a gift over the weekend. Over a few days, a few children worked together to build the kit and then began to experiment by launching a number of items across the room. Justin offered suggestions for minor adjustments to the components of the catapult and gave the children a measuring tape so they could measure and record distance as they launched objects. A couple of days later, the children assembled a castle in the block area to attack. As the other children asked to join in, Justin looked into different ways to make catapults and brought in materials for the other children so everyone could experiment with their own catapults. Every day he observed the activity, added new items, and evaluated what they were learning and how it was going. After about two weeks, they stopped playing with the catapults, and Justin knew it was time to move on to something else.

## Weekly Planning and Evaluation

Sharon works in a large program that serves anywhere from forty-five to fifty children on a daily basis. The children range in age from five to eleven, so they have varied interests. As a result, the program has developed a flexible routine with many activity centers; even the snacks and the playground are open most of the afternoon. Staff members are stationed at the messy or popular activity centers, and the children are encouraged to self-select their activities throughout the day.

At the beginning of each week, Sharon meets with the staff to discuss the theme, develop some new activities, and ask them to explore ways to enhance and expand the topics. At the end of each week, she checks in to evaluate how things are going, decide which activities should be rotated out, and begin planning new activities for the next week. She recognizes it is important for programs to evaluate their activity offerings to ensure that children are enjoying them and that they are meeting program objectives and goals.

## Monthly Planning and Evaluation

Tessa works at a medium-size program that serves about eighteen children ages six to twelve. The children come from two different schools, so they arrive at different times in the afternoon. Tessa has learned through experience that the most effective way to plan the day is to help the first group get settled, then serve a snack, followed by some flexible homework time. As those children move into activity centers, her coworker greets the second group, serves them snacks, and then helps them with homework time. The staggered schedule allows the staff to get to know the children and have more individual time with the smaller groups before the children move outside or into larger group activities.

Tessa plans a regular monthly planning meeting with her staff to develop the theme and ask for input. They have a lot of discussions with the children and share the activities that are popular at the moment so each staff member can bring ideas of things they can share. At the end of each month, they follow up with a discussion surrounding the evaluation of activities that have taken place. They collect feedback from the students through discussion and through anonymous activity surveys to find out whether children liked an activity and to get ideas for improving activity offerings. Collecting feedback on these activities and discussing how they were received, how they could be extended or enhanced, or whether to even offer them again is important knowledge to have in planning future activities.

## Scheduling

Each program needs to develop a schedule and routine based on the needs of the students it serves. Let the children be your guide as you work to develop a plan. They'll let you know if they need more time to relax or more active play outside before they are ready for snack. Keep the schedule flexible while ensuring they have enough time to complete activities and meet learning outcomes. Think about the following questions as you consider the schedule for your program:

- Is there adequate time for the children to relax after the school day?
- Is snack served in a relaxed manner, where children have time to sit and talk with each other?
- Is there adequate time for gross-motor and/or outside play?
- Are the children ready to move with transitions, or do they ask for more time?
- Do the children have opportunities to self-select activities?

## Conclusion

In this chapter, we have discussed how to integrate project-based, youth-centered learning that supports learning standards in your program. We have explored the cycle of curriculum, instruction, and assessment as it applies to school-age programs. We have learned how long-term activities or project-based activities can offer children valuable experience in problem solving, communication, and following through. Curriculum should be balanced, integrated, and driven primarily by the interests of children and staff. After reading the chapter, how might this change how you plan the curriculum in your program?

 SOLUTIONS

### Tenisha Needs New Ideas

Thinking about Tenisha and her small program from the opening vignette, it sounds like she could use a little support developing a curriculum and adding more advanced options. While it's fine to start the afternoon with snack, homework, and a few simple activities as the initial options, the children need more choices in activities for the rest of the afternoon. They have spent much of their school day moving as a group, and by the end of the day it's better to offer options. While it may seem easier to work in a smaller program, a small program offers different challenges, such as a mixed-age group with little in common.

Tenisha determined that she needed to develop a topic and plan some activities around something that was more meaningful to the children. She planned a group time in which the children brainstormed themes and shared their interests. Then she used her planning time to come up with specific activities and shared them in the days that followed.

Based on these discussions, she began to develop more learning centers that she stored in large bins and offered as additional choices for her small group. One bin, labeled *art supplies*, supported her in teaching a new technique or art idea, such as knitting, weaving, or watercolor painting, to the students who were interested. Another bin included games, which she rotated. A third bin included more advanced science activities and a science kit she had acquired. She began to recognize that, although this was a small group and the children knew each other, they had very different interests and wanted to explore them in different ways, rather than as a whole group.

## Addressing Parent Concerns about Activities

While family involvement can be good for programming, how can Terrance help a concerned parent understand how children's play in activities such as woodworking serves as a vehicle for learning? He could invite the parent to spend time in the program to join the children and observe the learning that goes on in these carefully supervised centers. He could talk with the parent about the developmental levels of manipulation, mastery, and meaning that grow as children create with wood or learn the operations and workings of small clocks and radios, and he could explain all the safety procedures the program has in place (Beaty, 2008). While this may not be all it takes to change the parent's mind, sometimes watching children engage in the process of these two centers can help a parent gain insight into the learning taking place. If this does not work and the parent is still adamant, Terrance could ask the parent for suggestions and explore other activities that might engage children. He might also ask the parent whether she has a skill to share; this may go a long way in warming the parent up to promoting children's hands-on learning.

## Meeting JJ's Creative Needs

Dakota has observed some staff practices that are not ideal in the arts and crafts area, and she has decided to address these issues in a staff meeting. As she sees it, they have three different things to talk about: the goals of the activity, the strict adherence to the week's theme, and the strict adherence to the time allotted for each activity.

The staff needs to review and assess the goals of creative art and their specific activities. Certainly, there are times when children may ask for supplies the program may not currently have, but the program has scissors that are easily accessible. When staff refuse to give children materials that allow them to enhance or expand their creations, this stifles the children's creativity. The process of the creation is often more valuable than the finished product. JJ had a specific purpose for the scissors, and it was consistent with the theme, so best practice suggests he should have been permitted the scissors, with supervision if necessary, to enhance his creation.

The second issue is the staff's strict adherence to creations reflecting the theme of the week. Theme-based activities can be fun but also can squelch the creativity of some children if the activities are too narrowly focused. The likelihood dinosaurs did not have manes should not crush JJ's creativity and prevent him from creating one. Staff should again look to the goals of the activity and, when assessing, be cautious not to squelch creativity when children drift from theme-related activities to ones they may be inspired to create during the process. Chapter 8 speaks more to enhancing children's creativity and respecting their divergent thinking and exploration.

The third issue is the strict adherence to set times as children rotate between activities. While a seemingly good idea, this practice can pose issues for children who do not wish to participate in an activity and for those who want to spend more time with an activity. Perhaps Dakota can change the program routine to allow the children to come and go between activities as they desire and as space is available. In this way, children's needs are being met and the program is more reflective of developmentally appropriate practice.

# THINK. ACT. REFLECT.

## Think.

Think about some themes or activities that you recall from your childhood educational experiences. Perhaps it was a special math unit during which the teacher organized a classroom store, or perhaps it was a science unit that included a lot of hands-on activities. Why do these particular activities stand out in your mind after all this time? Try to think of some concrete aspects that made them special.

## Act.

Brainstorm a list of potential project-based themes that might be meaningful to the children in your program. Sit down with them in small groups and explore the topics. As a group, select one that everyone seems particularly interested in. Brainstorm potential activities, discuss possible learning outcomes, and share ways you might assess those activities. Plan it out.

## Reflect.

Reflect on your initial childhood educational experience. Would you have enjoyed the theme that you selected as a group? Which activities stand out for you, and why?

section **2**

# Applying Child-Development Principles to School-Age Care

# chapter 6 | Physical Development

Lola is a director of an inner-city after-school program located in an elementary school. The children can no longer use the wonderful outdoor school playground because of recent neighborhood violence and a nearby shooting. The gym space is shared with the school's intramural basketball team and is not always available. How can Lola ensure that the children in her program receive at least thirty minutes of gross-motor activity a day?

School-age programs recognize that after a long day in school, children want to move around and have time to themselves. Children in these programs typically need some type of physical activity soon after arriving. Physical activity helps children develop coordination skills and strength and helps to release tension. This chapter will highlight the changes that characterize body growth and motor skills for school-age children, then examine central issues in children's development and provide suggestions for physical activities such as cooperative games. Reasonable expectations for physical development within specific age groupings are included.

Physical development is commonly divided into two major areas: growth and development. *Growth* is defined by the physical changes of the body, such as the increase in size, height, and weight that typically occurs as children grow. *Physical development*, on the other hand, defines how children gain control over their physical actions through muscle control. Growth and development go hand in hand because the development and improvement of physical skills depends on the size of the child and the muscular strength that follows a typical sequence.

Physical development is further differentiated by large- or gross-motor and small- or fine-motor skills. Gross-motor skills are the abilities required to control the large muscles of the body and may include running and jumping. Fine-motor skills are associated with grasping, holding, writing, and putting things together, such as small interlocking blocks. The development of these skills relies on core trunk control and shoulder strength that provides a stable base so the arm and hand can move with control. Without gaining strength in fine-motor skills, a child may be able to do small tasks and then might lack confidence to do other tasks. Improving gross- and fine-motor skills promotes children's cognitive and social development.

Being physically active promotes growth of muscles and bones and cardiovascular health and can help children develop a lifelong pattern of exercise. The CDC suggests that children ages six through seventeen do one hour or more of moderate-to-vigorous physical activial activity daily (https://www.cdc.gov/healthyschools/physicalactivity/guidelines.htm). Regular physical activity can be important for promoting lifelong health and well-being and can prevent risk factors for various health conditions such as heart disease, obesity, and type 2 diabetes. Many school-age children are unaccustomed to regular exercise and may even be overweight. Enjoyable games that require vigorous movement can go a long way toward offsetting this trend and may even kindle an interest in sports among children who have not had an opportunity to play.

Overall, school-age children grow 1 to 3 inches a year and gain about 5 to 8 pounds or more. The weight increase is due mainly to increases in the size of the skeletal and muscular systems, as well as the size of some body organs. Muscle mass and strength gradually increase as "baby fat" decreases. The increase in muscular strength is due to heredity and exercise. Children also double their strength capabilities during these years. Let's break down physical development by stage and age.

## Development from Five to Seven Years Old

Children this age make great advances in gross-motor skills and have increased muscle strength. As they gain greater control over motor skills, their movements are more precise and deliberate, although some clumsiness persists (Allen and Marotz, 2000). Most children have increased dexterity and eye-hand coordination, along with improved motor functioning, which facilitates learning to ride a bicycle, swing a bat, or kick a ball with accuracy (Allen and Marotz). We can often find large individual differences in young children's fine-motor ability. Some children, such as those born with chromosomal conditions such as Down syndrome and those exposed to alcohol during prenatal development, tend to progress more slowly than their age-mates (McDevitt and Ormrod, 2007). Some evidence indicates that certain fine-motor activities, such as cursive handwriting, may be easier for girls than boys. Fortunately, explicit instruction and practice can help children improve fine-motor skills, although some differences in dexterity inevitably persist (McDevitt and Ormrod).

Children develop best physically when they can be active at a developmentally appropriate level of unstructured free play. Programs can support physical development by offering children the opportunity to climb and jump on safe, properly sized equipment. In addition, provide children opportunities to practice physical skills, such as doing a cartwheel, dribbling a ball, and hitting a ball, and have staff offer gentle coaching when a child seems to need help. To support children who are insecure about their physical strength or ability, high-quality programs create movement stations, which provide opportunities for children to develop and improve specific skills. The stations can accommodate a wide range of skill levels, and children can select what they want to work on and improve, at their own pace.

While children may begin to join teams and learn the rules for formal games such as baseball or soccer, the strategies for offense and defense are still elusive, so instruction needs to be age appropriate. Picture a game of soccer where every player chases the ball the entire time, even the goalie. At this age many children prefer to just to kick the balls around. Offering them many balls to play with provides more opportunity for skill development than giving them one ball and asking them to wait their turn. Similarly, providing games with minimal rules and minimal "outs" encourages children to have fun and be successful.

## Development from Eight to Ten Years Old

In this age group, arms and legs grow longer, and body shape takes on a more mature appearance. Children this age range exhibit significant improvement in agility, balance, speed, and strength (Allen and Marotz, 2000). According to McDevitt and Ormrod (2007), children within this age range improve fine-motor skills. Their drawings are more detailed, as they are supported by physiological maturation and cognitive advances. They also begin to tackle such fine-motor activities as sewing, model building, and arts and crafts projects (McDevitt and Ormrod). As children progress through this age range, they become increasingly sensitive about their physical appearance and their self-consciousness increases as they get closer to puberty. Although many children exaggerate their own physical flaws, the reality is that appearance is influential in social relationships, and it does affect how children feel about themselves (McDevitt and Ormrod).

To support physical development in this age group, offer vigorous activities such as dancing, ice skating, swimming, riding bikes, and flying kites. Children this age often seek opportunities to participate in organized team activities and games, such as basketball, kickball, and soccer. By this age, rules of games make more sense, but the children will have varying levels of experience. Children with a basketball hoop in their driveway who love the game may know all the rules; other children may have never had that experience. When setting up games with the children, it's important to review rules, practice skills, and follow the game to help everyone at their respective level.

## Development from Ten to Twelve Years Old

Changes in physical growth and development are quite different from child to child during this period. Girls in particular grow more rapidly, and some may be experiencing some of the early hormonal changes associated with puberty, such as the development of breasts, hips becoming shapelier, and the onset of menses. It is important at this stage to present a positive picture of becoming a woman and to keep the channels of communication open. This age group can become more private about their lives. Boys tend to physically mature later than girls, but at this age boys may become exceptionally competitive and see social status as being tied to sports ability.

To support this age group's physical development, it is important to support physical activity that will promote a good body image. Children this age usually enjoy physical activities, including team activities. Have resource material regarding sign-ups for community or school program teams and provide ample time for this age group to engage in physical activity.

## Development from Twelve to Fourteen Years Old

Changes in physical growth and development are still quite different from child to child. A growth spurt usually occurs at this age. Boys begin to grow facial and underarm hair and may lag behind girls in height but will usually end up taller. Most girls are menstruating, and both boys and girls are showing physical signs of puberty.

Many children this age become less active as organized sport activities become more competitive and teams become more selective. Daily physical activity is important during this stage for children to develop strength, so it is important to focus on activities they show interest in, such as jogging, yoga, or cycling. Some twelve- to fourteen-year-olds may prefer individual activities, such as karate, yoga, aerobics, or swimming, rather than group sports and activities. In cases where the children have interests that lie outside the skills of the staff, outside resources may help. By engaging a karate instructor to offer a weekly karate class or asking a yoga instructor to help them get started with some basic poses, for example, or even by using instructional videos, staff can support this age group in their physical development—and their own as well!

To further encourage children this age, let them organize many physical activities and games themselves. Program staff should tolerate some bickering as children fuss over rules, negotiate and compromise, and learn other ways to get along. By permitting these children to organize and develop their own games, they will have the opportunity to learn to be good leaders.

# Sexual Development, Gender Identification, and Attraction

Physical development also includes the changes in the body as children reach puberty. In most cases, their bodies undergo a series of biological changes that lead to reproductive maturity between the ages of nine and fourteen. This is marked not only by the maturation of sex-specific characteristics but also by a growth spurt in height and weight. Girls typically go through the process before boys do, starting with a growth spurt, breast development, and the emergence of pubic hair (McDevitt and Ormrod, 2007). These changes are gradual; whereas, the start of menstruation is an abrupt event that can be either positive or scary, depending on the girl's awareness and preparation. Having sanitary products available and making sure that girls know where they are located may ease any initial stress and concern. During school hours, they know to go to a nurse for help, but it's helpful to have some emergency supplies, such as sanitary napkins in varying sizes and packages of new underwear in a couple of sizes, available in case of staining or emergencies.

Boys begin puberty between nine and fourteen years, when the testes enlarge and the scrotum changes in color and texture. About a year later, the penis grows larger and pubic hair appears, and then the growth spurt occurs. At about thirteen or fourteen years old, boys have their first ejaculation experience, often while sleeping. Boys seem to receive less information from their parents about this milestone than girls do about menstruation; therefore, little is known about their feelings about it (McDevitt and Ormrod, 2007). Later developments include growth of facial hair, deepening of the voice, and reaching adult height. Interestingly, in girls, puberty *begins* with the growth spurt, and with boys, puberty *ends* with the growth spurt.

Children begin to develop interest in the opposite and/or same sex at varying ages, depending on environment, psychological readiness, and values. Gender is an integral part of personal identity, and children who are unclear about their gender can be confused in their self-concept. According to Jason Rafferty and colleagues in their 2018 article in *Pediatrics*, "Being a boy or girl, for most children, is something that feels very natural. . . . [B]abies are assigned male or female based on physical characteristics. This refers to the 'sex' or 'assigned gender' of the child. Meanwhile, 'gender identity' refers to an internal sense people have of who they are that comes from an interaction of biological traits, developmental influences, and environmental conditions. This may be male, female, somewhere in between, a combination of both or neither." Self-recognition of gender identity develops over time, and most children's gender identity aligns with their assigned gender. However, Rafferty and colleagues assert, for some children, the match between their assigned gender and gender identity is not so clear.

In terms of gender development, most children can easily label themselves as a boy or girl by age three and by age four have a stable sense of gender identity. Some children, as Rafferty and colleagues explain, do not identify with either gender.

Both genders have some capacity for sexual arousal even before puberty. Children and preadolescents occasionally look at or touch one another in private places and play games that have sexual overtones. Except in cases of sexual abuse, sexuality before adolescence lacks the erotic features present in later development.

Although sexual maturation is a natural process, knowing how to best handle the sexuality of children is challenging for everyone: parents, teachers, staff, and children themselves. When parents and teachers do broach the subject of sexuality, it is often to speak about problems such as irresponsible behavior, disease, or unwanted pregnancy. With puberty and a growing interest in the opposite and/or same sex, programs may find some special challenges. Some programs have reported issues with curious children as young as eleven and twelve experimenting with the opposite and/or same sex during program hours. General awareness of the children in the program, coupled with close supervision, can ensure that nothing inappropriate happens.

Children and adolescents must come to terms with their emerging sexuality, either on their own or, in most cases, in collaboration with trusted peers. They must learn to accept their changing bodies, cope with unanticipated feelings of sexual arousal and desire, and try to cope with conflicting messages from home, school, religious groups, peers, and the media as to what levels of sexual intimacy are appropriate.

In school-age programs it is important not to make assumptions about children's sexual orientation or gender identity and to support children who question their sexuality or identify as LGBTQ+ (lesbian, gay, bisexual, transgender, questioning, and everything in between). A *lesbian* is a woman who is attracted to other women; similarly, *gay* refers to a man or woman attracted to the same gender. *Bisexual* refers to a man or woman who is attracted to both genders. *Transgender* describes people whose gender identity differs from the sex assigned to them at birth. *Questioning* describes a person, often a preteen or adolescent, who has questions about his or her gender identity or sexual orientation. Many LGBTQ+ individuals report being aware of their sexual orientation as very young children; others may not have been aware of their sexual orientation or gender identity until they were older adults. Families are not always supportive of their children as they identify their sexuality, and it's very important for staff to recognize these challenges, identify any personal bias, and respond in supportive ways

One after-school program had a nine-year-old boy enrolled whom the staff called "It." The children immediately followed suit and began to ridicule, bully, and harass this child, who was struggling with his gender identity. In this case, rather than support the child, the staff escalated a situation that quickly became a hostile environment for this child. The staff should have realized that this nine-year-old is just a child whom their program should be protecting and supporting. They should have immediately squelched any discussion or action surrounding homophobia, transphobia, and anti-LGBTQ+; curbed their own judgments; and built a warm, nurturing after-school community that promoted acceptance and diversity.

How can we help children struggling with gender identity? First and foremost, make your program a safe place, where anti-LGBTQ+ language is not tolerated. It is important for staff to be available to all children but especially to those struggling with gender identity. Staff should ask children how they wish to be identified and what name they prefer to be called. If a student discloses a struggle and staff are uncomfortable, encourage staff to support the child as best they can. Meet with school or community organizations to learn about ways to better support LGBTQ+ children, and learn to create an inclusive school-age program that highlights the contributions of minorities and LGBTQ+ individuals. Create a nondiscriminatory policy for your program that includes sexuality and gender identity.

# Physical Development and Children with Special Needs

Some children have long-term physical conditions, such as chronic illness, serious injuries, or physical disabilities, that may affect school performance, friendships, and leisure activities. Some chronically sick children show few if any symptoms, but others have noticeable limitations in strength, vitality, or alertness. Children with Down syndrome, for example, are more susceptible to sprains and dislocations because of poor muscle tone and excessive mobility in their joints. Children with Ehlers-Danlos syndrome, a connective tissue disorder, often have weak muscle tone and loose joints that are unstable and prone to dislocation and chronic pain. An innocent activity such as tug-of-war, for example, can easily dislocate a child's shoulder. Children with physical disabilities, such as blindness, cerebral palsy, congenital heart problems, or muscular dystrophy, have the same basic needs as other children for regular physical activity but may have specially adapted equipment, such as a wheelchair or crutches, and need an environmental layout that permits safe movement. Some children with physical disabilities, especially those with multiple handicaps, have cognitive as well as physical impairments, but many others have intellectual capabilities similar to those of their nondisabled peers. Because physical activity and exercise are vital to health and fitness, program staff must find ways to adapt physical activities for all children with special needs.

Some medical conditions, such as asthma and diabetes, may cause a child to tire easily and have low strength and endurance. Asthma is a chronic lung disease that involves episodes of airflow obstruction. Symptoms of an asthma attack include shortness of breath, wheezing, or tightness in the chest. According to the Asthma and Allergy Foundation of America (AAFA, 2019), there are about 6.2 million children

The Americans with Disabilities Act, Section 504 of the Rehabilitation Act of 1973, prohibits places of public accommodation, including child-care and after-school programs, from discriminating against a person on the basis of disability. Such places must afford "full and equal enjoyment" of the facility and services and must make reasonable accommodations for the individual. For more information, see http://www.adata.org

under the age of eighteen with asthma, translating in 2017 to one in twelve children. Asthma is the third-ranking cause of hospitalization among children younger than fifteen (AAFA). The condition may restrict the child's participation time. In situations like these, it's recommended that programs require a doctor's note so that staff best understand any limitations a child may have. While exercise doesn't cause asthma, different types of breathing during exercise or the pollen count and allergens in the air can trigger an asthma attack. Games such as volleyball, gymnastics, dance, and baseball are good choices for children with asthma, as they have short periods of movement followed by breaks. Programs should have a personal asthma action plan created by the child's pediatrician so staff can act quickly should an asthma attack happen. In addition, programs can ask parents of children with asthma to give the staff informal training on the signs, symptoms, and other relevant information of asthma, or programs can look for professional training in
the community.

Children with special needs are often overlooked or excluded when physical activities are planned or implemented. In most cases, the intention is not deliberate but more likely due to a lack of understanding of a child's ability. The benefits for physical play for special needs children are roughly the same as for all children: skill development, social-emotional well-being, and greater confidence. In addition, physical play offers special benefits to children with special needs, including managing functional decline, facilitating life-skill competencies, increasing independence, and enhancing socialization.

Most games can easily be adapted to include children with special needs, even if a child's walker slows her down or the child doesn't readily grasp the rules of the game on the first try. High-quality programs encourage all children to help each other and play together in cooperative ways. Think through some

School's Out: Challenges and Solutions for School-Age Programs

options before program hours, and plan for the physical development of the children in your care. For example, in one program the staff had set up a relay race. With two teams, one child from each team was supposed to dribble a ball across the gym, throw the ball at the basket until they were successful, and then dribble it back to their team so other children could go. The game was fun for a few minutes as the first children successfully dribbled the ball across the gym and quickly made a basket, but the next couple of children struggled and the entire team watched as they tried again and again and again. The enthusiastic shouting and cheering soon turned to shouts of, "Can't you even get a basket?!" Unfortunately, this version of the relay game quickly focused on those children who were shorter or had little experience with a basketball. A simple adjustment, such as setting out many balls and encouraging lots of children to shoot baskets on their own terms, with some baskets at a normal height and a couple set at a lower height, would offer a much more discreet opportunity to practice and play. Doing this not only promotes inclusion of all children with disabilities, but it also makes participation more fun for all the other children who are not as athletic or skilled physically.

Physical disorders that children may have include orthopedic impairments, such as cerebral palsy. This condition involves restrictions in movements because of muscle, bone, or joint problems. Children who struggle with mobility cannot move freely and safely in some physical-activity situations. With the help of adaptive devices and medical technology, many children with orthopedic impairment function well in after-school programs. Careful and creative planning is required for the safe use of walkers, crutches, wheelchairs, and motorized scooters in crowded spaces and while other children are moving. Accommodations are needed to allow more time and greater space for children using special equipment. Cognitive limitations and information-processing problems may affect a child's communication, attention span, or ability to follow directions, remember, problem solve, or carry out some complex activities. Providing careful directions and simplifying steps can help these children to understand games and participate with their peers.

Mindful programs include all children when deciding what games are played, for how long, and how often. When working with school-age children, it is important for program staff to participate in the games as well as organize them, as long as staff continue to supervise the group while playing. It is more fun for children if their group leaders participate in play with them.

# Cultural Considerations and Physical Activity

Consider the ethnicities and cultures of the children in your program, and include physical activities that represent everyone. High-quality programs offer children opportunities to learn skills and traditional games from their own and others' cultures. Many common games such as kite-flying and hopscotch appear in different cultural contexts but are modified in varied ways, creating local versions, using local resources, and called by different names, even within a single language. For example, *oonch neech* is a Pakistani version of tag. Chilean children play *Corre, Corre, La Guaraca*, a game similar to Duck, Duck, Goose. Quality programs seek ways to develop activities and games that are respectful of cultural heritage and values.

Children gain appreciation for their own and others' cultures by playing games from different countries. For example, in different regions of Brazil, the game of marbles is called *búrica* or *búlica* and is played with mudballs or cashew nuts (Gosso and Almeida Carvalho, 2013). One can imagine the confusion and resistance of Brazilian children if they are asked to use a beautiful marble for play. All over the world, games are often played as part of celebrations or for holidays. For example, Catch the Dragon's Tail is played during Chinese New Year celebrations. In San Juan, Puerto Rico, checkers games bring groups together in a common activity on Saturday nights. In some cultures, games teach children skills they may need for survival. For example, in Botswana the game of Stalker, much like hide-and-seek but with a blindfolded hunter and blindfolded prey, teaches the real-life skills of concentration and patience.

# Trends in Physical Activity and Obesity

According to the Institute of Medicine's *Educating the Student Body: Taking Physical Activity and Physical Education to School* (2013), few children in the United States—probably no more than half—meet the currently recommended standard of at least sixty minutes of vigorous or moderate-intensity physical activity daily. The proportion meeting the standard declines with age, with more elementary school children than middle and high school students achieving the goal. Boys are more likely than girls to meet the recommendation.

During the past thirty to forty years, the volume and intensity of daily physical activity among youth have gradually declined in schools. According to the Institute of Medicine, "Fewer than one-quarter of all states require physical activity outside of physical education for all grade levels, and only about 1 in 5 states require daily recess at the elementary level. Requirements for physical activity outside of physical education decrease significantly at the middle and high school levels, and recess policies apply only to elementary schools." Childhood obesity is a serious problem in the United States, putting children and adolescents at risk for poor health. According to the CDC (2019), in the United States the percentage of children and adolescents affected by obesity has more than tripled since the 1970s. Data from 2015–2016 show that nearly one in five school-age children and young people (six to nineteen years old) in the United States is obese. Obesity prevalence was 13.9 percent among two- to five-year-olds, 18.4 percent among six- to eleven-year-olds, and 20.6 percent among twelve- to nineteen-year-olds (CDC). Childhood obesity is also more common among certain populations: Hispanics (25.8 percent) and non-Hispanic Blacks (22.0 percent) had higher obesity prevalence than non-Hispanic Whites (14.1 percent) (CDC).

As discussed in chapter 3, high-quality school-age programs can play a role in helping children achieve and maintain a healthy weight by adopting policies and practices to encourage a healthy lifestyle. Through helping children eat more fruits and vegetables, practicing healthy portion control, offering fewer foods and beverages that are high in added sugar, and increasing the daily minutes of physical activity, children will learn healthy habits.

# Encouraging Physical Activity

McDevitt and Ormrod (2007) recommend some specific strategies that staff can follow to promote physical activity:

· **Be proactive:** Staff can incorporate physical activity into many activities.
· **Provide appropriate equipment and guidance:** Encourage children to safely engage in physical activity and exercise. Provide an open space and balls and other props needed to play games. Staff may need to intervene occasionally to minimize physical aggression, remind children to follow safety rules, and encourage children who do not readily join in but want to participate.
· **Make exercise an enjoyable activity:** By the time children reach middle school, many have had unpleasant experiences with physical exercise. As a result, they may associate exercise with discomfort, embarrassment, competitiveness, boredom, injury, and failure. Children are more likely to engage in physical activity if they enjoy it and find it reasonably challenging.
· **Plan physical activities with diversity in mind:** Not every child will be a pitcher, and not every child likes baseball. In fact, it's probably a minority of children who are drawn to competitive sports, but nearly all children can find enjoyment in physical activity of some form. Be sure to offer a variety, from dance to volleyball, and remember to modify activities for children with varying abilities, to maximize the number of children who participate.
· **Focus on self-improvement rather than comparisons with peers:** Focusing on one's own improvement is, for most children, far more motivating than focusing on how their performance compares to others. Focusing too much on competition with others may lead children to believe that physical ability is largely a matter of natural talent when in fact most skills depend on practice. Utilizing self-progress charts may benefit some children, but keep these private; do not post a chart for everyone to see.

## Adapting the Environment to Meet Physical Needs

Fine-motor skills, those that involve more finely tuned movements such as finger dexterity, are used in everyday life and are mostly indoor activities. Program staff should provide fine-motor materials in each interest area and reflect on how they can help the children to develop and use fine-motor skills in meaningful ways. For example, with younger children, writing, pasting and gluing, scissor skills, tying shoes, and maneuvering a mouse when using a computer require fine-motor skills. Promote fine-motor development through activities such as knitting, woodworking, doing puzzles, drawing, building with Legos and other manipulatives, beading, painting, tracing, making jewelry and lanyards, playing an instrument, and so forth.

According to Janice Beaty (2008), when children are presented with a new material, "they play around with it, exploring it with their senses." She calls this exploration *manipulation*. Next, she says, children learn how to work the material; this second level of use is *mastery*. They will repeat the correct use of the material over and over. The third level of exploration, one that many but not all children engage in, is *meaning*. At this level, children put the material to some new and different use. These three developmental learning levels— manipulation, mastery, and meaning—are referred to as the 3Ms.

Offer a well-stocked writing center that includes a wide variety of writing mediums. Provide a variety of materials in the art center as well. As children get older, they will move away from fat markers and crayons and will gravitate to thin markers and colored pencils for precision in their creation. Imagine the frustration of a creative child when only crayons are available! Limited materials can cause a lack of interest. Adding developmentally appropriate writing and drawing mediums such as colored pencils, colored pens, charcoal pencils, calligraphy pens, metallic pencils, oil pastels, and thin felt markers, along with materials such as white and colored paper, rulers, a paper punch, transparent tape, two-sided tape, envelopes, protractors, and templates, can give the writing and art areas renewed interest and spark children's creativity.

Gross-motor activity can be enjoyed both indoors and outdoors. Provide some basic supplies, such as basketballs, footballs, soccer balls, playground balls for kicking, jump ropes, cones, large plastic hoops, and an air pump. Consider including beach balls, balls of all sizes, and Frisbees too. Programs should have at least one colorful parachute! Children love being under them, running in circles, watching the silk billow, and collapsing among the folds when the parachute deflates and falls. Most parachute play consists of placing six to twenty children around the outside of a parachute, where they each take a firm hold of the edge and lift the parachute up and down. One fun game is to throw a beach ball on top of a taut parachute and encourage the children to create waves as they move the ball around but prevent it from hitting the ground.

Providing physical activity can be challenging for programs that have space limitations, during inclement weather, or when scheduling conflicts occur for the program's allotted physical activity space. Even in small classroom spaces, however, warming up, working out for fitness, and cooling-down exercises, as well as other movement activities, are doable. An activity such as navigating a classroom road map with turns and twists and actions such as crawling under a table or walking a wiggly rope path can be fun. Staff can engage children in playing popular game shows, learning rhythm through dancing, and doing other popular activities while standing in place. The book *No Gym? No Problem! Physical Activities for Tight Spaces* by Charmain Sutherland is a great resource for programs with limited space. Sutherland (2005) encourages programs with limited space to explore the possibilities: "You will not only find your way but also become more creative, innovative, and resourceful! Without doubt, a gym is a wonderful classroom for teaching physical education and activities. But don't doubt the possibilities and opportunities that you have to teach great physical education lessons and activities, regardless of your facilities. The options are endless."

In small programs where only one adult is available to supervise the outdoor playground area, he may have some special challenges. Plan toileting time for all children prior to going outside and have all outdoor supplies ready to go in a bag or basket. Staff should be able to view the entire outdoor area and respond within seconds to an emergency, so bring emergency supplies in a backpack. Give the children choices among games and activities. For pickup time, leave a note so parents know where to find you, and bring the program list with family contact information with you.

## Organized Indoor and Outdoor Games

Structured games, or ones that are planned and organized by staff with teams, can promote social development by fostering communication, negotiation and compromise, cooperation, and leadership skills. Outdoor organized games and sports offer the means for maintaining and enhancing physical strength, endurance, and agility. Capture the Flag, soccer, or kickball are popular activities and can encourage teamwork. At the same time, structured games can have a downside if they are organized in such a way as to promote unhealthy competition, put excessive pressure on children to perform well, or encourage athletically talented children at the expense of their less-gifted peers. Well-meaning staff can bolster children's athletic skills, but they can also rob children of the intrinsic enjoyment of indoor and outdoor organized games.

 **CHALLENGE**

Donnie, a nine-year-old, is new to the program. The children have been playing softball for about a month now and are fairly comfortable with each other and secure with the rules. At his first turn at bat, he misses, and a few children snicker. He quits and won't try again, although staff suspect he really wants to play. What can you do and say privately to Donnie to encourage him?

Less-structured games, individual activities, or physical activities that encourage cooperation while minimizing the need to win provide a nice alternative to competitive team games. According to Koralek and Foulks (1995), the four essential elements of cooperative games are cooperation, acceptance, involvement, and fun. Examples include the game Electric Fence, in which children work as a team to get everyone from one side of a long rope that's about 2 feet off the ground to the other side, without touching the rope. Another example of a classic favorite from a local camp is called Weights and Measures. Staff balance a large wooden board (2 inches x 8 inches x 8 feet) over a log, which serves as a fulcrum. A group of about ten children figures out how to divide the group and stand on the log, with the goal of balancing the two sides. In both of these examples, the entire group works as a team as they talk through the problem and try different solutions until they are successful.

Develop a repertoire of games that can be played with large groups of children. One large wooden board, for example, can be reused in a number of ways: balance beam, ramp, scale, or bridge. Write down the games children are familiar with, rotate through them, and teach new ones over time. Even the most enthusiastic participants of a current popular game such as Four Square will tire of it if it is offered every day. There are many books on outdoor action games for children, as well as online lists of games. (See appendix A.)

Consider the ages of the children in your program. Different games can appeal to different ages. For example, five- to seven-year-olds would probably enjoy Follow the Leader or hopscotch, but ten-year-olds would not. Many children enjoy a scavenger hunt with a list of items to collect, a treasure hunt with hidden clues or a map, or an obstacle course, as long as it is appropriate for all the varying ages and abilities in your program. Consider other active games, such as beanbag bowling, beanbag shuffleboard, and marbles.

> **?  CHALLENGE**
>
> Meilyn is the director of a small after-school program. The ages of the children range from five to eleven. She meets their needs during free-play time with various learning centers, such as science experiments, dramatic play, easel painting and art activities, manipulatives, and sensory activities. However, when it is time for large-motor activity and everyone heads to the gym to play an organized game such as Capture the Flag, kickball, or Crossfire, the older children become frustrated and the younger children have difficulty keeping up. Frequently, the older children throw a ball too hard or play too rough, causing a younger child to cry and quit the game. Gym and outdoor time have become a nightmare for the children. What can Meilyn do?

Another great addition to outdoor time is water play. Many children in school-age care are unaccustomed to playing with water at school. It may take creative leadership to encourage them to participate at first. Make sure everyone has a towel and a change of clothes, select a warm day, and have some water fun! Running through sprinklers, water-balloon games, sailing newly crafted milk-carton boats down a gutter, making mud pies or sand castles, sponge toss, sponge racing, and playing on a Slip 'N Slide can all be great fun for children of all ages. (Of course, be mindful of any rules around the types of toys and props you can use at your site.)

## Safety Considerations

As mentioned in chapter 3, safety is always a consideration when providing opportunities for physical activity. For programs that share school gymnasium space, staff should not allow children to play with equipment that requires special supervision unless they have the appropriate space, training, and staff to oversee its use. Avoid using gymnastics equipment, hanging ropes, hard balls, skateboards, and roller blades.

Check outdoor equipment and the playground area daily for safety. You might be surprised to hear what kinds of items staff have found in their outdoor spaces: fallen branches after a storm, wild animals, yellowjackets, or remnants of parties. You might find garbage, broken bottles, and other items in shared school playground or public play areas; these must be disposed of before children enter the space. Wooden frames, swings, bolts, climbing structures, and surfacing can all become worn, loose, thin, or splintered over time and should be checked regularly.

If the program is in a school, it is wise to check with the principal or physical education teacher to see what rules the children are used to following in the gym and on the school playground. In some cases, rules may need to be modified to suit the situation, but it is helpful to stay within the norms the children are used to when possible.

## Conclusion

Big changes take place in children's bodies as they grow and develop. With these physical changes come new opportunities to practice motor skills, develop healthy habits, engage in physical activity, and socialize with peers.

High-quality programs recognize that after a long day in school, children want to move around and have time to themselves. Children in school-age programs typically need to go outside or to the gym to stretch their bodies soon after arriving. Providing developmentally appropriate physical activities for children will support their coordination skills and strength and will help them to release stress and tension. Consider opportunities to provide cooperative games, and include cultural variations of games for added interest and to encourage activity in your program to support healthy physical development.

 SOLUTIONS

### Lola Is Dealing with Neighborhood Violence

In our opening vignette we learned that, due to neighborhood violence, Lola is not able to use the outside playground for the children's physical activity. Where a gym or outdoor play space is available, children can have an active play period. When large indoor and outdoor spaces are not available, program modifications have to be made. Some suggestions for Lola include holding relay races in the halls, creating obstacle courses, doing stretching exercises, moving to music, playing Simon Says, playing beanbag games, and doing other activities that provide exercise in a limited space. However, it's important that Lola first inquire about policy regarding relay activities in the building where the program is held. Depending on the building space, Lola may be able to negotiate with the school principal for additional space for her program that would be suitable for daily indoor physical activity. Longer-term solutions include adding regular opportunities for yoga or exercise programs through videos in the regular school-age space.

## Donnie Is New to Playing Softball

As new children join the program, it's important to get to know them and help them feel comfortable. In this case, if the staff had spoken to Donnie a little more about his interests and talents, they would have discovered that he is new to playing softball. Sending him up to bat without taking the time to introduce him to some of the fundamentals of the game and letting him practice some skills may have set him up for an uncomfortable situation. Please don't assume that second, third, or even fourth graders have played a game before. Instead, staff could have paired him up with a few other children to practice swinging the bat and hitting the ball first. To promote leadership and positive group dynamics, an older child may be interested in serving as a team leader or coach who could give Donnie a few pointers.

Even after some practice, however, children are likely to miss the ball, strike out, get embarrassed, and quit. How staff respond is an important aspect of team play. Responses should be private, sensitive, and encouraging. Some examples include, "If you want to skip your turn for now, that is perfectly okay. If you like, I can practice with you," or "It can be difficult to learn a new skill. If you like, I can go over the steps and then pitch you a few balls until you feel more comfortable." It's also helpful if programs can include choices of noncompetitive games. Also consider providing opportunities for children to learn new skills in a positive, noncompetitive, and supportive way.

Learning about gross- and fine-motor development and the link between children's self-esteem and physical development and then implementing ideas for promoting children's physical abilities will aid in all children's optimal growth and development.

## Meilyn Needs Help Supporting Mixed-Age Groups

Meilyn is doing her best to come up with physical activities for the indoor space, but it sounds like she needs some practical tips for working with mixed-age groups. First, she needs to have reasonable expectations for each age group. The children do not need to do physical activity in one large, organized group. She could offer a couple of options or could plan for some open-ended activities that are not so structured. For example, for the five- to seven-year-olds, she can provide some balls to kick around, or this age group can organize a small game. For the eight- to ten-year-olds, she may include some cones to keep their kicking focused. For the eleven-year-olds, more precision play with balls in a created maze could be fun. In addition, Meilyn should involve all children in the planning for this time of the program. In this way, she will learn about the children's interests and can better prepare for this time and the mixed-age groupings she has. While organized games serve a purpose, she needs to change things up to meet the developmental needs of her group.

# THINK. ACT. REFLECT.

## Think.

While children do like to play games they are good at, they can become bored with the same repetitive games, and not everyone likes to play the same games. Try to remember some of the physical activities that were part of your childhood. Were there any games that you were expected to play all the time? Perhaps it was dodgeball that the gym teacher played over and over or an organized game of softball your fourth-grade teacher scheduled every Friday. Try to remember a few of your favorite physical activities and a few that you didn't care for. Why do these stand out for you?

## Act.

Introducing new games and activities can spice things up! Find three new games to offer the children. Survey them to find out whether they know of a game they can introduce to the group, look for online resources, and be sure to include games from other cultures. For at least one week, try the new games and play them several times until the rules are clear. At the end of the week, poll the children to find out how they enjoyed the new games. Have fun with it and create a chart, tally, or ranking system for the new games you try.

## Reflect.

How did the experiment go? Did anything surprise you? What did you learn from the children's responses?

# chapter 7 | Social and Emotional Development

**C**ameron is an eight-year-old boy who told Lydia, the director of an after-school program he attends, that in school he is scared all the time because he is being bullied on the school bus, in the lunch room, in the restroom, and during recess. Lydia wants to help Cameron by giving him some strategies and to provide safety and support for this targeted child. What can she do to help Cameron?

High-quality school-age programs are not just about curriculum and keeping children safe. They are the result of staff training in understanding all areas of child development, especially social and emotional development. Staff of high-quality programs use this knowledge to guide children in making good decisions and give students the strategies they need to have successful peer relationships. This chapter will discuss social and emotional development as school-age children move into programs where independence, problem solving, curiosity, and resilience are encouraged as they develop a sense of self. In addition to providing examples of learning activities that support positive identity formation, the chapter will highlight opportunities for reflective communication and will address the concept of trauma-informed care.

# An Overview of Social and Emotional Development

*Social development* is a term used to explain the process of how children learn to interact with others. As children grow and develop, they learn and refine skills to communicate and interact. *Emotional development* refers to the ability to recognize, express, and manage feelings and to have empathy for the feelings of others. Young children, like adults, experience many emotions during the course of a single day. At times, children also try to make sense of other people's emotional reactions and feelings. As children grow older, they become more aware of other people's feelings, as well as their own, and they can better regulate their emotions.

*Self-concept* is our image of ourselves. *Self-esteem* is the overall way we evaluate ourselves, in other words, how we feel about ourselves. A major contributor to self-esteem is social support that comes from parents, peers, and teachers, but it generally will not compensate for low self-concept. For example, if eleven-year-old Manuela feels that good looks are important and that she isn't pretty, she will lose self-esteem no matter how much praise she gets from others. When children have low self-esteem, they are more likely to have poor peer relations, suffer psychological disorders such as depression, be involved in antisocial activities, and do poorly in school (Kail, 2014).

Children who are withdrawn or isolated may be overly concerned about performance in social situations. They may attribute rejection to their own personality deficiencies, which some believe they are helpless to change. Some children may misinterpret innocent interactions or discussions as personal affronts and internalize these false notions. Rather than try new ways to gain approval, they may repeat unsuccessful strategies or just give up.

Globally, self-esteem is very high during the preschool years but declines in the elementary school years as children compare themselves to peers (Kail, 2014). Interestingly, self-esteem often decreases when children make the transition from elementary to middle or junior high school, and from middle school to high school. Self-esteem becomes more differentiated in older children and adolescents as they evaluate themselves on more aspects of self-esteem, including different types of academic skills (Kail). Children with high self-esteem tend to be more willing to volunteer to help those who are less fortunate than they are. Volunteering is a prosocial behavior that helps build self-esteem.

Loneliness and social dissatisfaction are social issues some school-age children face. Interestingly, in a study that examined loneliness and social satisfaction of elementary school students in relation to type of after-school care, results indicated that children who were in self-care or were cared for by a sibling had greater loneliness and social dissatisfaction compared to their peers under formal after-school care (Demircan and Demir, 2014). This speaks to the importance for school-age programs to encourage the development of social skills and meaningful interactions among children.

Play is fundamentally important for learning twenty-first-century skills, such as problem solving, collaboration, and creativity, which require the executive functioning skills that are critical for adult success (Yogman et al., 2018). Social skills, which are part of playful learning, enable children to listen to directions, pay attention, solve disputes with words, and focus on tasks without constant direct supervision (Yogman et al.).

Another aspect of social skills is knowing how to solve problems. Competence is a child's view of himself as being able to master skills and complete tasks. Knowing what to do in a social situation and what to do to solve problems both contribute to a child's feeling of competence, which in turn builds self-esteem. School-age programs have many opportunities to model problem solving; they can also create situations in which children have opportunities to practice solving their own problems, for example:

- "We forgot to bring out the soccer net. Maybe we could set up the red cones to mark the goal areas."
- "Shawn can't reach the Legos from his wheelchair. How can we set up the Lego supplies so he can reach them?"

Staff of high-quality programs verbally go through problem-solving processes to let children hear their thinking and how they approach a problem. They accept the children's suggestions as brainstorming occurs. This is how children learn to problem-solve. Over time, the less children depend on adults to solve problems or give directions to their activities, the more independence and motivation they will show.

According to the Collaborative for Academic, Social, and Emotional Learning (CASEL) (2019), *social-emotional learning* (SEL) can be defined as the process through which children understand and manage emotions, set and achieve positive goals, feel and show empathy for others, establish and maintain positive relationships, and make responsible decisions. Staff can foster positive social and emotional development, attitudes, and behaviors by promoting and modeling cooperative learning and project-based learning. Through modeling, children can learn to recognize how they feel or how someone else may be feeling. Teaching children conflict-resolution techniques and utilizing peer mediation can help children to strengthen social skills.

Effective SEL approaches often incorporate four elements, represented by the acronym SAFE:

- **Sequenced:** connected and coordinated activities to foster skill development
- **Active:** active forms of learning to help students master new skills and attitudes
- **Focused:** a component that emphasizes developing personal and social skills
- **Explicit:** targeting specific social and emotional skills (CASEL)

According to CASEL, ideally programs will use SAFE approaches to support the social and emotional development of the children in their programs. For example, CASEL recommends the following:

- Modeling and coaching to help children learn to recognize how they feel or how someone else might be feeling
- Prompting the use of conflict-resolution skills and dialoguing to guide students through the steps of problem solving to teach them to apply skills in new situations
- Giving children practice through whole-group meetings to develop decision-making skills
- Teaching cooperation and teamwork through participation in team sports and games
- Cross-age mentoring, in which a younger student is paired with an older one, to build self-confidence and a sense of belonging and to enhance academic skills
- Teaching reflective listening by having one member of a pair describe a situation to his partner and having the partner repeat what she heard

# Understanding Peer Relationships

As children grow, they spend an increasing amount of time in social groups outside the family. Children learn life skills, such as how to get along with others and how welcome they are or are not in particular groups, from interacting with peers. Peers make an important contribution to children's development and become increasingly more important as children become older. Thus, the influence of peers is a vital factor in social and emotional development.

From a developmental standpoint, peer relationships serve multiple functions. According to McDevitt and Ormrod (2020), not only do they offer companionship, but peers also create contexts for practicing social skills, making sense of social experiences, and shaping habits and ideas. Friendships are especially important peer relationships that provide emotional support and foster motivation to resolve conflicts in mutually satisfying ways (McDevitt and Ormrod).

Because of its importance in the development of children and adolescents, peer acceptance is an important quality for staff to monitor. Children who are well liked, kind, trustworthy, and accepted in most peer groups have good social skills and can initiate and sustain conversations, are sensitive to subtle social cues that others give them, and adjust their behaviors to changing circumstances (McDevitt and Ormrod). In addition, these children listen carefully, manage open lines of communication with peers, are happy, and can control their negative emotions. They also tend to be quite prosocial, often helping, sharing, cooperating, and empathizing with others (McDevitt and Ormrod). For example, if a program's attempt at starting a monthly newsletter is frowned upon by most of the children, staff can engage popular children as leaders to change other children's attitudes and involvement. By selecting a couple of friendly children to lead the newsletter team, others are likely join in.

Some children are liked by peers, but they are not frequently considered a best friend. They are often described by peers as shy and engage in low rates of interactions. Others are rejected by their peers and are frequently selected for exclusion. Rejected children have more serious adjustment problems than those who are viewed as shy. Children who are rejected by their peers often have poor social skills, may continuously draw attention to themselves, and may be impulsive and disruptive (McDevitt and Ormrod). Some rejected children appear to peers to be immature, insensitive, inattentive, strange, or moody, and such children can often become the victims of bullies (McDevitt and Ormrod). Staff can help these children by teaching and modeling basic social skills, such as how to initiate a conversation, and by placing them in cooperative groups with popular children who will likely accept them. Staff can also help rejected children to accurately assess whether the intentions of peers are negative. They can privately role-play to discuss hypothetical situations involving negative encounters with peers, such as when a peer cuts ahead of them in line. For children who are shy or do not readily engage with peers, staff can help them learn positive ways to interact and to hold peers' attention, such as by asking questions, listening in a warm and friendly way, and saying things about themselves that relate to the interests of their peers.

# Building Self-Esteem and Confidence

The secret to developing good self-esteem is helping children focus on the positive and not letting fear of failure get in the way of embracing new challenges or meeting new people. Positive self-esteem, confidence, and good social skills are crucial for children's development. Children may be reluctant to try new things; staff can support children's efforts and provide the freedom and independence to be able to do so. For those who are easily overwhelmed, break the challenge into smaller manageable goals so children can see their accomplishments as they progress. Competence comes from practice. Give children the space, time, independence, and opportunity to expand their curiosity by problem solving and figuring things out for themselves. The more confident they become in their problem-solving skills, the more likely they will be to try new things or face challenges.

## Set Realistic Goals

Often, adults expect children to meet expectations that are not developmentally appropriate. Similarly, some children set unrealistic goals for themselves. Striving to meet age-inappropriate expectations can reduce children's confidence and self-esteem and can frustrate them. Remind children that setting unrealistic goals can likely cause disappointment, and teach them to set realistic and manageable goals:

- Show them how to break big goals into little goals, keeping the goals short term.
- Celebrate success.
- Build on existing goals, and talk about the goals to motivate results.

## Offer Developmentally Appropriate Challenges

Provide developmentally appropriate activities for your group of children so they can meet age-appropriate expectations. Foster confidence and self-esteem by offering daily outdoor time in the schedule. Outdoor play promotes risk-taking as children climb high, jump off things, and walk backward up slides. As they develop competence in their balance and gross-motor skills, and as their muscles develop strength, their confidence and self-esteem will grow.

We all learn through trial and error. Define mistakes as opportunities to learn and grow, and children will be more willing to experiment on their own, try new things, and not be so fearful of failure. It is important that staff never correct mistakes or criticize children for their efforts in trying new things. Encourage risk-taking and give children the independence they need to explore and discover. Provide constructive feedback that will nurture rather than dampen their enthusiasm for independence in the future. Use affirmations to support children's developing problem solving, confidence, and self-esteem.

## Let Children Do Things for Themselves

Some staff can be quick to intervene when a potential scuffle is likely to occur between children. Sometimes it is okay to sit back while observing and see how the children work out problems for themselves. When things go awry and peer rejection occurs, talk with children. Rejection is hard to deal with, but you can help children see how their strength and resilience grows when they experience rejection and learn how to handle it properly.

One of the key points in supporting children's self-esteem and confidence is to give children the independence to do things for themselves. For example, while some science or cooking activities may require close supervision, allowing children to perform the activities by reading directions or recipes and to learn by doing goes a long way in promoting activities that will develop their self-esteem. Overbearing staff can unintentionally squelch the independence, self-confidence, motivation, and self-esteem children need to try new things.

How do staff supervise without being obtrusive? Allow children the time, space, and independence to try new things. Be a facilitator encouraging children to try again after mistakes or unsuccessful experiences. Provide many opportunities for them to succeed. Compliment children on things they are doing very well. Avoid false compliments, as they do not encourage a child's best work. Avoid taking over an activity or giving too much guidance toward success. Inform parents or guardians of the child's successes. Not only does this please most parents, but they are likely to reinforce the child's self-acceptance through praise of his or her efforts.

When we give children the freedom and independence to explore, we are creating an environment in which children are more likely to engage in the self-regulating behaviors they need to accomplish their goals. Create an orderly and somewhat predictable environment to support children in their development. Children are in a better position to make wise choices and direct their activities appropriately when they can trust the daily program routine of identified blocks of time for working on activities. This helps children know what to expect and easily and reasonably anticipate certain outcomes in their work. Establishing regular routines for completing or working on tasks can help children work productively with minimal guidance from staff. Provide help and guidance only when children really need it.

# Independence and Children with Special Needs

Children with cognitive and physical disabilities may especially need opportunities for independence, as adults tend to monitor their behaviors and actions closely. Tailor independent activities to children's unique characteristics and abilities. For example, George, a child with cognitive delays, may be able to fetch a favorite board game from the program storage unit without close supervision, as long as the staff keeps eyes on him from a distance. Staff may allow Juanita, a child with visual impairments, a chance to explore the program before other children have arrived so she may familiarize herself with the daily activity choices and steady her bearings by locating wastebaskets, beanbags, and other portable items that are placed at the same location each day.

# Stages of Social and Emotional Development

By age five, children are aware of complex emotions, such as shame, pride, and guilt, and these can affect their opinions of themselves. They show an increased ability to reflect on emotions and begin to understand that the same event can elicit different feelings in different people. Moreover, they show growing awareness that they need to manage their emotions to meet social standards.

The sense of self also has a social aspect, as children incorporate into their self-image their growing understanding of how others see them. For example, an eight-year-old child who compares himself to some of his classmates during outdoor time may determine that he is not a good basketball player and may lose his athletic self-esteem. During school years, children's academic self-concepts become well defined as children have successes and failures in school and form beliefs about their abilities in math, science, history, and other content areas. These experiences contribute to their overall academic self-concept. Imagine the child who believes she is not proficient in most academic areas. She will have a negative academic self-concept. When self-esteem is high, children will be motivated to achieve. However, if self-esteem is based on success, children may view poor grades, failure, or criticism as indicators of their lack of worth and may feel helpless to do better. This helpless pattern includes self-blame, negative emotions, lack of persistence, and lowered expectation of themselves. This child will likely give up because she does not expect to succeed.

By middle school, children are aware of cultural rules for emotional expression. They have learned the difference between *having* an emotion and *expressing* it. They have learned what makes them angry, happy, fearful, or sad and how other people react to a display of these emotions, and they have learned to adapt their behavior accordingly. Emotional regulation involves voluntary control of emotions, attention, and behavior. Children who struggle to control their emotions tend to become visibly angry or frustrated when prevented from doing what they want to do. Emotional control increases with age; however, low control may predict later behavior problems.

*Empathy* is the ability to understand and share the feelings of others. It is important that children develop empathy, as it helps them to understand how others are feeling so they can respond appropriately.

Empathy can greatly reduce the amount of conflict in a child's life. Children tend to become more empathetic and more likely to help and demonstrate prosocial behavior in middle school. Such behaviors are signs of positive emotional adjustment.

High-quality programs encourage prosocial behaviors in children by providing activities such as role-playing so children learn to take the perspectives of others in certain situations. They encourage and recognize empathy toward others and encourage children to act on the basis of moral principles.

Let's break down social and emotional development by stage and age.

## Five to Seven Years Old

These children can begin to think about problems in a logical fashion, but they may have difficulty controlling their behavior in groups. Five-year-olds are friendly and outgoing most of the time and are becoming self-confident and reliable. According to Allen and Marotz (2000), their world is expanding beyond home and family and school. Friendships and group activities are of major importance. They continue to need adult comfort and reassurance but may be less open in seeking and accepting comfort (Allen and Marotz).

By age seven, children are becoming more aware of themselves as individuals, taking themselves seriously, and worrying about what peers think about them. They are more reasonable and willing to share and cooperate, and are better listeners. They are better able to follow through and can stay on task longer (Allen and Marotz). They are more outgoing, like to be helpers, and are less quarrelsome, although squabbles and tattling continue to occur.

Situations that promote positive emotional development include providing opportunities for children to identify, understand, and discuss their feelings and emotions; respecting the feelings of others; and providing an environment that is nurturing and celebrates diversity, as well as being inclusive to those with special needs.

To encourage prosocial behaviors in this age group, high-quality programs model and expect children to share materials, take turns, cooperate with others toward a common goal, and empathize with others. Reading a book about understanding feelings, having children share materials to make one end product, creating situations where turn taking is involved, and creating activities that involve cooperating, such as having children compete in teams to accomplish an end goal, are good ways to nurture positive social skills. Practicing praising others is also a good activity for this age group.

As children get older, they are able to more accurately appraise a stressful situation that may cause them anxiety and overwhelmed feelings, and they can determine how much control they have over the situation. Older children can generate more coping alternatives and cognitive coping strategies.

# CALM-DOWN BOTTLES

For children who become overwhelmed and anxious, calm-down bottles can help them feel less anxious and focus their attention. Children can easily make these as a science activity.

**Materials**

Clean plastic bottle with lid

Water

Glitter, sequins, foil confetti

Small objects

Glue

1. Fill the bottle with water.

2. Add glitter, sequins, foil confetti mix, and other small objects.

3. Glue the top on.

Children can shake and watch the calm-down bottle when they are overwhelmed.

## Eight to Ten Years Old

Eight-year-olds display great enthusiasm and are concentrating on improving skills they already possess and enhancing what they already know. They experience strong feelings of independence and are eager to make decisions about their own plans and friends (Allen and Marotz, 2000). They increasingly devote their interests and attention to peers and team or group activities, as well as to forming new interests in same-gender groupings (Allen and Marotz).

Most of these children are able to work without much adult supervision or direction and are learning to accept responsibility for their actions. By age nine, children are beginning to be able to see another's point of view and can empathize with children whose feelings have been hurt or who are different in some way. Their cooperative skills have strengthened and most have a best friend. Ten-year-olds need things to be fair; arbitrary rules can frustrate them. They are working to establish independence and individuality by wanting alone time and becoming private and can become noncompliant at home and at school.

To promote prosocial behaviors in this age range, encourage the children to play and create board games and long-term projects that will inspire cooperation, negotiation, compromise, problem solving, and working together to reach a goal. Support this age group's interest in the world by providing opportunities for activities such as building birdhouses or race cars, planting a garden, or inviting an owner of exotic pets to share her pets and her knowledge of ferrets, snakes, or hedgehogs.

## Ten to Twelve Years Old

Most children this age are confident in their self-perceptions and may test the program rules and authority. They have learned the two-way street of friendship and are more willing to adjust to one another's individual likes and dislikes. They are becoming more independent and responsible for their actions. They are learning to manage emotional changes brought on by puberty. They are developing more positive self-esteem and resilience by building on their strengths and accepting their weaknesses. They are developing leadership skills. Around age twelve, we see children's reasoning change, and they begin to take intentions into account when determining how badly someone behaved. Friends are becoming more important than ever, and most have found acceptance within a peer group. They are becoming more self-assured and are able to say no. They are beginning to be attracted to the opposite and/or same sex, and they are working toward handling issues about sexuality and relationships.

To promote prosocial behaviors in children in this age range, encourage volunteering and community service. These opportunities are ideal so children can begin to understand the idea of giving back to the community. Participating in a lengthy project that has a visible outcome, such as creating skits and making costumes to offer a springtime community production or organizing a food drive, provides leadership opportunities for children.

## Twelve to Fourteen Years Old

Social interaction is the most important thing in their lives. Younger teens are extremely busy with friends in school sports or clubs, and they think a cell phone is a necessity! The opposite sex is of interest to some members of this age group. Peer pressure and group pranks are not uncommon. Youths in this age group do not believe they need before- or after-school supervision; yet, after-school programs for this age group have become a successful and growing trend.

To promote prosocial behaviors in children within this age group, high-quality programs offer community-service activities, leadership opportunities within the program, and preparation for these children to earn a wage in part-time jobs in the future.

The ages of twelve to fourteen bring a whole range of new and confusing changes to many children in both their bodies and their personalities. This is a period during which a child's persona can change weekly in the form of a hair style, favorite music, and clothing. How we dress, speak, and act has a direct effect on the people around us, and how they respond to us tells us important things about ourselves. One of the crucial tasks in this period is for these children to succeed in finding a role that results in feedback from society that matches her perception of self. Twelve- to fourteen-year-olds who consider themselves to be competent, connected with society, and attractive to others will feel comfortable in roles that reflect those characteristics. Those who have learned to believe they are lazy, troublemakers, or no good will more likely take on demeanors that elicit those messages from people around them and reinforce their already negative self-perception.

As children in this age group move further into adolescence, they begin to work to make decisions and commitments around occupation, religion, philosophy, sex roles, and personal standards of sexual behavior. Psychologist James Marcia identified four statuses that involve the adolescent search for identity: diffusion, foreclosure, moratorium, and achievement. Diffusion and foreclosure are more common in early adolescence; moratorium and achievement are more common in late adolescence (Kail, 2014).

- **Diffusion:** Early adolescents do not show interest in occupational or philosophical choices.
- **Identity foreclosure:** Early adolescents have an identity chosen on advice from respected adults, such as parents, sport coaches, or clergy, rather than an identity that is the result of personal exploration of alternatives.
- **Moratorium:** Adolescents are still examining and exploring alternative identities.
- **Achievement:** Adolescents have explored alternative identities and are now secure in their chosen identity.

To support children this age as they begin their adolescent search for identity, staff should provide opportunities and encourage discussion that helps in the exploration. For example, have a career day so middle schoolers can learn about different careers. Encourage discussion, recognize their autonomy, and provide freedom within structure. When parents and staff set rules and enforce them without explanation, adolescents are less likely to easily achieve an identity.

# Supporting Social and Emotional Development

Creating a sense of belonging is the most powerful way to support social and emotional development in children. High-quality school-age programs provide a warm, supportive, nurturing, and responsive environment. Staff listen to children; allow children to contribute to the creation of program rules, curriculum choices, and other program decisions; and implement peer mediation.

Peer mediation is a process by which two or more students involved in a dispute meet in a private, safe, and confidential setting to work out problems, with the assistance of trained students. Use this approach to teach children conflict resolution, a valuable skill they can use throughout their lives. We will further discuss peer mediation in chapter 9.

In addition, high-quality school-age programs create curriculum that supports social and emotional development by empowering the children and promoting social inclusion, building a cohesive community, and ensuring resilience. Playing board games, for example, gives children a chance to practice social skills, such as compromise, negotiation, and turn taking. An engaging physical activity such as an obstacle course allows children to try new things and helps them to see what they are capable of, which supports self-esteem and feelings of competence. Programs that establish predictable but flexible daily routines help children feel safe and secure. Praising children for their accomplishments and encouraging children to praise other children supports a nurturing school-age community. Lastly, as mentioned previously, creating a quiet, cozy area for children who need to decompress after a long day of school or who just want to be alone goes a long way in respecting children's rights to downtime and privacy.

Additional activities that will help children value themselves as individuals, value friendships, and learn to demonstrate how kindness, compassion, and respect are important. Take a look at the following ideas.

## Bucket Filler

This activity example is inspired by the children's book *Have You Filled a Bucket Today?* by Carol McCloud. Each child designs his own lunch bag, and these are placed in a special area of the program. Children are encouraged to "fill a bucket" (in this case a lunch bag) to acknowledge acts of kindness when they see them. At the end of each week, children look in their bags to see who noticed their prosocial or kind behaviors. Staff can intervene privately to be sure each child has a least one comment in her bag, but if promoted with enthusiasm, children take this seriously and, often, staff do not need to intervene at all. Providing positive social-emotional opportunities for children will make them feel good about themselves and help them develop confidence. Children will form secure relationships with others and ultimately will be able to focus and learn. This strong and healthy foundation will lead to strong social and emotional development, confidence, and future academic success.

## Compliment Circle

Another example is having a periodic compliment circle. Have the children sit in a small-group circle, and start with a book or discussion and talk about compliments. Each child can turn to the child next to her to offer a compliment. This takes time and practice, as some children are very good at compliments, while others may struggle to find something kind to say. They may start with superficial compliments, such as, "I like your shirt." Over time (and with a lot of modeling from staff), the compliments become more meaningful, such as, "Thank you for giving me a hug when I was having a bad day." It shouldn't come as a surprise that children who have mastered the skill of compliments are well-liked by their peers.

## Including Older Children

To support social and emotional development in older children, provide opportunities for them to problem-solve with peers and complete a project as a way to reinforce collaboration and compromise. Encourage them to help younger ones with homework. Invite them to contribute ideas for special daytime events, such as poetry slams, Math Madness, or special guests. Notice and comment positively when they are considerate of the interests and needs of other children in the program. Older children respond positively to leadership opportunities such as a peer-mentoring program or being junior group leaders.

# Encouraging Resilience

You may have heard the term *resilience*, but what does it mean, and how does it apply to programming? Resilience is the ability to thrive despite adversities. For example, many children and adolescents find the challenges of poverty overwhelming and engage in drinking and drugs and may even drop out of school. However, many children and adolescents from poor families do well; they are hardy to life's hardships.

Resilience is an important lifelong skill for all children. The building blocks of resilience include attachment, self-regulation, and competency.

- **Attachment:** support from caring adults and positive peer interaction
- **Self-regulation:** the ability to respond to stress with poise; allows the student to absorb, identify, and manage strong emotions
- **Competency:** building abilities, from reading to math to cooking a meal; provides a sense of self-efficacy

How does resilience apply to school-age programming? High-quality programs nurture positive qualities, such as empathy, optimism, and forgiveness, and give children a chance to use these qualities. Staff notice and reinforce these qualities and avoid focusing on failure and negative behaviors. They teach by example, and they train all staff members to develop the same qualities. To make a difference in all children's lives, invest in each child's strengths, for it is from strength that they can tackle their challenges.

- Foster a sense of belonging in all children.
- Create a safe, nurturing community within your program that supports all children's backgrounds and current situations, and show children that all adults in the program care about them.
- Convey clear and consistent expectations for children's behavior while allowing them to express strong emotions, teaching them how to do so appropriately.
- Provide activities that encourage children to be leaders and to be able to use skills learned, such as cooking or sewing, in everyday life.
- Introduce children to their community agencies, libraries, zoos, and other programs, whether by field trips or having the community come to the program for enrichment opportunities.
- Communicate high expectations for all children's success and provide materials for them to succeed in school. Asking children to do their homework when they do not have a pencil or ruler is setting them up for failure. Having supplies at the homework table may be all that is needed for that child at succeed in school.

# Recognizing Stress in Children

All children experience some anxiety, a general uneasiness, a feeling of self-doubt, or sense of tension. According to the American Academy of Child and Adolescent Psychiatry (AACAP), anxiety in children is expected and normal at specific times in development. For example, young children may have short-lived fears, such as fear of the dark, storms, animals, or strangers. "Anxious children are often overly tense or uptight. Some may seek a lot of reassurance, and their worries may interfere with activities . . . Because anxious children may also be quiet, compliant, and eager to please, their difficulties may be missed" (AACAP, 2017). It is important to get to know all the children in your program and to identify ones who are overly anxious.

School-age children are just learning how to identify and deal with stress in their lives. According to the US National Library of Medicine (NLM) (2019), "Stress may be a response to a negative change in a child's life. In small amounts, stress can be good. But, excessive stress can affect the way a child thinks, acts, and feels. Children learn how to respond to stress as they grow and develop. Many stressful events that an adult can manage will cause stress in a child. As a result, even small changes can impact a child's feelings of safety and security."

According to the NLM, the following are some of the most common stressors that cause school-age children to worry:

- Worrying about schoolwork or grades
- Juggling responsibilities such as school and work or sports
- Problems with friends, bullying, or peer pressure
- Changing schools, moving, or dealing with housing problems or homelessness
- Having negative thoughts about themselves
- Going through body changes, in both boys and girls
- Adjusting to parents' separating or divorcing
- Money problems in the family
- Living in an unsafe home or neighborhood
- Deployment of a family member, for children who have family in the military
- Upcoming or recent permanent change of station, for children who have family in the military

School-age children are learning how to recognize what causes stress and how it affects their behavior. It is important to realize that things that might not be a big deal to adults can cause huge stress in children. It is not always easy to recognize

when children are stressed, but short-term behavioral changes such as mood swings and acting out can be indications. Others have trouble concentrating. Still others become withdrawn or spend a lot of time alone. A child who is stressed may overreact to something very minor, become clingy, or have drastic changes in academic performance. According to the NLM (2019), signs of unresolved stress in children include the following:

- Decreased appetite and other changes in eating habits
- Headache
- New or recurring bedwetting
- Nightmares or sleep disturbances
- Anxiety, inability to relax
- New or recurring fears
- Clinging, not wanting adults out of their sight
- Anger, crying, whining
- Not able to control emotions
- Aggressive or stubborn behavior
- Unwillingness to participate in family or school activities

We want children to learn how to manage their stress in healthy and positive ways. Keeping the lines of communication open with families will help you be on alert to whether a child may be experiencing a stressful situation at home or at school. As an important caregiver in the child's life, it is important to watch for signs that a child may be overloaded with stress so you can help her cope with it in a healthy way.

Children who have a number of coping techniques have the best chance of adapting and functioning competently in the face of stressful events. The following are recommendations for helping children cope with stress:

- Encourage children to express their anxiety.
- Let children know it is okay not to be perfect.
- Create problem-focused strategies, such as planning a study schedule and tutor support for a child stressed by an upcoming test.
- Provide emotion-based strategies, such as relaxation exercises, outdoor play, or describing their feelings to a friend, in an attempt to reduce anxious feelings.
- Encourage children to problem solve potential solutions.
- Model self-care and positive thinking.
- Reward behaviors that reduce stress.

Anxiety and stress can be a chronic struggle. Often, the source of a child's anxiety changes over time, so it may seem as though you are continually helping her to cope with stressful situations. With repetition of the stress-management techniques listed and with adult support, most children will learn to lower their own anxiety levels and cope with anxiety-provoking situations.

# Aggression and Bullying: How to Prevent and When to Intervene

One important issue for staff to be aware of is how to intervene when aggression or bullying is present. While the majority of these issues happen in schools in unsupervised areas, such as the bathrooms, hallways, playgrounds, lunchroom, and on the bus, they may spill over into school-age programs. Harassment, aggression, and bullying create a hostile environment through threats, intimidation, or abuse. It comes in many forms, but bullying is the result of regular interactions that cause a student to fear for his or her physical safety, cause physical injury, or result in emotional harm. At the same time, not all negative behavior is bullying. Being rude by inadvertently saying or doing something that hurts someone else, good-natured teasing where there is a natural give-and-take between friends, or generally mean behavior such as purposely doing something to hurt someone else once or twice is inappropriate and should be handled by staff but may not rise to the level of bullying.

Cyberbullying (Dooley, Pyzalski, and Cross, 2009; Lang, 2012; Li, 2008) creates a new and distinct issue because it holds more power over a child, can go viral with a broad reach that goes far beyond a small group of students, and is often anonymous, so some children who might typically remain silent may join in. Staff should be alert to how cell phones are being used during program hours, with the expectation that most students now have access to social media while playing on their phones.

Michele Borba, in her 2018 book *End Peer Cruelty, Build Empathy*, notes nine signs a student may be prone to bullying, but it is important to recognize that no child will demonstrate all nine signs:

- Lacks empathy, sensitivity, or compassion
- Likes to dominate and craves power
- Feels entitled or has a positive view of self
- Is obsessed with status
- Is intolerant of differences, excludes or shuns others
- Doesn't accept responsibility
- Is impulsive or quick tempered
- Taunts, intimidates, or harasses those more vulnerable
- Behaves aggressively toward others physically, electronically, verbally, or emotionally

We know that there are terrible consequences for the children who become targets. They may experience emotional distress, self-blame, loneliness, peer rejection, and/or withdrawal. They have increased anxiety, depression, suicidal ideation and attempts, and low self-esteem. Some desire to avoid school, and in some cases they may respond with extreme violence.

Adults are often unaware and do not see the problem, and it's important to recognize that students frequently do not report what is happening. Both boys and girls bully, but there are some differences. Boys direct physical aggression toward younger targets. Girls are more subtle and indirect with same-age girls, such as ignoring or excluding them from the group (Cowie, 2000; Nansel et al., 2001). Bullying can occur in preschool, but it peaks in grades four to seven, so school-age programs are well positioned to watch for signs, act by notifying families and schools as appropriate, and support children by teaching strategies. For school-age programs in middle schools, bullying peaks during middle school years and becomes more covert and difficult to spot (Borba, 2018). We begin to see relational aggression, which is harm caused by damaging someone's relationships or social status, thereby excluding the bullied child from a group. Boys and, increasingly, girls resort to more physical means, such as hitting, shoving, using intimidating body postures, and threats of violence to bully others (Borba).

## ? CHALLENGE

A new child to the program, ten-year-old Diego, a Hispanic boy, was having trouble being accepted by the other children in program. They would not let him enter their playgroups, and when he became assertive, the director made him sit in the time-out chair. His mother was so upset that, after talking with the program director, who claimed Diego was the one who had started all the trouble, the mother wrote a letter to the program's board of directors about the situation. She said the program director was racist and treated her child differently from the other children in the program, who happened to be Caucasian. What would you do if you were the program director?

The first part of effective bullying prevention is creating a safe and positive community to support all students' cognitive, social, moral, and emotional development (Borba). Creating a caring climate requires school-age programs to build a nurturing, responsive environment by encouraging and expecting respectful relationships between staff and students and encouraging students to relate to and appreciate one another. Responsive school-age programs use rules and logical consequences to provide a consistent approach to guiding children's behavior and fostering responsibility and self-control. Borba recommends whole-group meetings to build community and create a positive learning climate in after-school programs. Building inclusiveness into the program can also alleviate bullying. If they see bullying, children should be encouraged to tell an adult at home and an adult in school or a school-age program, if that is where the bullying took place.

Be aware, be present, and be positive. Greet all children by name and be a role model of dignity and respect. Acknowledge positive behavior, and encourage the children to work together and include each other. Show the children that your program is a safe space. Continually observe the program, and watch for those hot spots, such as the bathrooms, hallways, playgrounds, and meals, where bullying could happen.

Observe any children who tend to be on the fringe of activity, playing by themselves, or alone. Some children may just need some time to themselves after a long day at school, but some children may be alone because they need help joining an activity. Perhaps they are afraid to join because they don't know all the rules or fear they are not as good as their peers. Take time to get to know the children, finds their strengths and interests, and help them find peer groups where they connect.

If you determine that bullying is an issue for some children, either in your program or within the school setting, it's important to address it swiftly. Bullying doesn't go away without adult support. A variety of approaches can help, including teaching children to confront the bully, teaching potential bystanders to be upstanders, developing support groups, and nurturing skill development for both the bully (empathy and perspective taking, problem solving) and the victim (asserting themselves, coping strategies). Parents and administration should get involved as well.

Many great programs outline these approaches to deal with bullying, and many of them include interactive videos that you can watch as part of your daily activities to counteract issues with bullying through discussion and education.

- **NetSmartz:** An educational website sponsored by the National Center for Missing and Exploited Children, this site includes videos, presentations, and lesson plans for children of all ages, free of charge, with an emphasis on internet safety education. Visit https://www.netsmartz.org/
- **NSTeens:** This site, also supported by the National Center for Missing and Exploited Children, emphasizes cyber safety for teens. It includes videos about cyberbullying, gaming, and meeting offline. Visit https://www.nsteens.org/
- **The Alberti Center for Bullying Abuse Prevention:** The goal is to reduce bullying abuse in schools and in the community by contributing knowledge and providing evidence-based tools to effectively change the language, attitudes, and behaviors of educators, parents, students, and society. Visit http://ed.buffalo.edu/alberti.html

# Child Suicide

With suicide now the second most common cause of death among young people between ages ten and twenty-four (American Academy of Pediatrics, 2019), it's important to know the risk factors and be ready to support children. The American Academy of Pediatrics (AAP) defines *suicide* as death caused by self-inflicted injurious behavior with intent to die as a result of the behavior.

It is difficult for adults to understand what would motivate a child to take his or her own life. Changes in behavior are often seen as a phase the child is going through, just a part of being a preteen or adolescent. This may or may not be the case. Children and teens who are depressed have a higher risk of suicide. Symptoms of depression sometimes are obvious, such as appearing sad, hopeless, bored, overwhelmed, anxious, or irritable all the time. But some children are good at hiding their feelings or don't know how to share them. Since as many as one in every five teens experiences depression at some point during adolescence, the AAP (2019) recommends all children over age twelve be screened for depression at their yearly checkups.

According to the CDC (2019), "In the past decade, headlines reporting the tragic stories of a young person's suicide death linked in some way to bullying (physical, verbal, or online) have become regrettably common." Targets of cyberbullying are at a greater risk than others of both self-harm and suicidal behaviors, with students who experience bullying or cyberbullying being nearly two times more likely to attempt suicide. Approximately 18 percent of youth (one in four girls and one in ten boys) report self-harming at least once (Meagan Meir Foundation, 2019).

Four out of five completed suicides give clear warning signs of their intentions (Jason Foundation, 2019). This means that, if we learn the signs and know how to respond, we have an opportunity to help 80 percent of those teens who are contemplating suicide (Jason Foundation). Some signs include suicide threats such as "I hate my life," previous suicide attempts, preoccupation with death or suicide, depression, giving away possessions, taking excessive risks, and problems paying attention (Jason Foundation).

To support school-age children and youth, keep supportive and nonjudgmental lines of communication open, especially if they are at increased risk. Pair at-risk children with friendly children, because sometimes having one good friend will make all the difference. Take the time to get to know all the children and build trust, then be sure to get them help if you think they're having thoughts of suicide.

One final technique is reflective communication. When children come to us with problems, it's common for adults to interrupt and minimize their feelings, offer some advice, or attempt to solve the problem for them. Unfortunately, this rarely works and does not teach children how to work through problems. Reflective communication is different; it is an exchange of ideas. It occurs when adults really listen and then attempt to highlight and reflect what a child is saying. While it may take some practice, reflective communication helps children know that someone really understands what they are feeling, that their feelings are normal, and they are valued. For example, an adult might listen as a child complains about how she feels as though no one likes her. The adult might respond, "It sounds like you're feeling left out." The adult can acknowledge the child's feelings and confirm that it's normal to feel this way. Then, together, they might discuss some possible solutions. Reflective communication is a great way to check in and build relationships.

# Adverse Childhood Experiences and Trauma-Informed Care

Experts in the field have begun to understand the effects of trauma and adverse childhood experiences, also known as ACEs. Let's explore how we can meet the needs of all children through trauma-informed care in school-age programs. ACEs describe all types of abuse, neglect, and other potentially traumatic experiences that occur to people under the age of eighteen. ACEs include single experiences, such as a traumatic car accident or house fire, and ongoing experiences, such as an alcoholic parent living in the home. ACEs have been linked to risky health behaviors, chronic health conditions, low life potential, and early death (CDC, 2018). As the number of ACEs increases for an individual, so does the risk for negative outcomes. The presence of ACEs does not mean that a child will experience poor outcomes, but there is a neurological response to trauma, and each individual responds differently. Children's positive experiences or protective factors can prevent them from experiencing adversity and can protect against many of the negative health and life outcomes even after adversity has occurred. With this knowledge, more programs are attempting to understand and respond to mental-health challenges with what is now termed *trauma-informed care.*

Trauma-informed care is the result of training and professional development, so staff can better understand and respond to the needs of children who may have experienced trauma. Trauma-informed care includes many of the best practices that are being shared throughout this book. Staff arrange the physical environment in a way that helps all program participants feel safe and secure. Staff enjoy spending time with the children and help them build relationships with each other to feel connected. Program policies and procedures support children and families, and staff are knowledgeable about community services and can refer families that need support. An effective program increases on-task behavior, increases a perception of safety, and encourages children to respect personal space. Trauma-informed care includes setting clear rules and expectations, active supervision, encouraging appropriate behavior, and developing a clear continuum of response (Scheuermann and Hall, 2008). When staff understand social-emotional development and provide activities that help develop these skills, the end result is trauma-informed care.

## Conclusion

Socialization is a process by which children learn to get along with one another and in society so they can function in it. The earliest lessons begin at home, from parents, grandparents, and siblings. As children enter school, the agents of socialization become peers, the media, teachers, bus drivers, after-school staff, and adults in the community such as coaches, religious-education teachers, karate sensei, or ballet instructors. Outcomes of socialization include positive behaviors, attitudes, and emotions, as well as confidence in language, culture, ethnicity, and gender identity. During this process, some lifelong assumptions about the world are formed.

High-quality school-age programs become especially influential in the socialization process, as well as building resilience in children. What can you do differently today that can have a positive effect tomorrow?

 **SOLUTIONS**

## Lydia Is Challenged by Issues of Bullying

Lydia is concerned about a child who told her that he is getting bullied at school. She knows it's important for her to report this situation to both his parents and school officials, but there are things she can do in her program as well. Children who bully tend to target other children who are isolated from their peers. One good friend can buffer the pain of peer rejection and the effects of bullying. Lydia can create situations in her program to help Cameron build relationships and acquire a friend or several friends. She can do this subtly by forming study teams, encouraging Cameron to join program clubs of interest, play board games, and join sports teams during physical activity time. Lydia can also privately coach Cameron in appearing assertive: using strong posture, using a strong and steady voice, learning to say no, and walking away confidently (Borba, 2018). Lydia can also encourage Cameron not to go into hotspots alone, notice surroundings, and always let a trusted adult in school, in the after-school program, and at home know if bullying is occurring.

## Helping Diego Establish Friendships

When Diego first arrived to the program, the program director and staff should have welcomed and accepted Diego in ways that would show both Diego and the children that he was accepted. A "Welcome to the Program" party and letting the children get to know Diego and his interests would be a good start to creating a warm, nurturing after-school community that is inclusive to all children.

Let's talk about the time-out chair. This is simply not an appropriate method of guiding children's behavior. Isolating a child from others in the group never works, and it certainly does not teach better skills. Instead, it makes the child angrier, prevents staff from building a relationship with the child, and leads to more behavior problems. At age ten, children can be reasoned with and discussion can occur about how to more appropriately handle conflict. More prosocial discipline strategies will be shared in chapter 9.

When parents came to staff or program directors with their concerns, rather than place blame on the child, the program director should have listened respectfully and found ways to include Diego in play and group activities. Teaching children *access rituals*, appropriate ways to successfully enter groups, helps children be successful socially.

# THINK. ACT. REFLECT.

## Think.

In this chapter, we shared a number of ways staff can support social and emotional development. In a high-quality program that meets the needs of young children, staff have already developed a number of strategies to support the children in their care. Think about the strengths in your program. What are some of the everyday things your program does to help children develop resilience?

## Act.

Using some of the resources provided, look for some additional activities that you can use to help children recharge and heal. Remember, team activities help children learn how to work with others, build trust, solve problems, and work toward a common goal. If you currently work in a program, select one of the activities and try it.

## Reflect.

Think about one of the children in your program who struggles in the area of social-emotional development. Perhaps this child has trouble making friends or has a quirky personality that seems to irritate the other children. Reflect on what this child experiences in your program from her perspective. Based on what you learned in this chapter, what could you do to provide the child with extra support?

# chapter **8**  |  Cognitive Development

**A**manda is the head teacher in an after-school program. Several children in her program, Chikondi, Logan, Liam, Jasmine, and Carmen, show interest in science and nature. The program has little funding for supplies to support a science center. What can Amanda do to support the interests of these young scientists?

Children are naturally curious. They constantly want to make sense out of their experiences and, in the process, construct their understanding of the world. As school-agers become more confident, they want to be challenged with interesting activities that enhance what they are learning in school. This chapter will include suggestions to build a curriculum to support cognitive and language development through project-based learning that includes supporting creativity and divergent thinking. Developmental milestones and reasonable expectations for different age groups will be included.

# Cognitive Development

Cognitive development is the process of learning to think and reason. Psychologist Jean Piaget identified four stages of cognitive development: sensorimotor, preoperational, concrete operational, and formal operations. Each stage is characterized by a different way of thinking and knowing, incrementally more complex than the last, and every child passes through each stage in the same order.

- **Sensorimotor:** From birth to about age two, children in the sensorimotor stage depend on their senses and physical movement to provide all their knowledge.
- **Preoperational:** Between ages two and six or seven, children are in the preoperational stage. Characteristics of this stage include *animism*, in which they believe in inanimate objects having lifelike qualities. They may say such things as "Grampa's truck is tired" when it will not start. Another characteristic is *egocentrism*, which means they not only believe the world revolves around them, but they cannot consider another person's perspective. Another characteristic is *centration*, the narrowly focused thought of the preoperational child. They tend to focus on only one quality of something and not the whole thing. For example, if you present to them two measuring cups, each filled with 1 cup of water, and you pour 1 cup into a tall vase and 1 cup into a baking tray, when you ask they will tell you there is more water in the tall vase, even though they saw that both measuring cups held the same amount of water. Understanding the limitations of the preoperational child's thinking can aid after-school staff in mediating disagreements between children at different levels of thought—for example, between a kindergarten child and a second grader.
- **Concrete operational:** Children usually move into the concrete-operational stage at age six or seven through about age eleven, and logical thought appears in concrete and familiar things. In the previous example, where the preoperational child focuses on the tall vase, a concrete-operational thinker will think through that both measuring cups had equal amounts of water, and therefore, both containers hold the same amount of water despite the different size and shape of the containers. This is called *conservation*, the principle that some characteristics remain the same despite changes in appearance, and includes concepts such as volume, weight, mass, and displacement. Staff can support this cognitive stage by providing many hands-on activities that include classification (sports cards into teams or positions), seriation (making orderly arrangements from small to large or vice versa), and reversibility (activities that allow the child to think through a series of steps and then reverse the steps to the starting point).

- **Formal operations:** Lastly, most middle and high school children are in the formal operations stage. Here, the focus of thinking shifts from what *is* to what *might be*. Situations do not have to be experienced to be imagined, as people this age are beginning to acquire deductive reasoning. This age group can think hypothetically, consider alternatives, and analyze their own thinking. Since they can think about worlds that do not exist, they often become interested in science fiction and fantasy. After-school staff can create science fiction or fantasy book clubs, drama clubs that create plays and stories of science fiction or other genres, and Lego clubs where students can create space vehicles, buildings, and cities of other worlds.

According to psychological theorist Lev Vygotsky, cognitive development occurs through the child's conversations and interactions with adults and more-skilled peers. These people serve as guides and teachers, providing the information and support necessary for the child to grow intellectually. Language, then, is critical for cognitive development, as it provides the means for expressing ideas and asking questions.

One of the best ways to encourage children's problem solving is for after-school staff to show their own interest in learning about the world and to share their interests. In addition, staff should offer children opportunities that encourage thinking, reasoning, questioning, and experimentation. Activities could include a science center with daily experiments that children can lead. Staff can ask open-ended questions to inspire discovery and learning. One easy and inexpensive experiment is having children place three raisins into a clear plastic cup containing a clear carbonated drink such as Sprite. Watch their amazement as the raisins begin to lift off the bottom of the cup, rise to the top, and then fall back to the bottom, repeating this cycle for several hours until the carbonation goes flat. This can spark much discussion, thinking, and reasoning as the children try to figure out how this works. (Hint: The carbonation gets into the folds of the raisin, lifting it. When the raisin gets to the surface the carbonation is spent, and the raisin drops, gathering carbonated bubbles in its folds that will lift it again once it reaches bottom.) This experiment can be extended by also trying a prune. Children will come to realize that a prune is too heavy for the carbonation to lift it.

# Language Development

A child's first form of communication is crying, soon followed by smiling, cooing, babbling, and pointing. By their first birthday, children begin using recognizable words and, by age two, are stringing together two- and three-word sentences. During the preschool years, their vocabulary grows and sentences become longer, but the children do make common errors. *Overextension* occurs when young children define a word too broadly, such as using the word **car** to include trucks and buses. *Underextension* is when children define words narrowly—for example, using the word *car* to define only the family car. These errors disappear as children have more exposure to the language. By the time children are age five or six, they use language that seems adultlike in many respects. They understand and use grammar correctly, and by middle school further improvements in language take place. Children's vocabulary learning is fostered through experiences, including being read to and reading to themselves. Throughout the elementary and middle school years, children learn thousands of new words, create complex sentences, and learn to speak with others appropriately. They become pragmatic as they choose words, modify sentences, or change voice inflections for the listener in a particular situation. They can code-switch, for example, changing the form of their speech to formal when addressing adults and then switching to slang with peers.

Programs can promote language development by encouraging conversations during snack times, having group meetings, labeling storage shelves and learning centers, encouraging everyone to contribute to planning and discussion, encouraging reading, and having children express thoughts about the books they read. Some examples of ways staff can promote language development, as well as social skills, include the following:

- Teaching and modeling how to read nonverbal cues
- Teaching and modeling how to listen, without interrupting, while others speak

- Teaching children to see another person's point of view
- Modeling how to praise others and give others compliments and positive feedback

All children want to have friends. Those who have poor language and equally poor social skills have a difficult time making friends. Think about ways to integrate these skills into everyday activities.

# Writing

Writing is an integral part of the language arts. Programs can promote children's writing skills by providing a writing center stocked with plenty of writing mediums, such as pencils, colored pencils, chalk, crayons, fat and thin markers, blank writing books, pads, and plenty of paper—both lined and blank—for creative writing. Children may not like to write when required to for an assignment, but they may like to write for a fun reason. Make writing engaging by developing a monthly program newsletter for families, and include work written by children, such as poetry, program news items, an interview, or a short story.

Provide paper pads and pencils in every learning center to encourage children to write for purposes that are relevant to their activities. For example, they may want to keep score at the board-game center, jot down a range of ideas in the dramatic-play area, or collect data in the science center. Incorporate writing naturally into play, such as encouraging children to create a script for a puppet show or make recipe cards of favorite snacks. Board games such as Scattergories and Apples to Apples are opportunities for children to increase vocabulary that will aid them when they practice writing. While spelling and grammar are important, focusing too much on those aspects of language will squelch creativity in young writers.

# Reading

Encourage children to read, and provide a selection of books that meet all age groups. For low-budget programs, consider borrowing books from the local library or school library to provide children with a rich selection over the course of the school year. Another way to build a library in your program is to ask families to donate used books.

Create a cozy area with a blanket or rug and washable pillows or beanbag chairs. Add a basket of books to create the right environment to encourage reading. Most children who struggle or do not like to read will eagerly listen while a staff member reads a book. By reading up to a cliffhanger or an exciting part of a story and then stopping for the day, many children will be eager to pick up the book and proceed from there. Trips to the school or local library will also encourage children to read. Consider inviting a local children's author come into your program to speak about their book, to promote the fact that reading can be fun.

## English Language Learners

School-age programs play a critical role in the lives of linguistically and culturally diverse children. The staff's attitude is crucial in making the program accepting and appreciative of diversity. Maintain an additive philosophy by recognizing that English language learners need to acquire new language skills instead of replacing existing linguistic skills. Provide a stimulating, active, diverse linguistic environment with many opportunities for language use in informal play experiences, such as puppetry, social interactions, and science discoveries. Be sure to label centers and objects in English and in the children's home language.

Avoid ignoring individual differences with regard to language-learning time frames. It is a myth to think that children can learn a language quickly and easily. Children learn languages *differently* than adults do, not more easily. Avoid rushing the process. They need time to acquire, explore, and experience second-language learning. Accept children's attempts to communicate as trial and error and part of the learning process. Give children opportunities to practice both their first language and English language skills. Having English language learners teach interested children and staff their native language can build respect and acceptance.

# Creativity

There are several different definitions of *creativity*. While we usually associate the arts with creativity, any subject can be approached in a creative manner. Creativity, in this case, is the ability to produce work that is original, appropriate, and useful (Woolfolk, 2019). Having rich knowledge in an area is the basis for creativity, but for many problems, that "something more" is the ability to restructure the problem to see things in a new way, which leads to a sudden insight (Woolfolk). Creativity is a way of thinking, acting, and making something original that is valued by that person or others. Similarly, divergent thinking is the ability to propose many different ideas.

Everyone possesses a certain amount of creativity. Children seem to have a natural ability to come up with creative answers, creative approaches, and creative uses of materials. They must be free to develop all these natural abilities that make each child uniquely different. Unfortunately, many adults would like children to conform, and as pressures from adults grow, children find it less and less rewarding to express interest in topics, to be curious, and to be creative in exploring the world around them. Children learn quickly that they will be rewarded for certain kinds of behavior. If the rewards are granted for quiet, uncreative behavior, children will act in quiet, conforming, and uncreative ways. They will stop asking questions. They will stop exploring.

Children want to express themselves openly, and they want to bring out new ideas and have new experiences. Children benefit from creativity in many ways. When they can explore, discover, and create, they learn to seek answers, solve problems, and think divergently. Children learn by doing. They need real hands-on experiences with real objects to explore and make discoveries through their senses of touch, taste, smell, seeing, and hearing. Children learn from each other by imitating, by making mistakes, and by repeating and practicing the same skill over and over until they master it. Most importantly, children learn by cause and effect: "What would happen if I . . ." All these ways children learn require hands-on, open-ended interactions with materials, a creative mind, an inviting space, and the opportunity to use the materials in ways they can explore and discover.

## ? CHALLENGE

Hazel is a director of a small after-school program. She offers a variety of activities but none that are messy; therefore, painting, sensory, and collage activities are not offered. She does offer wonderful science experiments. However, she leads the experiment, not letting the children touch the materials, and she explains the process and results to the children. The children claim they are bored with science. What would you say to Hazel?

How can school-age program staff promote creative thinking? They are in an excellent position to encourage creativity through their acceptance of the unusual and the imaginative, modeling divergent thinking, and using brainstorming. Since evaluation always inhibits creativity, to encourage creativity staff can encourage children to trust their own judgments, emphasize that everyone is capable of creativity in some way, encourage open-ended projects where children determine what they will do, and be advocates for creative thinking by promoting brainstorming sessions and considering all possibilities suggested. Staff can support reflective practices, the ability to reflect on one's actions, so children can take time for ideas to grow, develop, and be restructured. Reflection doesn't mean having children just jot down what they did or plan to do; rather, it means to encourage children to mindfully review what they did or plan to do, to make more sense of it.

What does creativity look like in a program? Providing open-ended child-centered activities is a great way to inspire creativity. Providing a generous block of free time daily when the appropriate space and materials are available for children to do what they wish is a good start. Ask open-ended questions in ways that permit children to freely express opinions and ideas about what they are working on. Encourage children to share their experiences, because when children are being creative, they are flexible, original, confident, and adventuresome. They can redefine situations and are willing to work at things for a long time. Staff can help children develop a willingness to express creativity in many ways, such as teaching them that change is good and that many problems have multiple answers. When children have the opportunity to go at their own pace and figure out their own way of doing things in a relaxed atmosphere, they are likely to become more creative.

Three-dimensional art can inspire creativity in children. Materials can include modeling clay, playdough, cardboard constructions, and other forms of sculpture. Some low-cost three-dimensional activities children can engage in include the following:

- Using paper towel rolls to construct something of their imagination
- Using shoe boxes to constructing dioramas of outer space or a fantasy city
- Creating masks with balloons and papier-mâché
- Using cardboard to create puzzles


It is important to consider the materials you provide for children to adhere objects together. One program took the children on a nature hunt. They eagerly gathered pinecones, wildflowers, small twigs, and other items to create a nature collage. The enthusiasm was soon crushed when the only mounting material available was construction paper and the only adhering items were glue sticks, which did not hold these items to the flimsy construction paper. Providing cardboard trays or sturdy paper plates and stronger adhering material, such as rubber paste or glue guns used with supervision, would have produced a more favorable outcome.

Creative activities will be more successful when the children have a variety of materials to choose from, such as the following:

- Paint
- Spools
- Yarn
- Googly eyes
- Construction paper
- Boxes in a variety of sizes
- Egg cartons
- Oatmeal cylinder containers
- Old playing cards
- Puzzle pieces
- Yogurt containers
- Milk cartons
- Scrap pieces of cloth

The more materials available, the more elaborate the creations will be. Provide proper adhering materials, including paste, white craft glue, yellow wood glue, glue sticks, glue dots, staples, tape, fabric adhesive, and those that include supervision such as superglue and a hot glue gun. Remember, not all adhesives are equal in bond strength. Consider the durability of the items that need adhering, for optimal success.

# Developmental Milestones

Let's break down cognitive, language, and creative development by age and stage.

## Five to Seven Years Old

Cognitively, these children are eager to learn the answers to "why" questions, as they have an unending thirst for knowledge. They still need to work with tangible objects (manipulatives), such as using counting bears, to grasp number concepts. They are beginning to understand time, but struggle to understand past and future. They feel an increasing awareness of right and wrong and may tell on peers who they feel are not doing the right thing. The ability to have complex thoughts improves at this age, and curiosity about the world will increase.

In terms of language development and communication, these children seem to ask endless questions. They are interested in the meanings of words and have rapid language development. That said, they can be intolerant of different accents and languages. The number of sight words they know will grow, their vocabulary will increase, and they are learning to spell but not always correctly. They are learning punctuation, capitalization, and other sentence structures. They enjoy reading simple chapter books.

To support this age group in cognitive development, offer puzzles, counting and sorting activities, paper-and-pencil mazes, and games that involve matching letters and words with pictures (Allen and Marotz, 2000). Making homemade butter to spread on bread or crackers for snack combines both math and science fun. Children can learn to read a measuring cup, measure the fresh cream, take notes and observe the change, use a stopwatch to time the change or shaking of the container, and research how fat molecules in the cream get shaken out of position and clump together to form butter, leaving water molecules behind. Jumpstart (www.jumpstart.com) has many low-budget science activities for children in this age range.

To support this age group in language development, include simple chapter books in a basket in your cozy or reading area. Reading to this age group is a great way to expand language and critical-thinking skills. Writing short stories is another favorite for this age group, but they will need help writing. Puppets, dolls, paper dolls, and costumes can expand communication skills in dramatic play. Including reading and writing materials in all interest areas, such as pads and pencils to record science results in the science center, will aid in promoting writing development.

Recommended books for this age group include but are not limited to old favorites such as *Young Cam Jansen and the Lost Tooth* by David A. Adler, *Frog and Toad Together* by Arnold Lobel, *Horrible Harry in Room 2B* by Suzy Kline, the Amelia Bedelia series by Herman Parish, and *Junie B. Jones and the Stupid Smelly Bus* by Barbara Park. See appendix B for recommended books for this age group. You can also ask your local public librarian for additional suggestions.

## Eight to Ten Years Old

Cognitively, these children like to collect and catalogue things such as baseball card collections. They understand explanations and rules and enjoy following rules to the letter. They may be very critical of their own performance. To support this age group, provide (and join in) games that require a moderate degree of strategy, such as checkers, dominoes, card games, and magic sets (Allen and Marotz, 2000). A simple deck of cards or Brain Quest cards can provide hours of fun. Having children create math riddles is a way to make math more enjoyable. Scholastic (2019) shares an example of a fairly simple riddle: "I am a perfect square, divisible by two and three. The sum of my digits is nine. Who am I?" (Answer: 36.) Scholastic offers many wonderful math activities for this age group at https://www.scholastic.com/parents/kids-activities-and-printables/activities-for-kids/math-activities-for-ages-8-10.html

Note that while many websites offer math-problem worksheets, these are not developmentally appropriate. We want children to enjoy hands-on math and science activities and experience the wonder of exploration and discovery.

In terms of language development and communication, children this age like to socialize with peers. They often exaggerate, boast, and tell tall tales. They are intrigued with learning secret word codes and using coded language (Allen and Marotz, 2000). Basic cryptograms are perfect for this age group and enhance math and problem-solving skills. Many free websites offer downloadable easy-to-medium-skill cryptograms to get the children started. Once the children understand how cryptograms work, they can enjoy making their own and decoding others'!

Recommended books for this age group include but are not limited to *Wonder* by R. J. Palacio, *The Tale of Despereaux* by Kate DiCamillo, *Charlotte's Web* by E. B. White, and the Diary of a Wimpy Kid series by Jeff Kinney. Also, this age group enjoys telling jokes and riddles, so have plenty of joke and riddle books available. See appendix B for more recommended books for this age group.

Tongue twisters are a great way to practice and improve pronunciation and fluency and can be a great deal of fun for this age group. You can easily find simple tongue twisters online. Some favorites include the following:

- Six thick thistle sticks. Six thick thistles stick.
- Eleven benevolent elephants
- Peter Piper picked a peck of pickled peppers. A peck of pickled peppers Peter Piper picked. If Peter Piper picked a peck of pickled peppers, where's the peck of pickled peppers Peter Piper picked?
- A proper copper coffee pot

- Toy boat. Toy boat. Toy boat.
- Which wristwatches are Swiss wristwatches?

## Ten to Twelve Years Old

Cognitively, these children show proficiency in particular skills and talents. They appreciate other people's points of view. Ten-year-olds will transition toward greater independence in managing and organizing schoolwork and homework, requiring less supervision from staff in getting homework done. As mentioned earlier, older children in this age group may be able to think in hypotheticals and abstract terms. Problem solving and logic will become easier for older children in this age range. The prefrontal cortex of the brain, which plays a role in impulse control and organizational skills, is still immature. They may question rules and beliefs they previously accepted.

To support cognitive development in this age group, children can make a compass of their own and learn about magnetic north and direction. This age group has the patience for long-term science projects that involve hypothesizing, observing, and documenting about nature and other aspects of science. For example, they may enjoy exploring a question such as, "Does adding sugar to a green plant affect its growth?" or "Will plants grow more or be unaffected by polluted soil?" Education.com has many low-budget science-fair projects for ten- to twelve-year-olds.

In terms of language development and communication, this age group uses a lot of slang and "fad" words. In addition, they often speak with the fluency of adults, having a strong command of language and communication skills. They will begin to understand proverbs, idioms, and sarcasm, and they are learning to determine tone in a conversation. Many enjoy reading more complex and lengthy chapter books.

To support this age group, provide a selection of chapter books for children, and have a book club to discuss and critique books chapter by chapter. These types of opportunities can go a long way toward strengthening children's language and critiquing skills.

Recommended books for this age group include but are not limited to *The Screaming Staircase* by Jonathan Stroud, the Percy Jackson and the Olympians series by Rick Riordan, *The Book Thief* by Markus Zusak, *The Giver* by Lois Lowry, and *Front Desk* by Kelly Yang. See appendix B for recommended books for this age group.

## Twelve to Fourteen Years Old

As mentioned earlier, these children can think logically, abstractly, and hypothetically; however, they can still have some difficulty thinking about the future. They can struggle to think about consequences before they act. They may think they are unique and no one understands them. They may also think they are invincible. This illusion of invulnerability may lead them to take foolish risks, such as experimenting with drugs and alcohol or having unprotected sex.

In terms of language development, communicating with friends, whether face to face, electronically, or in social media, is very important at this age. Depending on how much they read, they can have extensive vocabularies. They may become less literal and more figurative.

Exploring morality is a normal part of the developmental process. Since their friends are very important to them, they may explore a new style of clothes, other religions, or a way of life so they can be like their friends. They are interested in learning what exists beyond their school and community.

High-interest hands-on math activities in which they can collect data, analyze, and form conclusions are best for this age group. In terms of science activities, much like ten- to twelve-year-olds, this age group enjoys long-term science projects in which they can hypothesize, document, and come to conclusions. Education.com has many science-fair projects for this age group https://www.education.com/science-fair/middle-school

There are also several online websites for STEM (science, technology, engineering, and math) activities for this age group.

Recommended books for this age group include but are not limited to the Chronicles of Narnia series by C. S. Lewis, the Harry Potter series by J. K. Rowling, *A Good Kind of Trouble* by Lisa Moore Ramée, as well as old classics such as *Treasure Island* by Robert Louis Stevenson, *Johnny Tremain* by Esther Forbes, *Robinson Crusoe* by Daniel Defoe, and *Swiss Family Robinson* by Johann David Wyss. This age group also likes magazines, and many can be found geared to their interests, such as *Shine Brightly*, *Trains*, and *New York Times Upfront*. See appendix B for recommended books for this age group. In addition, twelve- to fourteen-year-old students love mysteries and thrillers. The list of recommended books in appendix B is a great start to helping this age group strengthen their reading skills and establish the habit of reading, especially if you provide a book club where the children can lead discussions and mindful critiquing.

To further support this age group, offer meaningful, goal-oriented projects that they can work on in groups, which allow them to spend time together. A variety of clubs work well for this age group, such as book, chess, dance, painting, karate, cooking, math, and rocket-building clubs. Be sure to add "interest areas" to your staff employment application, so applicants can alert you to activities that staff may enjoy developing into a club (Bumgarner, 1999). Clubs should only last forty-five minutes to an hour on the days they are offered. Much longer than that, program directors report, and the participants' enthusiasm and enjoyment starts to diminish (Bumgarner). Programs can give students in this age group the responsibility to develop their own club names, rules, and activities. This age group also enjoys organizing and participating in special events, such as community service neighborhood cleanups and working with younger children as homework or activity tutors. This age group can also enhance their leadership abilities by planning and facilitating activities for the younger children in the program.

# Using the Environment to Support Cognitive, Language, and Creative Development

It is important for children to be able to think, reason, and learn. When children know how to learn, they gain self-confidence and develop the skills they need to explore, try out ideas, solve problems, and take on new challenges.

To support children's cognitive development, school-age program staff can:

- expose children to new ideas;
- talk with children about what they are doing;
- ask open-ended questions;
- encourage children to make decisions and problem solve on their own;
- involve children in planning and evaluating the program's routines and activities;
- accept and respect children's ideas, suggestions, and solutions;
- provide resources, such as dictionaries, atlases, almanacs, and books from the local library, that reflect special interests;
- create discovery boxes on topics such as magnetism, weather, and static electricity;
- provide opportunities for children to participate in and learn about their community; and
- reach out to community resources to expose children to meaningful new experiences.

To support children's language and creative skills, program staff can:

- suggest that interested children keep a journal;
- encourage children to write and perform plays, skits, and musicals;
- encourage children to write and share poetry and short stories;
- supply materials, time, and space to allow children to pursue and develop creativity;
- encourage children to start a program newspaper or a chess, checkers, or creative writing club;
- provide materials that help children to learn to classify, sequence, and understand cause and effect; and
- help interested children research topics of their own choice.

## Gender Considerations

While science and math have traditionally been regarded as "male" domains, girls like science, math, and problem solving too! Don't exclude them. Good after-school programs increase girls' interests and offer effective and engaging activities, along with encouragement and information about scientific careers. These are key elements in any science- and math-friendly after-school environment and may be especially important for girls in promoting confidence in exploration, problem solving, divergent thinking, and discovery. Likewise, do not exclude boys from writing stories and engaging in poetry.

## Cultural Considerations

Cultural beliefs and practices clearly influence children's scientific knowledge and reasoning skills. Japanese children, for example, are more likely than European children to think of plants and certain nonliving objects as having some sort of "mind" that thinks (McDevitt and Ormrod, 2020). Further, according to McDevitt and Ormrod, "Schools in China tend to encourage respect for authority figures and to downplay differences of opinion among experts. Possibly as a result, high school students in China are more likely than students in Western countries to believe that science is simple rather than complex—that it involves discrete facts rather than interrelationships and unresolved issues."

Ethnic and cultural groups differ considerably in their emphasis on engaging young children in reading activities. Some African American groups focus more on oral storytelling that on book reading (McDevitt and Ormrod, 2007). Immigrant Hispanic parents often place higher priority on promoting their children's moral development (teaching right from wrong) than on promoting early literacy skills (McDevitt and Ormrod).

School-age programs must be sensitive to what children's early language, literacy, and cognitive experiences have been and must use them as the foundation for providing reading, writing, and problem-solving activities that are developmentally appropriate. High-quality programs can support children by having books that represent a variety of cultures in the cozy or reading area, most especially the cultures represented in the program. In science, math, and problem-solving activities, giving children the autonomy to determine their own conclusions, and accepting them, supports cultural differences in scientific thought.

## Religious Considerations

Religion is also a consideration as children develop theories about the world. According to McDevitt and Ormrod (2020) "Some children are apt to think that supernatural forces (such as God or the Devil) are largely responsible for natural disasters such as hurricanes. Adolescents' acceptance or nonacceptance of Darwin's theory of evolution is closely connected to what their religion has taught them about how human beings and other living creatures came into being." In programs, it is important to respect, not challenge, the diversity of thought and not force unwanted instruction, discussion, or opinion. For example, when discussing hurricanes, staff can focus discussion on descriptions of hurricanes, rather than on explanations of why these occur. If children ask how hurricanes occur, they can certainly explore and research different theories with no right or wrong assertion validated.

## Disability Considerations

Children with hearing impairments may be at a disadvantage when learning to read, in part because their general language development may be delayed. Some children with reading disabilities such as dyslexia have considerable difficulty learning to read and write. Children with cognitive impairment have trouble remembering, learning new things, concentrating, or making decisions that affect their everyday life. Cognitive impairment ranges from mild to severe. Clinical diagnoses of cognitive disabilities include autism, Down syndrome, and traumatic brain injury (TBI). Less severe cognitive conditions in children include attention deficit disorder (ADD), dyslexia (difficulty reading), dyscalculia (difficulty with math), and learning disabilities in general. To support these children:

- break down activities they are interested in into small, manageable parts, and support their need for extra time;
- create opportunities for students to interact by designing some relationship-building activities; offer opportunities for children to engage in reading together, so children with speech disabilities can hear fluent reading and can practice;
- be available to offer additional instruction in promoting reading, language, science, and math activities; and most importantly,
- make these learning activities fun!

## Conclusion

High quality school-age programs offer hands-on activities, experiences, and opportunities that encourage curiosity, discovery, exploration, and problem solving in an effort to support children's cognitive, language, and creative development. They encourage children to make decisions and solve problems on their own with minimal assistance. Program staff can serve valuable roles as both resource providers and participants as they introduce new activities that support learning and curious minds.

 SOLUTIONS

### Amanda Needs Help Developing Science Activities

In our opening vignette, Amanda had noticed that a number of the children in her program had a real interest in nature and science, but she didn't have enough materials available to do much. She was trying to find ways to engage these young scientists in many activities on a low budget. She really wanted to invest in a good set of magnets, because she knows that they can translate into hours of fun learning about their properties. Her director agreed and was willing to make the purchase, but he reminded her that nature is free and challenged her to go outside to see what she could find.

She decided to take the children outside, armed with nature reference books from the school library, so they could compare different types of pinecones and study moss, ferns, trees, rocks, insects, and birds to engage inquiring minds. Amanda could also check the library for books on science experiments for children that would use common and inexpensive household products. Similarly, googling "Steve Spangler" and exploring other science-for-children websites can provide Amanda with daily science experiments on a budget. The American Museum of Natural History has a free engaging and interactive-science website called Ology (https://www.amnh.org/explore/ology). PBS Learning Media (https://pbslearningmedia.org/) offers activities in anthropology, archeology, astronomy, biodiversity, genetics, paleontology, and zoology. Using a tablet or program computer for the children's interests could enhance their knowledge of different fields of science.

It is important for Amanda to remember to let the children lead the topic of interest in science and to try to provide exploration and discovery opportunities for the children as often as possible. Amanda should take both boys' and girls' interests seriously and not exclude or favor boys' interests or those of girls. Lastly, Amanda should look to the community for the possibility of free or low-cost resources. For example, by inviting a local backyard beekeeper to the program, children can learn that a beekeeper is called an apiarist; keeps bees to collect their honey and other products that the hive produces, including beeswax, flower pollen, and bee pollen; and keeps bees to pollinate crops.

## Anthony Needs More Materials

Anthony is certainly on the right track providing exciting and thought-provoking science activities, and the children seem eager to participate. By just setting out more supplies so children do not have to wait to explore and discover would go a long way toward increasing children's enjoyment. He had already spent most of his budget at the beginning of the year, so he decided to ask the families for help. He started by creating a huge list of science-based items and challenged families to see what they could find in their junk drawers at home. He was able to gather a wider variety of materials with the help of families who brought in items such as measuring cups, an old food scale, solar calculators, turkey basters, film canisters, rulers, and twist ties. Over time, he started adding the new materials with some tips on how they might be used.

## Helping Hazel Transition to Hands-on Activities

Hazel offers a variety of activities, but she is hesitant to provide anything messy. It's important for Hazel to recognize that activities such as painting, sensory, and other messy activities are vital in school-age programs for children to develop their creative ability. In addition, messy activities can calm children who are stressed after a long day in school. Perhaps Hazel could offer one messy activity a day and establish some ground rules for respectful use of materials until she feels more comfortable.

In terms of science, it will likely be difficult for Hazel to simply leave materials with directions for children to manipulate, explore, and discover things on their own, but this is how children learn. Certainly, supervision is warranted, and a staff member should be close by; however, the role of the staff member is to ask open-ended questions and to encourage exploration and discovery. If Hazel facilitates the experiment herself and then explains the results, children are not learning by discovery; their sense of wonder is being repressed.

This is why they are bored with science. Hazel will need to learn to trust the children to manipulate the materials, explore, and discover the wonder of science—and to handle materials responsibly.

## Too Much Journal Time

Journals are a fantastic literacy activity, but Sandy's director makes a point of requiring a structured journal time immediately after school. Children have had a long day in school, mostly sitting. While some children may want to enter the program and engage in journaling or completing their homework first thing, other children's physiological needs may need to be considered. Many may need to use the toilet, have a snack, and then engage in some gross-motor games either in the gym or outdoors. Once these children have run off some steam, then homework and journaling can be offered as a choice—but not as a mandatory activity. The director should note that ten to fifteen minutes of journaling is long enough after a long day of school, and the children are likely to have homework, as well, which should take priority over journaling.

# THINK. ACT. REFLECT.

## Think.

Community members can offer a great deal of resources to give children the opportunity to explore science, art, woodworking, the outdoor environment, language, and just about any subject. Develop a list of local businesses, community programs, and organizations in your community. Add some of the skills and talents of your friends and family. Survey the children's parents for interesting hobbies or occupations they are willing to share. For example, someone might know a local artist, dog trainer, or electrician who repairs lamps. Think about experts who might have something to offer the children in your program, and generate a list of possible leads.

Next, survey the children in your program to find out what they would like to learn about. Since children don't really know what they don't really know, they are likely to need some examples or prompts. For example, they are unlikely to have any experience with string art, but it's a great activity that they are sure to enjoy, if someone can gather materials and show them how to get started. Offer some suggestions to gauge interest in different areas. Consider their developmental stages and which activities are age appropriate. Could the artist come in to show them a new technique? Could the electrician show them how to wire lamp kits?

## Act.

Based on the list of local businesses, community programs, and organizations you located in the community, and on the interests of the children, identify someone in the community whom you can contact to come in to present something. Coordinate and invite this person to teach the children the skill or share information about the interest area.

## Reflect.

Observe and comment on the guest and her activity at the next staff meeting to determine the success of this event and whether to keep this resource for future visits. How did the activity enhance the program? Did the children's activities change as a result of the new experience?

# section 3

## Creating a Comprehensive Program

**M**arisa will be the director of a new after-school program at a public elementary school. She has limited experience gained from working in school-age programs and summer camps while earning her degree in child development. How can she be sure she has enough knowledge to create a successful, high-quality program?

# chapter 9

## Building Behavior Skills in a Caring Community

**S**ylvia has worked hard to get her program organized, but now that she has time to sit back and observe, she has noticed some issues. There is a lot of bickering among some of the children, and others seem to prefer to play by themselves and have not made any real friends within the program after several months. She wonders what she can do to encourage them to interact in more friendly ways.

Within the context of a school-age program, one of the most challenging aspects of programming is positive guidance and developing a positive classroom community—so how can we make that happen? This chapter will review the important aspects of program development that support positive behavior and offer solutions to common problems. We will explore topics such as cooperative games and activities that help build relationships.'

# Establishing Program Rules, Routines, and Transitions

## Rules

Rules and limits help adults and children agree on which behaviors are acceptable and which are not. When children know adults will enforce rules and expectations consistently, children feel free to explore and experiment. Each program should work with the children to develop a defined set of classroom or program rules. Children are more likely to respect rules they help create and are more likely to understand the reasons why rules are needed if they discuss and help set them. Develop your program rules with the children in the first days you are in operation, circulate them to parents and staff, and reference them regularly over the first several weeks until they are clear. As a general rule of thumb, rules should be worded positively and should state what the children *should* be doing, rather than what they *should not* be doing. Some examples of common rules include the following:

- Be respectful of other's belongings.
- Use kind words.
- Cell phone use is limited to the program office.
- Clean up your area before you leave at the end of the day.

Rules should be clear, consistently reinforced, and reviewed regularly. Post them in a highly visible area and embed them into daily lessons and activities. Practicing the rules can be a useful strategy. For example, if there is a classroom rule about language or kind words, chart some examples of kind words, and discuss which words are not acceptable. Swear words are an obvious no, but what about words such as *fart*, *spaz*, *dork*, *jerk*, or *idiot*? It may seem awkward to have such specific discussions, but these negative words are often overheard at home and in the school hallways, and children need to know exactly which ones are and are not acceptable in the program, and why. Talk about alternatives, how these words make people feel, and the consequences for using them.

Don't forget rules related to using the program environment. If specific problems or issues arise, you can always add new rules as needed. For example, if too many children begin congregating in the bathroom areas or rushing out of the program at pickup time and leaving a mess behind, you can talk about these issues with the children and come up with rules to address the problems. At the same time, it is important to have just enough rules. When there are too many rules, children can't remember them. When there are too few rules, the children will be unsure of their limitations and the environment may become unsafe and unorderly. As a general guideline, plan for about five or six rules. Recognize that there may be different rules for different age groups. Rules should reflect children's abilities and stages of development and should reflect children's increasing maturity and their ability to handle more freedom and responsibility.

Over time, remind the children of the rules as a preventative strategy, and when problem behaviors occur, redirect the child to review the rules. Remember to acknowledge children who demonstrate good rule following.

## Routines

Establish routines and procedures that support positive classroom climate. As the children and staff plan and practice these routines, the procedures will become habits, and over time it will become easier to run day-to-day operations. Examples of common routines include the typical schedule, as well as procedures for bathroom time and snack time. One program might take groups of children to the bathroom at set times; another program may have a bathroom in the room that children can use freely. Staff should take time to teach the children the standard procedures and should reinforce them over time until the children know exactly what to do and can follow them independently. Adding visual cues, pictures, or signs with pictures that illustrate what to do in small sequential steps may help. Introduce the routines and general expectations during a neutral time, and provide a rationale to ensure buy-in from the children.

Routines are the consistent sequence that children follow throughout the day. As an example, when the children arrive at the program space each day, they will typically stop at a locker, cubby area, or designated lunch table to drop off their bags. Then the children might sign in, wash their hands, and sit down at a table for snack. Practice and remind the children what to do as they enter your program each day. This practice will help them remember the routine and transition more easily into the program.

Take note of any spots where the children are having trouble. For example, if the bathrooms are a problem area because the children tend to linger there, a teacher might take small groups into the bathroom to practice the routine of handwashing and can reinforce the expectation of returning to the classroom promptly. Other programs might need to practice voice levels during group time. Some programs teach the children the level method: level 1 is a soft whisper; level 2 is a normal, indoor voice; and level 3 is a loud, outside voice. They remind the children which level they are to be using at which times. Large programs will need to practice their procedure for quieting the children and getting their attention through practiced clapping or dimming the lights.

For successful routines, it is vital to develop a schedule that promotes the engagement and success of school-age children. Look to balance active and quiet time, small- and large-group time, and staff- or child-directed activities. Teach children the expectation of each routine and when changes occur, such as early dismissal or a field trip, prepare the children ahead of time for transitions. Remember to give extra support to children who have difficulty following the routine and children who struggle with change.

# Transitions

Transitions and routines go hand in hand to promote a positive program climate. Transitions are the time when the children bring one activity to a close before moving on to something else, such as cleaning up the activities to move everyone outside. Transitions require some planning, as they can be the most problematic portion of a day. Frequently, large-group transitions can bring out negative behavior between children and adults as the room gets busy, conversations get loud, and children are asked to clean up before they might be ready to move on. Staff can minimize the stress if the number of large-group transitions is kept to a minimum. Instead, emphasize individual transitions or gradual opportunities for children to end one activity and start another. As an example, rather than expecting every child to eat snack at the same time, which requires a lot of waiting, teachers can set up a snack buffet that allows children to go over to pour a drink and make a plate during the set times of snack service. Plan for transitions by:

- minimizing the number of transitions the program has each day,
- creating a consistent (but flexible) schedule so children know what to expect and when,
- minimizing wait time by providing gradual transitions so children who are ready can move on to the next activity while others finish,
- providing a five-minute warning to prepare children for the coming transition,
- teaching children what is expected during specific transitions, and
- aiding children with verbal supports and cues.

Children who have cognitive disabilities or mobility issues can present unique challenges during transitions. It is best to give them the time they may need without rushing them. Take some time to plan transitions that are appropriate for the setting to help ensure they go smoothly.

From the start of the new school year, it may take a number of months to build a culture based on these rules, transitions, and routines. Try to avoid comments such as, "You should know better," or "How many times do I need to tell you?" While we may have heard these comments frequently as children, they are not particularly helpful. Young children are still learning, and their brains are still growing. It may take many repetitions for younger children to remember all the rules, so practice patience. Youth, on the other hand, may have a clear understanding of the rules but will continue to test the limits in some situations or ignore rules they feel are unfair. Try to focus on the positive, reinforce the rules and procedures at every opportunity, and believe that positive words work.

Giving directions is an important part of guiding children's behavior in a positive way that will ensure children's success toward good behavior. State the behaviors you want to see. "Walk, please" says the behavior you wish to see, but "No running" tells children the behavior you do not want to see and leaves them with other choices to consider, such as skipping or hopping. Before you give directions, make sure you have the children's attention. Be direct and remember to give short, simple, clear commands. Much like creating rules, give positive directions and give children the opportunity and time to process and respond to your directions. When appropriate, give a child choices for following directions. Lastly, always follow through with positive acknowledgement of children's behavior or response to your direction.

# Building Relationships

Everyone struggles with classroom management from time to time, so it's important to understand that the key to good behavior starts with staff following the rules, modeling manners, and building relationships with children. The relationships that we build with children are the foundation of everything we do. It is important to build these relationships early on, rather than waiting until a problem occurs. Take time to get to know each child. Take a look at their schoolwork, ask about their interests, and find out how they spend their time. Sit with them as they are eating snack, and find times to work next to them and play games with them. This is particularly effective with youth, who really appreciate it when someone shows an interest in the things they enjoy—even if it is not something that is particularly interesting to you. Giving children attention when they join activities, cooperate with others, share, and care for the school-age environment and materials are other positive techniques that help build relationships. When staff model caring, cooperation, and respect by showing appreciation and encouragement, and when they avoid using insincere praise and threats to control children's behavior, they are teaching children to communicate, cooperate, and build relationships.

Similarly, staff should refrain from any kind of teasing or sarcasm. While very common culturally, these are sophisticated forms of humor that can be very hurtful for children who may not yet fully understand the nuances of language. Children may joke along, but these forms of humor are more likely to make them feel uncomfortable with the complicated feelings that come from these types of interactions. Good-natured teasing from a group of good friends might be fun as everyone laughs, but it's not nearly as much fun when the same person is always on the receiving end or when the topic is something sensitive or embarrasing. Children can't always navigate the distinction between good-natured teasing and jokes that embarrass or humiliate and may miss social cues that they have gone too far and hurt someone's feelings. Staff should model only positive, authentic forms of social interaction.

 CHALLENGE

In an after-school program located in a community center, Lexi, the program director, was confused as to why she did not have good relationships with children's families and why there were so many challenging behaviors in her program. Darla, the licensor from the state, identified a bulletin board by the program's entrance as a potential issue. The bulletin board functioned as a daily message board for families about their child's behavior. At pickup time, parents were expected to locate the name of their child's program leader on the bulletin board to see if their child's name and any issues were listed. If you were Darla, what would you say to Lexi?

Children learn and develop in the context of relationships that are responsive, consistent, and nurturing. Children with the most challenging behaviors need a positive relationship with staff the most; yet, if staff aren't careful, their behaviors can prevent the child from benefitting from that relationship. Staff attention and time are important to children, and staff need to be sure that each child is getting attention at times other than when children are engaging in challenging behavior. The following are some additional ways to offer positive interactions in building relationships with school-age children:

- Greet children by name when they arrive in the program each day.
- Engage in one-to-one interactions at eye level.
- Use a pleasant, calm voice and warm, responsive physical contact when appropriate.
- Sit with the children during meals or snacks.
- Follow a child's lead during play.
- Listen to children.
- Acknowledge accomplishments, good ideas, and positive behavior.

Positive relationships with children enhance social and emotional development, help children develop good peer and adult relationships, help reduce behavior issues, help children develop positive self-esteem, and result in higher rates of positive child interactions in your program.

## ? CHALLENGE

As children enter the program each day, Deja recites negative behaviors that occurred during the previous day. She has a clipboard on which she keeps a running list of children's misdeeds throughout each program day. Deja uses rewards, such as stickers and washable tattoos, to motivate the children to follow the rules, handing them out as the children enter program—if their previous day's behavior qualifies. Marquis, Wyatt, and Abigail never seem to receive rewards, and their behaviors never seem to change. Lately, there has been an outbreak of challenging behaviors from many other children in the program as well. What would you recommend to Deja?

# Handling Challenging Behaviors

When you work with children, you know that it is likely that some challenging behavior will occur. As children act out, it's hard to know where to start. Punishment is not particularly helpful, as it can often escalate the actions and can create distrust between children and staff. School-age children are more interested in impressing their peers than the adults in the room, and punishment such as restricting a child from an activity, keeping them off the playground, or placing them in time-out can frequently backfire and create unpleasant responses. Instead, staff need to focus on building relationships within the context of the program, even as children are acting out. If the program is a fun place to go, where children feel safe and appreciated, negative behavior tends to fade out. Positive guidance techniques help staff deal with behavior in a positive manner that guides and teaches, rather than dwells on the negative aspects of misbehavior.

Positive guidance strategies take into account that children are learning how to manage their feelings, how to respond when they have disagreements with peers or adults, and how to problem solve. With these strategies, staff can help children learn the skills to interact with others and manage themselves in positive ways. These approaches and techniques include the following:

- Acknowledge feelings
- Provide active supervision
- Respond thoughtfully
- Engage in reflective communication
- Teach conflict-resolution skills

## Acknowledge Feelings

Children can become overwhelmed by their feelings. Take time to talk with them, label their feelings, accept their feelings, and help them learn resilience. It's important for them know that we all feel frustrated, sad, or angry sometimes. Accept their feelings, then teach them appropriate responses. Acceptance doesn't mean we need to accept a negative behavior; it means we need to acknowledge and accept the feelings behind the behavior, then talk about appropriate responses to those feelings.

## Provide Active Supervision

Active supervision is the highly proactive practice of moving continuously around the classroom space, scanning all areas of the setting, and interacting with the children. It doesn't mean staff need to be walking around as guardians but rather scanning the room while discreetly listening to conversations. When teachers sit down to play a game with children, they choose their location carefully and sit with their backs to the wall. They look up regularly to scan the room. They are aware of what is happening and intervene before a situation gets out of hand. Sometimes just simple proximity to a situation is enough to help children know you're there.

Victor is a program director. Parents often find their children lined up against the wall in time-out when they arrive to pick them up each evening. Children are typically told to sit in time-out when they exhibit challenging behaviors and are rotated in and out of the position against the wall. The staff do not discuss the behaviors or the reasons for them with the children. The children seem to just gladly go back and forth during the program. If you were Victor's supervisor, what concerns might you address with Victor?

## Respond Thoughtfully

Not all techniques work all the time. Encourage staff to use good judgment, their knowledge of child development and individual children, and a positive mindset as they decide how to respond to challenging behaviors.

### Planned Ignoring

Sometimes it's helpful to ignore minor student misbehaviors when the main motivation of the behavior is attention. Keep busy but stay close, discreetly listen in, and wait for an opportunity to notice appropriate behavior.

### Direct Eye Contact

Making direct eye contact with a child may be enough to let her know you are there and paying attention. Couple the eye contact with a smile or a nod of encouragement.

### Signaling and Nonverbal Cues

Nonverbal cues, gestures to prompt a desired behavior or response, can be effective. For example, if a child misses the trash can when throwing out a napkin and begins the walk away, the teacher might gesture from the floor to the trash can with a nod. When the child exhibits the desired behavior, remember to acknowledge that with a smile or wink.

## Redirection

In many situations, misbehavior can be redirected by giving the child directions and moving them on to something else. For example, if several children have been creating a clubhouse that is causing a lot of commotion, the staff member might set up a game outside that she knows will interest them. This redirects all their energy into something else, and they can regroup and revisit their clubhouse activity later.

## Positive Reinforcement

Use genuine praise when you notice someone being kind or exhibiting positive behavior. Try to find praise that is specific, and focus on the behavior you like to see—for example, "Thanks for helping her reach the top shelf!"

## Allowing Children's Choices

Staff can help children make informed and responsible choices by reminding them to think about how their actions may affect others. Give them a few positive options, and ask questions that guide children to make good decisions. When children make a choice, allowing them to experience the logical and natural consequences of their behavior, when appropriate, helps them learn the consequences of their actions. For example, if a child chooses to quit the game she's playing because she doesn't like her cards, the other children are unlikely to ask her play something else. This is a natural consequence for behavior. Quitting the game means you have to sit out. Talking to the child about the choice and how she feels about the consequence, then problem solving another plan may help the child develop problem-solving skills over time.

## Group Meetings

In terms of building behavior skills, daily meetings offer a really good opportunity to gather the children together to reinforce rules, introduce new materials or changes to the program, acknowledge children's accomplishments, or discuss new activity topics or themes. The meetings should be brief and enjoyable, so large programs may need to find alternatives to one really large meeting. For example, they could have "circles," where they divide up into smaller groupings based on age, interests, or arrival time.

When specific problems persist, group meetings provide an opportunity to practice conflict- resolution techniques, help children resolve differences, and model appropriate ways to handle disagreements. It's helpful to practice these techniques over time with simple problems, rather than try to introduce problem solving in the heat of the moment.

# Teach Conflict-Resolution Skills

Staff should encourage children who are in conflict to resolve their own differences and should only step in when needed to discuss the issues and help the children work out a solution. Otherwise, the staff should listen and observe while the children are working to resolve the issue. Staff can suggest negotiation, compromise, and reasoning to help children find a resolution; however, they should neither impose their solutions on the children nor lecture the children. Staff can help children express their feelings and understand how their behaviors affect others. Once children learn conflict-resolution skills, their solutions are often reasonable and fair, and they do not try to solve disagreements by bullying or acting aggressively.

Staff should pay attention to whether there are times when conflicts are most likely to occur. There may be simple changes they can make to prevent these conflicts from occurring. Joanie notices that Michael and Tyrese are squabbling every day as they enter the program and engage in activities. Upon talking with the boys, she learns that their class has early lunchtime at 11 a.m. They are likely hungry by 3:30 p.m., causing them to be irritable. She decides to change snack time to when the children enter program, rather than after some activities occur. This solution can meet the boys' nutritional needs and likely stop them from squabbling.

At the same time, staff need to be cognizant of conflicts where children need help and support. Often, children who tattle are an example of this. Sometimes the same child approaches staff to tell on a friend over and over again. While this can be a little frustrating for staff, they need to recognize that children who tattle are frequently asking for help. Sending the child back to "use his words" or "mind his own business" is not going to work because he needs assistance to resolve the issue he is experiencing. Perhaps he doesn't know what to say, or he is using his words but he is not being assertive enough and the other children are ignoring him. In both examples, the staff need to offer some support. Help the child use his words, give him the right words to use, or encourage him to stand up for himself, based on the situation.

## Peer Mediation

Peer mediation is a form of guidance in which youth help their peers solve a problem. In this way children can be empowered to learn to resolve issues by themselves. This method enhances language and communication skills, self-esteem, and skills such as cooperation and collaboration. Peer mediation reinforces positive social and emotional traits, such as respect, empathy, tolerance, patience, and the ability to resolve conflicts peacefully. For the mediators, the process enhances leadership skills as well.

What does peer mediation look like? It is a voluntary collaborative process by which two or more children involved in a dispute meet, away from the other children in program, in a safe and confidential area to work out problems with the assistance of one, two, or even three other child mediators.

Peer mediators are not judges. They do not take sides, and they do not make a ruling. They help students in a dispute listen to each other. In most cases, peer mediators work in pairs with students who are having a dispute, with an adult nearby. In the process, the mediators help the children in the dispute become clear about the issues and concerns of the matter, come to better understand one another, and arrive at a mutual agreement about how they want to handle the situation.

Instituting a peer-mediation program takes some practice, so training for staff is essential to the success of the program. Fairness is very important to school-age children, and it is imperative that mediators are focused on listening and are calm and fair.

Mediation includes the following steps:

- Each child tells his or her side of the story, uninterrupted.
- Each child restates the issue or concerns of the other.
- Each child identifies the problem or problems.
- If the problem still exists, they arrive at a mutually acceptable solution.
- If the problem no longer exists, children are asked if there were other ways to solve the problem than the one they chose.

Most programs begin with peer mediators who are the older children of the program, such as middle schoolers or those age ten or older, as they have gained some of the cognitive skills necessary to make more advanced social and moral decisions.

# Dealing with Persistent Behavioral Issues

To help children develop self-discipline, it's important to think about the reasons behind any persistent behavior. Program staff should take notes, think about what might be triggering the behavior, and make note of who is involved. Is there a specific child, activity, or time when issues arise? Persistent behavioral issues generally fall within three broad categories: strong emotions, unmet need, or lack of fit. Let's look at these a little more closely.

## Strong Emotions

Some behavior is the result of feeling strong emotions. Children may come into the program after a generally bad day at school. They may feel frustrated, overwhelmed, or confused about schoolwork or may be having trouble with peers and are struggling to fit in. Perhaps their life at home has spiraled out of control, and they feel helpless. We may not always know what is happening in their life or what to say in each situation, but giving children time to decompress and select their activities may be enough to help.

As an example, think about a time when you had a miserable day. Perhaps you forgot your lunch at home, spilled coffee on your new shirt, and then locked your keys in the car. After a full day, you are exhausted, but you take the bus to another place only to have every second of the afternoon structured. Structure is probably the opposite of what you need. What would really help after a tough day? Maybe a few minutes alone on the couch? Maybe some quiet time to go through your planner to better organize for tomorrow? Children feel the same strong emotions, and they are still learning the skills of self-regulation. They need a little support as they learn how to alleviate stress and tension.

When children are feeling strong emotions in stressful situations, creative opportunities allow them to express their feelings. Sensory activities, such as pounding clay, rolling out playdough, or pouring sand, are relaxing. Older children might enjoy writing, painting, music, or going for a walk. Mindfulness, a growing trend that may appeal to youth, is a method of handling emotions by paying attention to them. It includes sitting, relaxing, and simply focusing on your own natural inhaling and exhaling of breath. For more information on mindfulness and simple steps to get started, visit websites such as www.mindful.org.

## Unmet Needs

An unmet need might include the need for attention or the need to belong, or it may be that a child is simply hungry and really needs something to eat before she can settle in. When children have an unmet need, staff need to find out how to help meet that need. For children who have a physical need, such as hunger, moving up the snack time might help. For children who need attention, it's likely that they will continue to act out until they have had an opportunity to make connections and build relationships.

In one program, staff noticed that Chelsea was often alone. During transitions she'd disappear into the bathroom instead of helping clean up her area. After some observation, staff determined that she didn't have any close friends in the program, and she was heading to the bathroom to avoid transitions. They decided to assign her specific tasks and paired her with an outgoing student named Cliff in the hope they would build a friendship. Over time they noticed that Chelsea was getting more involved in the program, with Cliff inviting her to join the program's Minecraft Club.

## Lack of Fit

The lack of fit frequently points to issues within the program itself. When challenging behavior persists, it can be the result of a program that isn't the right fit, such as an environment, routine, or choice offerings that are not developmentally appropriate. This doesn't mean the children need to change; it means the program needs to adapt the structure and activities to meet the children's needs. Some children act out because they are frustrated with too much structure after a long school day. Others may act out because the program is lacking structure, and they are not sure what to do. Similarly, some children may need active play, while others just need to relax. Reflecting on the developmental needs of the children may lead you to some possible solutions within the structure of the program. Younger children have different needs than older children, and programs have to adjust accordingly.

In one program, the staff complained to their site supervisor, DeShawn, that the children were frequently complaining about being bored and acted out by clogging the bathroom sinks with paper towels and picking at the rubber edging around the tables. DeShawn noted that the daily activities included coloring sheets, a memory game, and Chutes and Ladders, among other preschool games. With a group of middle schoolers in attendance, it wasn't surprising that they were bored. DeShawn suggested the staff review the appropriateness of the indoor environment and activity offerings as they relate to the ages and stages of the children in care. He made some recommendations, including adding more sensory materials and activities, such as making their own playdough, having a noncooking activity for snack (fruit parfaits in Greek yogurt) so that the children could make on their own, offering a science activity the children could explore and discover on their own, and clipping Sudoku and other developmentally appropriate puzzles out of the newspaper for the children. (Many local newspapers will donate copies to schools for educational purposes.) In addition, DeShawn agreed to negotiate with the principal for outdoor and gym space. The next step was to arrange for observations using the SACERS as a guide and set some long-term goals for program improvement. Over time, the environment changed, and children were much more content in the program.

# Alerting Parents to Challenging Behaviors

Staff can usually deal with challenging behaviors during program hours. For the child who got frustrated because she was losing and dumped the game board, the response might be to leave the mess on the floor for a little while as a staff member talks with the child and acknowledges her feelings of frustration first. Then once the child has calmed down, she and the staff member can return to the area to clean it up together. There's no need to notify parents of every little situation.

When issues persist, it becomes increasingly important to involve parents if techniques described in this chapter are not effective in improving a child's behavior. High-quality programs work to build relationships with parents throughout the school year before these issues come up. Staff document their strategies and prepare for the important, but often challenging, conversations. The following are some steps to take when staff need to speak with parents:

- Set a time to talk when you and the parent are not rushed.
- Find a private place to speak, with a comfortable chair for the parent.
- Start with something positive about the child.
- Describe the situation, giving two or three concrete examples of what's been happening and locating difficulties by specific times of the day, places, activities, or routines.
- Avoid casting blame or using language that implies that the source of the problem lies in the personality of the parent or child.
- Ask the parent how he or she feels about the situation. Try to gather information from the parent that will help you to understand his or her point of view.
- Brainstorm together a whole series of possible solutions. Program staff and parents should do this together, with no one's suggestions ignored or dismissed.
- Discuss the pros and cons of each suggestion. This can be a time when you educate the parents about issues such as the limits set by state regulations. This is also a time when both you and the parent can share what has worked and not worked with the child before.
- Come to a consensus or mutual agreement about which solutions you will try and how long you'll try them, and discuss how you will put these into action. You can include the child in this part of the discussion.
- Agree to meet and/or talk again to evaluate how these solutions are working. This gives you a chance to change your approach, if necessary.

Unfortunately, some parents may view programs for school-age children as a service (in some communities, a free service), and motivation for parents to be partners with program leaders may be low. That said, school-age programs should try their best to promote partnerships with parents. Staff who are rigid, give parents the brush-off, do not communicate clearly, tell rather than listen, conceal information (forgetting that children can talk), or enforce policies and procedures inconsistently prevent partnerships with parents. Staff behavior that promotes partnerships with parents includes caring, flexibility, setting clear expectations, listening, providing options, and following through.

# Strategies to Guide Children's Behavior

We have shared a number of techniques, and a different combination may work in different situations. Remember that knowledge of child development supports good practices. Let's break down how to guide children by age.

## Five to Seven Years Old

- Encourage small-group activities.
- Encourage children to use thinking skills to solve their disagreements.
- Provide duplicates of popular games and plenty of materials.
- Play games with children so they learn the rules of the games.
- Be available when children are ready to share their feelings or concerns.

## Eight to Ten Years Old

- Ask children to explain rules for made-up games.
- Compliment children when they make good choices.
- Teach children conflict-resolution skills.
- Provide outlets for reducing stress.
- Include opportunities for children to form interest clubs and lead meetings.

## Ten to Twelve Years Old

- Give children responsibility so they feel more grown up and independent.
- Teach children conflict-resolution skills.
- Encourage children to review their plans before carrying them out.
- Teach children how to present and support their opinions.

## Twelve to Fourteen Years Old

- Teach conflict-resolution techniques.
- Incorporate a peer-mediation program that teaches middle schoolers how to be peer mediators.

## Conclusion

To guide the behavior of school-age children effectively, program staff should understand the factors that contribute to the way children behave and the developmental characteristics that may play a part. High-quality programs begin with program development that includes rules, emphasizes building relationships, and focuses on positive guidance techniques. They integrate games that encourage and support positive behavior and cooperation and will ensure that the children learn to really enjoy the program and each other. In addition, having realistic expectations of children's ability and providing guidance that reflects developmental characteristics help guide children's behavior. In cases where the same misbehavior occurs repeatedly, staff take time to analyze possible reasons and offer support.

 SOLUTIONS

### Sylvia Addresses Issues with Bickering

In the opening vignette, Sylvia was noticing that many of the children in her program spent a lot of time bickering, and some preferred to play by themselves because they had not made any solid friendships in the program. Sylvia was on the right track with her room arrangement and activities, but it sounds like many of the children in her program need more support developing social skills. If she spent a little time each day focusing on social-emotional development, it would go a long way toward helping children learn how to initiate interaction with their peers. Children need to develop social skills that help them work and play cooperatively and productively with other children. To do this, Sylvia needs to provide a nurturing and supportive environment to help children feel secure in themselves, value other people, and enjoy positive social interaction. She can set up areas that encourage children to socialize, such as having a cozy area with soft furniture, magazines, and books, and she should provide enough time for children to be able to socialize. She can work to build a sense of community among the children by encouraging them to help one another, and she can provide ways children can belong to groups. This can be easily done by incorporating clubs that reflect children's interests, such as a Harry Potter book club, a chess club, a photography club, and a knitting club. Sylvia should address any issues of bullying and teasing immediately, and the staff should teach and model acceptance of all individuals. Lastly, Sylvia should allow all students to express themselves without fear of social repercussions.

## Lexi Uses a Bulletin Board as Punishment

Lexi was having issues with discipline, and Darla, the licensor from the state, identified a bulletin board by the program's entrance as a potential issue. Public behavior charts are simply not an appropriate way to handle children's behavior or communicate with parents. It seems the program staff were expecting parents to take on the role of reinforcing limits in the program and reprimanding children for misdeeds. This sends an unfortunate message to families and children that the program staff are not equipped to handle basic behavior management. Public guidance messages do not inspire trust and are likely ignored. Lexi's use of the bulletin board was likely the cause of repeated misbehaviors. Posting a list of misbehaviors violates a child's and family's right to privacy regarding behavior issues.

Darla should work with Lexi and the program staff to determine potential issues in hopes of coming up with some solutions. Darla can gently suggest the removal of the public behavior messages. She can help the program staff begin to establish or review program rules with the children, making sure they are developmentally appropriate and allowing children's input in rule making. Discussing each rule with the children helps them understand the reasons for the rules and lets children develop consequences for rule breaking. Darla should also encourage program staff to build relationships with parents and to speak privately with them when larger guidance issues occur, but to handle smaller issues within the program. The rule of thumb in building relationships with children: Guide privately, praise publicly.

## Deja Struggles to Make Her System of Rewards and Punishments Work

Five percent of children are motivated intrinsically to follow rules, and 90 percent are socially motivated. Only 5 percent need extrinsic motivation, such as tangible rewards, to follow rules. Why discourage intrinsic motivation from 95 percent of the children because 5 percent may need or desire tangible rewards? Additionally, school-age children are unlikely to find stickers and tattoos very motivational, and reward systems take a lot of effort to manage. When staff are upbeat and make programming fun and engaging, children will want to behave.

In Deja's program, more challenging behaviors are occurring. It is likely the children are no longer interested in the stickers or tattoos, so the staff have to keep upping the reward ante, which can eventually get expensive. In addition, Deja needs to be concerned about Marquis, Wyatt, and Abigail, who never seem to receive rewards. How are their needs being met? If children cannot begin each program day with a clean slate, what is the motivation for following the rules? Deja and her staff need to reevaluate the way in which they are guiding children's behaviors and work toward building relationships with children. They should review and work on rules with the children's input and discussion, be responsive to children's needs and interests, and provide a supportive environment where children can learn and practice acceptable behaviors.

## When Victor Uses Time-Out

Time-out is not an effective way to guide school-age children's behavior. First, the children may like time-out, especially if they are seeking attention. Victor seems to be rotating the children in and out so much that they may view it as a break. Second, children may learn to behave to please adults, not to get their needs met or to develop the inner controls we call *self-discipline*. Time-out can destroy a child's trust in the program staff and the child's social relationship with others. It negatively affects self-esteem and destroys the supportive and nurturing school-age community. Time-out backfires in most programs because children learn very quickly that "if they are willing to do the time, they will do the crime." Consequently, rules no longer apply to them. This may be another reason why the children gladly come and go from the time-out place against the wall.

Two problems are occurring here. Victor is not modeling appropriate positive guidance skills, and the children, therefore, are not learning to get along and follow directions. Frequently, a child is placed in time-out for a punishment, with little discussion as to why the child is being isolated. In fact, in this situation, the children are placed against the wall for a set period of time and ignored until their time is complete, and then they are released. In doing so, Victor is closing off communication and missing an opportunity to teach the children behavior skills. Further, the children are not learning positive ways to interact with peers, such as listening, negotiation, compromise, discussion, and problem solving. The children are simply being removed. Nothing positive comes from this. Victor's supervisor should encourage Victor to seek training in positive guidance skills that help children learn to control impulsivity and take responsibility for their actions. He and his staff need to reframe the program by focusing on positive guidance, teaching the children the skills they need to be successful, and implementing more activities related to social-emotional learning. Victor should guide behavior by establishing predictable routines, setting clear rules with children, and modeling kindness and respect.

Let's look at the children in his program. The vast majority do not misbehave; they behave like children. They do not do things to be bad. They do things because they are impulsive, are still learning, and may not be getting a basic need met. Even typical children and youth have difficulty making friends, but those difficulties are magnified when children have difficulty relating to others or struggle to control their behavior. These children may have difficulty expressing themselves or giving words to feelings. Perhaps they never learned how to follow rules, take turns, negotiate, or cooperate with others. Instead, they may lash out in ways that keep other children at a distance and make it difficult to develop friendships. Staff may also find it difficult to build relationships, so they have to work even harder to remain professional and help these children find more effective techniques for relating to other children and adults. Staff may find that many of the techniques shared in this chapter are helpful, such as talking to children about the consequences of their actions, setting and enforcing clear limits, coaching them, and modeling acceptable language.

# THINK. ACT. REFLECT.

## Think.

Think about the role of a host at an expensive cocktail party. She has planned a perfect menu, ordered flower arrangements, sent out invitations to twenty important guests (who don't all know each other), and prepared her home with a perfect flow. The guests are beginning to arrive. What might the host do to ensure the party is a success for the guests? What kinds of things does a successful host do? Create a list.

## Act.

Now pretend you are the perfect host in a school-age program. Instead of twenty guests, you have twenty students. They are different ages and have different abilities and interests. Your job is to plan a menu, plan the activities, and prepare the environment with a perfect flow so natural groups can emerge. Look at the list you created. What does the host do to create a successful event that you can apply in your school-age setting?

## Reflect.

Some parties are an amazing success. Others are a lot of work, where the hostess is running around taking care of things and none of the guests seem to be having very much fun. Please use the following guiding questions to reflect on how you are doing in your program:

- What strengths do you have as a host, and what areas can use some improvement?
- What are some conflicts that arise in your program, such as during transitions, and are there any positive guidance strategies that you could use to resolve those conflicts?
- Are the conflicts related to disagreements about resources?
- As a classroom host, reflect on how your program atmosphere reduces conflict.

# chapter 10 | Developing Family Partnerships

**M**atthew's parents are divorced, and his mother has residential custody. According to the custody agreement, his father picks him up from the after-school program every Wednesday and alternate Fridays. One Monday, Matthew's father comes to the program and attempts to leave with Matthew. The program staff have not had any communication from Matthew's mother acknowledging the change. What should the program staff do?

High-quality school-age programs are aware that their clients are not just the children they serve but their families as well. The programs are designed to be sensitive to the schedules and requirements of working parents while respecting the culture, diversity, and dynamics of all families. This chapter will highlight the diverse family models and explain how to develop and enforce policies and procedures that support families while responding to common challenges. Respecting culture and diversity and reviewing ways to communicate with families will also be discussed.

# Defining Families

The family has had a basic and universal role in society as a support system. Traditionally, the nuclear family, with a mother, father, and children, was the most common. Extended families included one or more relatives, such as grandparents, living with the nuclear family. As society has changed, the definition of *family* has evolved to incorporate a number of diverse family models.

Blended families are formed when two single parents, one or both with children, marry and form a new family group. These may be divorced parents who remarry and combine their families, sometimes even having additional children. In these cases, the children from the first marriages can have two moms and two dads and quite a large extended family. Single-parent families have just the mother or father, but not both, living with the children. Interracial families include a family member from a different race or culture, such as spouses who belong to two different socially defined races. In the United States, same-gender individuals are able to marry and adopt and also may bring children from former relationships into their partnerships. Foster-parent families consist of parents who care for children other than their own for temporary periods of time. In this case, the family unit is always evolving.

In addition to the variety of family models, changes can occur in families that school-age program staff need to be aware of, so they are able to support the children and, in many cases, the parents as well. A new baby, moving to a new home, family illness, death of a loved one or pet, or a parent going back to work can disrupt the household for a time and can influence how children respond or behave. No single type of family can guarantee that children will not need some special assistance from the program staff at some time. While each family model has different needs, an understanding program staff can be an asset to all families.

To best serve children and families, program staff need to be aware of the forces that affect family life today. Economic forces can cause a need for both parents to work outside the home. Often, this means that a stay-at-home mom has to go back to work. Interestingly, there is a trend of stay-at-home dads, fathers who do not participate in the workforce and stay at home for a period of time to raise their children. According to the US Census Bureau (2015), the estimated number of stay-at-home dads in 2014 was 211,000. These married fathers with children younger than fifteen have remained out of the labor force for at least one year, primarily so they can care for the family while their wives work outside the home. In 2014, these fathers cared for about 420,000 children nationwide (US Census Bureau). When parents enter the workforce, after-school care, understanding, and knowledgeable program staff are needed as families and children adjust to the change.

Political forces can also affect family life. For example, provision of special services to aid families can include food stamps and other dependent-care benefits that can affect family life. Poverty is high in the United States, with roughly 15 million (21 percent) children living in families whose annual income is below the federal poverty threshold. The federal poverty threshold is a measurement that has been known to underestimate the needs of families. Using research that shows that families need an income of about twice the federal poverty threshold to cover basic expenses, 43 percent of children in the United States live in low-income families (National Center for Children in Poverty, 2018).

Social forces, such as smaller family units, nonnuclear families, and families who live far from their relatives, are affecting families. We are now seeing many smaller families than generations ago, and many more nonnuclear families. We are also seeing more families with high mobility, whose grandparents, for example, live in another state. In some situations, the sense of a family unit is disrupted, and the familial support systems may not be there. In the end, program staff should understand that no two families are alike, and each will treat their children differently based on their personal experiences. No single set of behaviors or experiences leads to optimal child development. All family models are flexible, culturally diverse, and adaptive to ecological and economic conditions.

# Working with Diverse Families

It's natural to feel some bias against people and groups that are different, but it's important for practitioners to reflect on this bias to work to understand their feelings and understand others, as a pathway to building relationships. One teacher, Thalia, was uncomfortable speaking with a mother who had limited English skills, so she spoke with the daughter and asked her to translate for her mother. Over time, Thalia noticed that the lack of communication was becoming a problem when she observed how the daughter seemed to be taking advantage of the situation and misrepresenting some of the program rules to her mother. Thalia began to ask questions to the daughter, who explained that her mother was taking a class at the local school but wasn't doing very well. She began to appreciate how hard it must be to learn a new language, and instead of getting frustrated, Thalia asked the administrator to find some help translating program materials into other languages. She made a communication board with common phrases in the languages spoken in the program for the children, staff, and families, to encourage experimentation with language. School-age programs need to understand, value, and respect the beliefs, attitudes, and religious, economic, and cultural backgrounds of each family. Further, good programs create an environment where all kinds of children can thrive and succeed.

In the National AfterSchool Association *Code of Ethics* (2009), introduced in chapter 1, it states, "We will participate in practices that respect and do not discriminate against any child by denying benefits, giving special advantages or excluding from program activities on the basis of his or her race, ethnicity, religion, gender, sexual orientation, national origin, language, ability or their status, behavior or family beliefs." While this may seem obvious, subtle discrimination and bias is still pervasive in school-age programs. It may appear in how groups are selected for activities, in the toys or books provided, or how holidays are addressed. It's natural for staff to plan activities or select materials based on their personal experiences. That's a great place to start. But they also need to work to understand and include different perspectives.

As an example, an after-school teacher was recently asked to develop a reading-and-relaxation area in her program. Someone donated a round carpet and small comfy couch, and another family donated a bag of used books from home. The teacher used magazines to make a collage poster. It was a beautiful center, but the site director noticed how the images in the books were all very similar. While not purposeful, the teacher had developed a center that represented herself, excluding the diversity within her program. The site director encouraged the teacher to stop by the library to find a collection of books that represented different races, cultures, storylines, and abilities. The site director set aside a portion of the budget to purchase a broader selection of books, and they made sure to purchase some that depicted images of a wider variety of cultures.

In looking into practical strategies for implementing acceptance and tolerance into the classroom, Andrew Miller (2011) offers several suggestions in his article for Edutopia that might prove helpful:

- Get to know your students. Build on and learn about their backgrounds and cultures.
- Find places in your current curriculum to embed multicultural lessons, ideas, and materials. (Please note that for this to be most effective, it must be a continuous process, not merely the celebration of Black History Month and then all is forgotten.)
- Allow controversy. Open your classroom up to respectful discussions about race, culture, religion, and other differences.
- Make sure you have books, activities, and materials that represent all the children and families in your program.
- Staff should reflect the cultures of the program and the wider community population whenever possible.
- Avoid characters from television or popular culture, as they tend to reinforce stereotypes.
- Immediately address any issues of bias or prejudice with the children, such as when someone is called a name or excluded from a game.

Cultural bias can be unconscious, since we grow up with our set of norms, often assuming this is how it is in the entire world. High-quality after-school programs respond to differences without judging them to be inferior and work together with families to overcome disagreements or misunderstandings. Focus on transformative education, where two people or groups come together and everyone is changed by the encounter (Gonzalez-Mena, 2008). Transformative education comes from respectful interactions and ongoing dialogues acknowledging that our experiences with one another are important (Gonzalez-Mena). When we stretch to understand different points of view, we become transformed by each other's life experiences to a different level of knowledge and sensitive multiethnic care (Gonzalez-Mena). Now let's look at policies and procedures that will be sensitive to all families and their needs.

# Developing and Enforcing Policies and Procedures

As discussed earlier, programs should evaluate reasonable and effective criteria when developing school-age program policies and procedures. In chapter 2, we explored all the important components of a staff handbook. Many of these same components should be outlined and shared in the form of a parent handbook as well. In addition to the program's mission, philosophy, goals, and objectives, parent handbooks should clarify the policies and procedures from families' perspectives and be parent/family friendly—in other words, be suitable for all families. Content should include the following:

- Admission and withdrawal policies
- Hours of operation
- Tuition and costs
- Transportation
- Nutrition
- Behavior-management policies
- Child-illness and medication policies
- Schedules
- Calendars

Programs that ignore parents' working hours, commute time, and need for child care during school holidays and teacher in-service days add stress to already stressed families (Bumgarner, 1999). Programs are more effective and successful when they are seen as advocates rather than adversaries of parents (Bumgarner).

The purpose of a handbook is to outline responsibilities and communicate expectations for the daily operational functions of the families it serves. Administrators should confer with families and children as they develop or revisit details and guidelines. The goal is to provide clear policies and procedures that address common possibilities for potential problems, such as late tuition or late pickup, while remaining as supportive to families as possible. It is important that parent handbooks reflect your concern for parents' needs, such as having the program open on some school holidays that are not usually included in the business-holiday calendar and maintaining hours that are long enough to serve parents who commute some distance to work (Bumgarner). Parent handbooks may also outline opportunities for family participation in the program. Let's look more deeply into a few policies that should be designed to support families.

## ? CHALLENGE

Denise is a laboratory technician at a local hospital. She cannot leave her shift until her replacement comes in. In most cases, she works first shift and is at her children's after-school program for pickup with plenty of time to spare. However, on occasion during sudden inclement weather, a traffic delay, or other circumstances that cause her shift replacement to be late, Denise can arrive late to pick up her children. Her program has a late-fee policy. This week, her shift replacement was uncharacteristically late three times due to car troubles, causing Denise to be thirty minutes late past closing. Denise simply cannot afford the accumulating late fees, and the program staff were becoming visibly irritated with her, despite Denise calling to alert them she would be late. If you were the program director, what would you do?

## ? CHALLENGE

Ms. Clark is always late picking up her children. The program closes at 7 p.m., and the parent handbook is clear about the closing time and fees that occur from being late. She eagerly tosses the late fee at Aiko, the site supervisor, and continues to be about an hour late every day. Aiko has regularly reminded Ms. Clark of the closing time, to no avail. As a site director, what can Aiko do?

### Hours of Operation

High-quality programs are sensitive to the schedules and requirements of working parents. Programs can research local businesses to find start and close times and can take this information into consideration when designing schedules. Where are the parents employed, and when do typical shifts start and end the workday? Programs can also procure the school-district calendar so they know the days when school is not in session, as well as half days with early dismissal or holiday breaks.

Once they develop a calendar time frame for the program, programs can consider some other factors. Some programs schedule activities for after-school hours, but activities can also be scheduled for the morning hours before school, when many parents are either commuting to work or are already at the workplace. In addition, consider learning, enrichment, and recreation activities that your program can provide during school holidays and summer breaks. See chapter 11 for specific recommendations for summer programs.

## Cost

Cost is an important factor for working families and is a consideration for policy. Researching local businesses' employment salaries will help you determine the range you may charge for tuition and any multiple-child discounts you may wish to offer. Could the program, for example, make accommodations for the likelihood of enrolling more than one child? Work hard to design cost-effective programs that can meet the needs of elementary school children, as well as middle school students. Accommodations for multiage siblings, whether by serving many age groups directly in the same after-school program or arranging for linked, age-specific programs, is critical (US Department of Education, 1999). The key is not necessarily that siblings be in the same program but that all children in a family can be served by an after-school program in a convenient and cost-effective manner (US Department of Education).

Policy or some type of payment contract should make clear the weekly fee and accepted methods of payment. In some cases, automatic withdrawals from bank accounts have become the trend, which relieves program staff of having the awkward discussion of trying to glean late or accumulating past payments.

## Transportation

Transportation to programs is a stressor for many families. Often, schools bus children to various locations for after-school care. Some programs offer transportation and provide vans that wait outside a school for the children. In these cases, policy and procedures should be in place for when children are absent, when school is unexpectedly dismissed early or late, and when school is on break or holiday.

### Nutrition

Nutrition is an additional stressor for some families. The mere fact that most children attend school-age programs directly after the school day means that, often, their lunch boxes are empty. It is recommended that eligible programs take advantage of the United States Department of Agriculture's (USDA) federally funded Child and Adult Care

Food Program (CACFP). This program provides reimbursement for nutritious meals and snacks for eligible children who are enrolled for care at participating child-care centers, day-care homes, and after-school programs (USDA, 2019). Each day in the United States, more than 4.2 million children receive nutritious meals and snacks through the CACFP (USDA).

It is important to be culturally sensitive when drafting a nutritious snack menu, to be sure to be aware of any food allergies or cultural limitations for a particular food.

# Communication with Families

Program staff should make it a goal to partner with parents to create and maintain open communication about the children in their care. Parents and families are children's first teachers and caregivers. Parents can share insights and information that program staff may need to work with their children and can give advice regarding interests and approaches that are effective with their child.

Programs need to involve parents and families as partners and should communicate with them regularly. This should begin with a new-family orientation once a family is admitted into the program. High-quality programs include an orientation with a guided tour of the program, an introduction to teaching staff, and an opportunity to ask questions of the administrator (Talan and Bloom, 2011). Provide a folder to parents containing the parent handbook and other necessary paperwork. This will go a long way toward promoting positive communication with families. Orientation should not only be a one-way street. Solicit information from families about their child's developmental history, interests, likes, and dislikes. Learn whether a language other than English is spoken at home and the family's preferred method of communication. In programs where some families speak English as a second language, staff should work with administration to be sure important news and program information is translated into their native language. Some programs have discovered that texting or emailing families can be effective, as families can use a translator app to communicate. The use of Remind, a popular free app, allows staff to send out texts to larger groups while keeping their personal cell-phone numbers private.

Initiate and maintain open communication with families that is clear, reliable, honest, and ongoing. Building trust and rapport with families takes time. Staff should learn the names of family members and something about them. Ideally there should be a system in place to connect to new families roughly thirty days after orientation to be sure they feel their child or children are acclimating well and to learn whether they have any questions or concerns. Connect with families through informal conversation, family meetings, newsletters, bulletin boards, notes that go home with children, mailed letters, email, phone calls, and so forth (Talan and Bloom). Hold periodic parent-staff conferences that accommodate parent's schedules, because they offer opportunities to share information about each child's progress and to make plans for the future. Don't always contact for bad or negative issues; parents need to hear wonderful stories, accomplishments, and good deeds too.

 CHALLENGE

Mikayla comes to pick up her son from the program and notices grass stains on her son's pants. She goes directly to Renata, the site director, and states rather gruffly that she is very unhappy that his pants have stains. She says she is fed up and is removing her son from the program. If you were Renata, what would you do?

High-quality school-age programs organize and involve a parent advisory team to provide direction for the program. Together, staff and the advisory team discuss topics such as specific plans for meeting the needs of children and coordinating communication among staff and families through written information, meetings with families, and frequent informal discussions.

# ACKNOWLEDGE, ASK, ADAPT:
## COMMUNICATING WITH FAMILIES TO RESOLVE ISSUES

**Acknowledge: Reflect and Listen**

- Communicate awareness of the issue.

- Convey sincere interest and responsiveness.

- Involve the family in seeking a joint solution.

**Ask: Learn about the Family's Point of View**

- Gather data and clarify.

- Pay attention to verbal and nonverbal responses.

- Restate what you think the family members are saying.

**Adapt: Work with the Family toward a Solution**

- Listen for areas of common agreement.

- Negotiate around important issues.

- Seek win-win solutions.

(Adapted from Mangione, 2013)

# Parent Involvement

It is the administrator's role to promote positive partnerships with families in their program and to offer family-friendly supports, such as a family-resource library, care for mildly ill children, social functions for family and staff, tuition scholarships, and child care during school parent-teacher conferences.

Beyond support, the success of a school-age program depends on both family and community involvement. Many school-age programs utilize family and community volunteers. By making parents a part of the program, there is more of a sense of community and fewer parent-staff misunderstandings. Involving families in the program, both in day-to-day activities and in overall planning, supports and encourages parents' participation, and the children's development is dependent on this. At the same time, children are enrolled in school-age programs so working families can do their jobs and trust that their children are in a safe, nurturing space during work hours. Therefore, it's important for programs to respect the supportive nature of their role and to have realistic expectations of what parents can and should do. While it's great to have parents come in to lead activities, recognize that time may be an issue and they may prefer simple, less time-consuming ways to participate.

Programs support family involvement by including them in program decision making. If your program offers orientation sessions for new families at the beginning of the school year, incorporating a few seasoned parents into orientation may provide information to new families from the parent perspective and also can encourage a support system among parents. Other examples include regular surveys to gather feedback, opportunities for parents to volunteer and get actively involved in the program, and a parent advisory board that can help guide the mission and philosophy of the program. Family and community members with an investment, however large or small, in a school-based after-school program will tend to be more interested and involved in their own children's learning, in the learning of all children in the program, and in the life of the school as a whole (US Dept. of Education, 1999).

When staff build relationships with families, it gives them an opportunity to learn about the children in their care and to provide resources and support as needed. In terms of participation, there are many different ways families can get involved, but it takes time to plan for parent involvement. Inviting them to come in to talk about skills, demonstrate an art technique, build birdhouses, or decorate cupcakes are just a few examples. Other programs might plan an evening or weekend activity that includes dinner. The goal should be finding ways they can participate that are enjoyable or lighten their load and simplify their day, rather than adding another layer of work and responsibility.

As an example, one program found that they were having an influx of children from immigrant families in their after-school program. Recognizing that winter clothing was going to be an issue for these families, who were arriving from warm climates, one program set up a clothing exchange. Over a few weeks, staff worked with school administration to locate clothing donations, and families within the program donated items that were too small for their own children, as well as toys they had outgrown. A few parents volunteered to work with staff to sort and label the items. As they arrived to pick up their children, some parents made arrangements to stay a few minutes to sort the items, and then they opened up a "swap shop" to distribute the items. All families were encouraged to take what they needed, and items were set aside for families who could not attend.

# Conclusion

Developing partnerships with parents and families begins with an understanding of families and the important role they play and requires a firm foundation of thoughtful policies and procedures. Beginning with the first contact, high-quality after-school programs develop ways to help families get to know the program staff and find ways to keep them informed of changes and upcoming events. Respecting culture and diversity, while finding opportunities for families to participate in the program, will ensure positive partnerships.

 SOLUTIONS

### Who Can Pick up Matthew?

In our opening vignette, we read about Matthew, whose parents are divorced. His father arrived to pick him up on a day that was not his regularly scheduled day, and the staff were not sure what to do. In most cases the program staff cannot allow the father to take the child in this scenario. They have to follow the court documents, which should be on file with the program. They should call the mother, and if the father refuses to leave, they may have to call the police. Any change in the court papers that may occur over time should be on file at the program. It is strongly recommended that your staff learn state and local laws regarding custody. Check with your local police to see what they suggest. In many states, this solution will not be found in licensing regulations for school-age care, as licensing agencies typically defer to the police and legal system to take the lead.

### Denise Is Rarely Late

On occasion, Denise is delayed at work and can arrive late to pick up her children, causing late fees. Since being late is uncharacteristic of Denise, let's imagine how she must feel. She cannot leave work until her replacement arrives. Her father is usually her backup in the event she cannot leave work, but he is away traveling. She is frustrated with her coworker and stressed as she drives to the program, and then she is greeted by irritated faces demanding a late fee. She understands she is late, that staff want to go home and are now thirty minutes over their clock-out time, her child is upset, and she is feeling miserable. It's a difficult situation for everyone.

In spite of our best efforts to develop a climate of open communication and committed partnerships, parents and staff will occasionally have uncomfortable issues to deal with. It is of the utmost importance that these issues be handled with respect. Staff should understand the program's policy for resolving conflicts with families. Are staff free to work out the solutions directly with parents, or should the program director or administrator be notified and included?

Developing partnerships with parents requires open and frequent communication, understanding, and, at times, compassion. Things happen. On the third occurrence, a compassionate director may have sent her staff home and stayed with the child and then greeted Denise to ask if there is anything the program can do to make things easier for her until her father returns. The director may be able to provide the name of a reliable neighbor Denise could meet and interview as a plan B when her father is out of town. Finally, understanding Denise's financial situation and waiving the late fee for this uncharacteristic behavior can go a long way toward supporting the family during difficult times.

## Ms. Clark Is Always Late

While it is important to respect and honor the parents of children in their program, despite the best efforts of site directors and staff, parents sometimes violate policy. The role of the administrator is to step in when the director of the after-school program is at her wit's end. Aiko should make her administrator aware of the problem and ask for help. The administrator should be present the very next day, and when Ms. Clark offers the late fee, the administrator should signal the staff to take the children away from the immediate area so they can speak privately. The administrator should first ask whether there is a problem that is causing the late pickup. If there is an issue, the administrator can work with the parent to find viable solutions. If the parent is simply running errands child-free after closing hours, then the administrator should remind her of the policy. Unfortunately, there are times when programs need to let families go; while not ideal, program policies must be honored.

# LATE PICKUP: TWO DIFFERENT SOLUTIONS

Here we see the same problem, a parent being late at pickup time, with two different solutions being recommended. Ms. Clark is always late and seems to blatantly disregard Aiko and the closing time, eagerly offering late fees and continuing to be late. Denise, on the other hand, is rarely late and responsibly has her father pick up her child when she cannot. However, with her father out of town and her coworker's car acting up, she was late three times in one week. Developing partnerships with parents requires open and frequent communication and, at times, compassion, rather than the strict adherence to policy. Our recommended solutions in these cases are just that—recommended. There are no steadfast solutions to challenges because all situations have staff, children, or families often needing support, guidance, or understanding and, in some cases, objective strategies for problem solving. Even after generating a solution in working with families on a problem, things can go wrong. Checking in with families to discuss how the possible solution is working for the family and being ready to adapt the solution if warranted can go a long way toward maintaining positive relationships with families.

## Mikayla Is Unhappy with the Program

Mikayla is ready to pull her child out of the program, but it is clear that she is not just upset about her son's pants. You may have heard about the straw that broke the camel's back. While each complaint or issue may seem small (even too small to report), eventually these complaints add up. This seems to be a last-straw reaction. The grass stains are the latest in a series of unpleasant issues that have made Mikayla feel she can no longer tolerate this situation. It is important for Renata to try to keep the line of communication open by asking Mikayla to meet her the following day to discuss this situation. This will give Mikayla a chance to cool down and will give Renata a chance to interview her staff. Renata needs to find out whether there have been any issues or occurrences that may seem small but, when put together, could add up to a larger problem.

It is also a good time to review policy and procedures and to establish routine check-in with families. Having a suggestion box or an anonymous periodic survey of families to get program feedback can help maintain communication with families. While staff may greet parents each day, it is unlikely they would know what could be brewing if staff do not try to communicate with families. Some families may say everything is fine, if asked directly, even if it may not be.

Renata met with Mikalya the following day and learned that last week her son had been excluded from a game and was being bullied during school hours. In addition, Mikayla's son is allergic to dairy products, but the program had served dairy products for snack twice last month.

With regard to the allergy issue, this information enabled Renata to review the program menu and to post children's allergies to remind the staff to avoid serving foods that could trigger allergic reactions. She also decided to provide alternate snack choices for children with allergies, so no child would go without a snack.

Renata should encourage staff to monitor children's interactions more closely, to make sure that children are not being excluded. Renata could arm Mikayla's son with some strategies to strengthen himself against bullies, and she could encourage Mikayla to report the bullying to school officials.

Renata beefed up day-to-day communication with parents with a genuine interest in making sure there were no other issues festering. To achieve this goal, she implemented personal conversations, telephone contact, brief notes, a suggestion box, and surveys.

# THINK. ACT. REFLECT.

## Think.

One of the mothers, Mrs. Greene, insisted in coming into the after-school program daily, interfering with the program staff and children. Shira, the lead staff member, at first tried to have Mrs. Greene play board games with children, but none of the children would participate. Meanwhile, Mrs. Greene's son was running around disrupting the other children and activities, and she was engaging staff in social discussions, often placing herself between the staff and their view of the children. When program staff tried to intervene regarding her son's behavior, Mrs. Greene exclaimed, "It's okay! He's with me!" and the boy continued to run around being disruptive. Mrs. Greene continued inserting herself with program staff to "help," often reprimanding other children, especially those who reacted negatively to her son's disruptive behaviors. The program staff complained to Shira about the situation. Finally, Shira told the mother that parents were to volunteer in the program only by invitation, and they thanked her for her contribution, stating it was another family's turn. She came in the next day anyway.

What would you have done? Pause to think about some possible solutions.

## Act.

To determine an appropriate response, let's do some research and consider the options. While taking into consideration the 2009 National AfterSchool Association *Code of Ethics*, which can be found at www.naaweb.org/images/NAACodeofEthics.pdf, are there any ethical principles that support program staff in their effort to dissuade the mother from coming to the program every day?

It seems Shira's program has a parent handbook, as there is a volunteer-by-invitation-only policy. Does your program have a parent handbook? If so, does anything in the parent handbook apply or could anything be included in the parent handbook that might help with or prevent this situation in future?

Are there any items in the regulations for your state that might be of help in this situation?

Using one of these suggestions to determine a response, explain your recommendation and why.

## Reflect.

Based on the solutions you recommend, reflect on your role as a professional and on how you can be sensitive and supportive of parents and families while following ethical and professional programming.

# chapter 11 | Providing a Summer Camp

**M**aria had grown fairly confident in her new role as the director of the before- and after-school program held in the local school building. But as the only person in charge, she was feeling very nervous about the transition to summer. Instead of running the program in the cafeteria, she would move to a playground behind the building. She had a picnic table under an awning and free use of the bathrooms just inside the nearest door of building, but the space felt awkward, and she wasn't sure how to get organized so it felt like a real school-age program.

While it is typical for school-age programs to provide some activities during short program hours throughout the school year, providing summer camp offers a whole different set of challenges. Practitioners must try to redevelop the program and switch from a partial-day program to a full-day program and possibly hire more staff. Other programs operate solely in the summer, so new staff need to be trained and be ready to get to work right at the beginning of the summer session with a full curriculum. This chapter will explore the challenges of running a program that operates during vacations in the school year or through the summer. Since the program day is extended, it must provide more structure and activities. While we will not delve into the specific challenges of programs that include an overnight component, many of the suggestions for setting up daily activities for a day camp in the summer are similar, whether the children are there from 9 a.m. to 5 p.m. or are staying overnight.

Summer camp programs are varied. Many are run out of child-care centers and serve families in the community year-round, with expanded services for a full-day school-age program during the summer. Other programs are run by community recreation departments and pop up in the community to serve working families during the summer, so the same children might attend fairly regularly all summer. They may be under a larger recreation-department umbrella with an administrator who runs a variety of programs, including swim lessons at the local pool, tennis lessons in the park, and activities for adults at the senior center. Additionally, a variety of youth programs that emphasize enrichment activities and run on a weekly basis are available, such as theater camp, photography camp, zoo camp at the local zoo, or science camp at a museum. These programs might have specific program hours, such as 9 a.m. to 12 p.m. or 9 a.m. to 3 p.m. each day. Families might drop off the children in the morning and pick them up in the afternoon over the course of a week or two.

Each type of program has a different set of challenges, so programs need to develop their goals based on the needs of the community and the children who are expected to attend.

- What is the purpose of the program?
- Who is the likely audience?
- Why would families choose to send their children to this particular program?
- Will the same children attend the entire summer, or will a different group register each week?

The answers to these questions should help drive the planning process. For the purpose of discussion, we'll review the options for programs that have very broad and flexible goals.

# Scheduling

Set up the framework by developing a fairly consistent schedule for the day that allows a balance of activities. Start by thinking about arrival and departure times, and consider what time you expect the program to get underway each day. Your program may open at 6 a.m., but do you expect the majority of children to arrive by 7:30, 8:30, or 9 a.m.? Will they depart anytime after 3 p.m., or do you expect the majority to be there until 5 or 5:30 p.m.? These times can make a big difference in the schedule of the day.

Children who arrive by 7 a.m. may have different needs than children who arrive closer to 9 a.m. What will the early birds do as they wait for others to arrive? While it's common to start out with a few tabletop activities or simple coloring, that's not usually enough. Think about what activities will be made available before the program gets underway.

Next, schedule a large block of time for learning centers or choice activities. It is preferable to offer a large block of time in both the morning and afternoon in full-day programs. For the remainder of the day, plan to include large- and small-group activities, active and quiet, indoors and outdoors. Add in meals and snacks and an afternoon rest/reading time, and the day is complete. Following a routine that allows for some flexibility is ideal.

Enjoying time outside during summer camp is great, but plan for the typical climate in your part of the country. Time in the direct sun should be limited to morning and late afternoon, and children should have access to a shaded area, awning, or tent. Provide water throughout the day, and all children should apply sunscreen regularly as per licensing requirements. Also plan for days when the weather is rainy, stormy, humid, or just plain uncomfortable. Can you rearrange the schedule? Will the program move to an indoor space? Will the program close under certain conditions?

## ? CHALLENGE

Tiandra is happy with her summer camp, and the children are great, but the space she has been assigned in the large church building is not air-conditioned, and this has been an unusually warm summer. The weatherman is hinting that the heat will continue for the next few weeks. Even with the windows open all day, the children are getting cranky, and the supply of freeze pops is getting low. Tiandra is concerned that it's getting too hot to operate her program, and she doesn't know what else to do.

## Selecting a Theme

Think about summer themes that would be fun and interesting for school-age children. They are not required, but themes help tie together a series of activities and can build on the school curriculum to support summer enrichment and learning. Themes may vary greatly depending on the focus of the program, community events, and interests of the children. The following are some popular summer topics:

- Sustainability and the environment
- Nature and science

- Insects
- Animals
- Summer Olympics and sports
- Survivor challenges
- Gardening
- Carnival or fair

The list goes on and on. Brainstorm topics that will appeal to both boys and girls of the ages in your care. While everyone might enjoy kicking a soccer ball around for an afternoon, the single topic of soccer is unlikely to appeal to everyone for an entire week. Try to select a broader topic that will integrate activities that are both indoor and outdoor, active and passive, and include a variety of content areas, such as science, math, language arts, social studies, and the arts.

Some programs like to select a different theme each week, and that's one option. But for programs that have the same children all summer, it's helpful to plan themes that last longer and weave together in meaningful ways, rather than starting and stopping a new topic each week. Once you have selected the theme, it's helpful to review relevant learning standards and develop some outcomes the program would like the children to achieve. Then start to research activities that can support those outcomes. What can the children explore that will enhance their learning and development? Refer to the chapters in section 2 for a reminder of age-related development.

Summer curriculum expands as the children have more time to plan and complete activities. Quick games, such as Connect Four and checkers, can be switched out and replaced with longer games, such as Clue or even Monopoly, as the children have more time to start and successfully complete the game. Planning and practicing a theatrical performance, building Lego robotic kits, or learning to sew with a sewing machine are much more manageable in a full-day school-age program when children don't have to transition through activities so often. Use the large blocks or learning-center time to your advantage as you work on building the curriculum.

Activities can be planned in ways that allow the children to have choices. While some children enjoy structured physical games outside, such as Capture the Flag, other children may prefer to just shoot baskets or kick a ball around without the aspect of competition. Some children may prefer to just sit on a blanket and read. Finding a balance that allows them to control some aspects of their day is preferred.

As an example, one program developed a theme based on the book *Treasure Island* by Robert Louis Stevenson. The teachers read a few chapters from an abbreviated version of the book to the large group each day as they relaxed on the large carpet after lunch, or the teachers had the children read a little on their own. Then they discussed the content and learned vocabulary words (language arts). The oldest children researched the history of real pirates versus the storybook versions and shared what they discovered. The children enjoyed a lot of activities based on buried treasure (dramatic play), making maps (social studies, art), and counting coins (math). They made ships out of recycled materials and tested them in the kiddie pool to see which ones could float (science). They played Capture the Flag (gross motor). For snack they made pirate snacks (which closely resembled snack mix) and drank "grog" (which resembled fruit juices). Many other games and learning center activities were rotated in and out throughout the summer, but the topic of *Treasure Island* added a fun component and tied them together.

Another program developed the topic of the Summer Olympics that lasted much of the summer. They divided into small groups and selected different countries for a research project. They started by visiting the library and reading books about their selected country, locating some notable aspects of the country (language arts). They researched a few athletes from the country so they could follow their stories. They learned the rules of their sports and played several of them (gross motor). They located their country on maps and explored some of the cultural characteristics of their country (social studies). They searched for popular foods, found recipes, and sampled some of the foods from their country (science). They listened to popular music (music and movement), looked at the work of famous artists, and searched for examples of common styles (art). They learned about some of the American athletes and watched some of the actual Olympic Games on television. They put together large presentation boards and then had a special culminating night where they shared their presentations with families.

Please note that while this group accomplished a lot during the summer, these were not structured learning activities. Staff offered prompts and some challenges each day. The children enjoyed the constructive work because it was timely and meaningful, but they made decisions about every aspect of their projects. The Olympic Games were left on to view during the day, and the group enjoyed watching for a particular sport, athlete, or country flag. The staff followed their lead by offering support, borrowing books from the library, purchasing supplies, and arranging the sharing night.

# Making the Outdoor Space Work for You

How do you build a program that is primarily outside? Some programs open in the summer and only use an outdoor area. Other programs are inside all year but have the luxury of moving the program outside in the summer. Working outside all summer may seem like a dream, but it requires a lot of planning in terms of space and materials. Children have more time during an extended day, and the standard playground activities are not enough to keep them interested and challenged.

Staff need to plan for the daily activities and have materials readily available, so they are not pulled away from the group to go inside and locate what they need. In previous chapters we learned about the typical learning areas: arts and crafts, music and movement, blocks and construction, dramatic play/theater, language and reading activities, math/reasoning, and science/nature activities (Harms, Jacobs, and White, 2014). While it may seem fairly straightforward to plan and organize these learning centers inside, it takes additional planning to provide similar activities for a summer camp or full-day program that is run outside.

First, think about the learning areas, the ages of children in your care, and the number of children in the group. How many choices do you need to have available each day? For large programs, you should have at least five to seven learning areas available. Smaller programs may opt to rotate through a few learning areas on a weekly basis, based on the interests of the children. For example, you won't need seven learning centers open for five children.

Next think about how you can set up these areas outside. Usually a picnic table can serve as a home base for one or two learning areas, and hopefully you have a few picnic tables to work with. They will serve as the focal point for the arts and crafts center, science/nature, or a manipulative area with board games. The book or quiet area can be situated on a blanket, with pillows nearby. Some staff might use a series of bins and carry them out every morning to set up, with one bin for each learning center. Other programs might prefer the use of a few carts that can be rolled out and used by the children. Either option is fine as long as it is working for the staff and the materials are rotated based on the interests of the children. Let's look at a few examples of how programs make good use of space for the learning-center activities in their new outdoor summer-camp spaces.

## Tiny Tune Camp

This program has a small group of about eight children every day, ranging in age from five to seven years old. They are assigned a picnic table under an awning behind a child-care facility. Most of them grew up in the program, or they have younger siblings in the other classrooms. Their teacher, Shamalia, complains that her biggest challenge is how the children are quickly growing tired of the child-care routine. Now that some of them have attended school, they long for "big kid" activities. In response, she has developed a schedule of activities that alternates between whole group and smaller groupings, with a variety of choices. She starts with the whole group at the table for a morning snack and discussion, then she lets them choose from a couple of activities. Throughout the rest of the day, she provides something quiet at the picnic table, while an alternative active game is going on in the play yard.

On this particular day, she reads a book after snack, then the children choose between arts and crafts or blocks and construction on the sidewalk. Later, they play a large-group game, then the children choose between a science/nature activity at the table or a language/reading activity on a blanket under a tree. Since she is the only staff member, Shamalia has to prepare everything in advance and has to keep everyone together for toileting and mealtime. She follows the schedule fairly closely, but she recognizes that the children have different interests, so they always have several choices. The key to her success is developing a curriculum that mirrors school activities, rather than the preschool games and puzzles that they find in the child-scare classrooms. Instead of picture books, she asks the local librarian for suggestions and borrows some chapter books. Instead of Candyland and matching games, she teaches them card games such as Flinch and Rummy.

## City Club

Cheryl is the program manager of a summer camp that is run by a community organization in the city. The program has about twenty children, and she is lucky to have three rooms set aside in the community center for their use during the day. During the school year, they spend most of the day in one large room set up with six tables, but in the summer they can also utilize the computer room and a small room adjacent to the main space. In addition, there is a small gym and a large green space outside. Her biggest planning issue is how to move children through those separate spaces in way that allows freedom while still ensuring the program is organized and safely supervised.

She decides to make full use of the three rooms by divvying up the learning centers into different rooms. In the computer room, she sets up language and reading activities on a bookshelf and a soft area for relaxing. In the main room, she sets up arts and crafts, blocks and construction, dramatic play/theater, math/reasoning, and science/nature activities. The small room has carpeting, so she decides to use that as the group meeting space, but it can double as the music and movement area. She adds some pillows there, as well, so children can listen to the radio and hang out in the space if they choose. She sets up a schedule for the day that uses the main room as a home base, with other rooms open during alternate times. The staff are stationed in all the open areas, so there is always at least one person in each room. As the children move from room to room, the staff ensure safety. They use the gym daily, and when it is open, they alternate between structured games and individual activities that appeal to both younger and older children. Physical activities are encouraged, but Cheryl does not require the children to participate. Her biggest challenge is safety in the outside green space. In the summer she likes to plan games outside, but there has been some violence in the nearby community recently, so they only go outside if safety is assured and the security guard at the community center is available to provide extra support.

## Big Kids' Club

This large program averages about thirty-five to forty children a day. Matt is in charge of this program, which is located in a church facility, and he works hard to develop activities that will keep all of the children engaged. Together with the three staff members, he has initiated learning centers, and a different staff member is assigned to lead some of the choice activities each day. Matt begins the day by leading a brief large-group meeting on a carpeted area, where he may read a book and talk about the topic of the week, introduce a game, or have some social-emotional learning activities. Then the children can select from among the learning centers. Since the program is so large, Matt's biggest challenge is transitioning smoothly from one activity to another so the children do not need to wait for new activities to begin.

On this particular day, one teacher is doing a cooking project, another is leading a creative art activity, and the third teacher is moving around the room to assist where needed. As the day progresses, Matt makes an announcement and offers to bring some children outside to play a game. Some children stay inside with staff; others choose to go outside to play. Eventually all the children move outside with the staff as the inside activities come to a close, and other activities are initiated outside. Since the group is so large, Matt's goal is to be sure they always have access to several different options. As one activity wraps up and children leave the area, staff clean the space and get something different started. The activities are fluid, so transitions are gradual and children do not need to wait for something new to begin.

# Field Trips

Field trips offer a nice alternative for programs that have the same children all summer while their parents work. A field trip offers a break from the daily routine and allows the children to visit local parks, museums, and activities during the warm summer months. However, it's important to remember that the cost of school-age care is already very steep for many families, so adding on the cost of special trips may present an unnecessary burden. Programs should weigh their options very carefully and include families in the planning process as they consider potential field trips. Look for cultural activities that support and enhance learning and the program goals, rather than something that's just entertaining. While laser tag, go-carts, and arcade games might be really fun, they are expensive and don't offer much in terms of learning. Are they worth the expense?

Taking children swimming at a local park or community pool is a common summer activity, but anything water related can be dangerous, and there are many aspects of safety to consider. There is no way for staff to assess children's swimming skills in advance, and children have varied experience in the water. Some may have had years of lessons, some may have had only limited experience in an above-ground pool, while some may have never been in a pool deeper that two feet. When asked, children are likely to overestimate their swimming ability. Unless staff are trained as lifeguards and have experience, the program should rely on professionals and should consider locations where certified lifeguard supervision and a staff person certified in cardio-pulmonary resuscitation and first aid is included. Water parks offer limited supervision, and it can be very hard to keep track of groups of children, so they are not recommended for school-age programs, as the liability is too great. Many states have regulations regarding taking children to swimming pools, lakes, and other bodies of water, and these regulations should be adhered to. When swimming is included as part of the program activities, the program should get signed statements of permission from the parents.

Many communities offer free lunchtime concerts and events or discounted tickets. Cultural programs, such as art museums, zoos, historical villages, national parks, and theaters, tend to have special discounted programs during the summer. Many art museums across the country open their doors free of charge on Free Art Friday, the first Friday of every month. In rural communities, there may be a local llama or alpaca farm that would interest the children or perhaps a blueberry farm where they could pick blueberries to take back to the program to make treats. Program families may have new ideas or connections to people who can offer interesting field trips. Let them provide some guidance.

Venues change from year to year, so a park that has been a great field-trip location one summer might undergo some problems or be under construction. Someone should preview the venue (or browse social-media feedback) whenever possible to be sure it's still a good location, and the staff should come up with alternatives and a backup plan in case it is not. As an example, children in one community regularly visited an aquarium in a nearby city during the summer, followed by an afternoon in the park next door. One summer they arrived to discover that many of the exhibits were under construction, so the aquarium visit ended quickly. The playground next door was partially roped off, with another summer-camp program already using the open portion. The program staff were not prepared with any other options, and they were not familiar with the area, so the children ate lunch on the bus and came back early. The entire day was a bust.

Field trips can be fun, as long as they have been carefully planned and staff have set guidelines for children. The following are just a few of the aspects staff should consider:

- **Food:** Will lunch and snacks be provided, or will families pack a lunch?
- **Sunscreen:** Will children apply sunscreen in advance at home? If so, what are the plans for reapplication (as it should be reapplied every two hours or according to the package instructions)?
- **Money:** Will children have an opportunity to purchase souvenirs or ice cream at the location? How will staff respond if someone shows up with twenty dollars to spend while someone else has nothing?
- **Supervision:** Will parents be allowed to volunteer? If so, how will staff ensure safety? Will the group travel together or break up into smaller groups?
- **Staff:** All field trips that include an activity where emergency medical care may not be readily available, such as hiking or a trip to the farmer's market, should bring along a staff member who possesses a current first-aid certificate and CPR certification.
- **Communication:** How will parents who are not attending communicate with the program while they are on the field trip? How will program staff communicate with parents? How will staff communicate with each other during the field trip?
- **Weather:** What happens if inclement weather is expected? When will staff make the decision to go ahead with plans or cancel? Is there a rain date or backup plan?
- **Transportation:** Transportation is frequently the most expensive aspect of a field trip. While small programs may be tempted to have staff or parents volunteer to drive, research liability carefully, and follow any licensing requirements. Local trips within walking distance, the use of public transportation, or renting buses reduces liability.

In many cases it's more cost effective to bring someone or something into the program rather than travel somewhere. In some communities, the local library has a traveling van that can visit with a program and offer a lending library. In other communities, the zoo or nature center has programs that bring animals for a visit. Local theater groups, magicians, or puppeteers may have something that is age appropriate for an afternoon visit. Work with your local networks to see what options are available, then figure out how they might fit into the summer curriculum.

In one community, the recreation department organized an annual theater camp in the park, where the children put together a musical or play over a two-week period. On the last day, they performed a free afternoon outdoor performance. Another program was able to walk their group of children over to the park to see the performance. It became a summer tradition—one program performing, another program watching. What can you find in your community?

# Competitive and Cooperative Games

Competitive games are typically sports activities where teams play against each other and keep score to determine who will win and who will lose. School-age children enjoy structured games with rules because they know exactly what is expected and can ensure fairness. Typically, they learn the rules, play the game, and then adapt the rules as they play together. While competition is a healthy side effect of team sports, it is frequently discouraged in school-age programs unless carefully supported by staff. Good sportsmanship is a learned behavior that takes a lot of modeling, encouragement, and experience. Sportsmanship comes from team-building exercises where children learn to appreciate playing together on teams with varied skill levels.

When dividing up teams for structured games, such as kickball or soccer, it's important for staff to divide the teams with an appropriate balance of boys and girls and a variety of skill levels. Asking the children to select their own teams is discouraged, as the strongest players are always selected first, while other children are singled out game after game. Children with special needs, limited physical abilities, or social issues always lose in those situations. Instead, staff should divide up the teams discreetly in advance, so the group can transition smoothly into the planned activity.

Be sure to provide a balance of cooperative games. Cooperative games allow everyone to succeed in different ways and help build a sense of community, as children are encouraged to help each other rather than beat each other in a competition. It's a great way to build a positive and supportive program community. Many examples are available online, but here are a few of our favorite cooperative games.

## The Human Knot

This game is versatile in that multiple group sizes can play. Form groups of about ten children each. Have each group stand in a circle, facing inward, standing shoulder to shoulder. First, instruct everyone to lift their left hand and reach across to take the hand of someone standing across the circle. Next, have everyone lift their right hand and reach across to take the hand of another person standing across the circle.

To play, the group must communicate and figure out how to untangle the knot and re-form the circle without ever letting go of any hands. The game typically takes ten to fifteen minutes to complete, depending on the age of the children. When you are done with the Human Knot activity, you can ask some debriefing questions if you wish, such as: "How well did your group work together?" "What strategies did your group adopt?" "How did it feel to solve the game?"

# Electric Fence

Tie a long rope (at least 20 feet) between two trees at least 2 feet off the ground (even higher for children who are older or more skilled). The goal of this game is to encourage the team to communicate and work together to help each other over the rope. Time them all as one team, so they can work for a quicker time on another day or larger programs can keep track as other teams attempt the same challenge.

To play, challenge a team of children to get all of their members over the "electric fence" without touching it. If someone does touch the fence, the entire team needs to start over. At first, they typically think the task will be easy, as a few of the taller children jump over the rope, but fairly quickly they realize they need to talk through potential options to be sure everyone gets over safely.

# Hula Hoop Relay

Relays can be fun, but two teams are racing against each other, and the teams are watching as players run back and forth across a field. Relays can be stressful for children who are slower than others because everyone is watching as they struggle. Hula Hoop relays provide a great opportunity to rush, but no one is put on the spot. To play, you'll need a hoop or two, then line the children up. As they hold hands in a long connected line, each child works to pass the hoop across his arms and over his head, then on to the next child, until they move the hoop down the line. For beginners, it may be helpful for one child to maneuver the hoop for the children as it moves down the line.

# Pinwheel

Gather a group of about ten children in a circle holding hands. Select one person to let go of the hand of one of his neighbors; that person becomes the leader. Ask the leader to walk around the inside of the circle, still holding the hand of the person next to her, curling the group in, until the group forms a tight circle. Then the children can either hug and cheer or the leader can reverse directions so the group spins out in reverse.

# Conclusion

While it is typical for programs to provide some activities during the short program hours during the school year, it's often a challenge for practitioners to redevelop a program as they switch from a partial-day program to a full-day program. In this chapter we shared ideas for developing a summer program that offers a lot of flexibility while challenging children with a rigorous curriculum during the summer months. For more help developing a summer-camp program, visit the You for Youth website (https://y4y.ed.gov/summerlearning).

In 2016, the US Department of Education's 21st Century Community Learning Centers (21st CCLC) program launched the Summer Learning Initiative. On the site (https://www2.ed.gov/programs/21stcclc/index.html) you'll find additional resources about the planning process. You'll also find tools and insights from 21st CCLC grantees who received training and coaching through the Summer Learning Initiative to help them plan, design, implement, and assess high-quality summer learning programs. How do programs in your community compare?

 SOLUTIONS

## Maria Needs Help Moving the Program Outside

In our opening vignette, Maria was concerned about moving her program outside for the summer. Every program has a unique space, so Maria decided that the first step would be to go to the new space and try to envision how she could make the environment work for her. She discovered that the back door was actually close to the storage area where she kept her supplies, and the bathroom was just inside the doorway. She realized that moving her program outdoors wouldn't be as hard as she thought. There was one picnic table under the awning and a few more scattered around the playground area, so she got permission to move two of them closer to the awning, with another one close by on the blacktop area.

Next, she began to develop the daily schedule. In her climate, the morning can start out cool and the grass can be dewy, so she decided to start the day with a group time, followed by learning-center activities in the blacktop area, and planned playground time later in the morning. Most of the children currently enrolled were about five to seven years old, and she expected many of them to remain through the summer. She started brainstorming themes that she knew would interest them and asked for their feedback. Now she needs to consider perishable materials for her arts and crafts and other activities and how this and other materials would factor into her budget or operating expense. In addition, after looking at enrollment, Maria would need to determine how much additional staff she may need and during what hours of the day. She should look to community resources that may come to her camp program for enrichment activities. Lastly, Maria should create a parent-and-child survey to get feedback at the end of the summer program that would guide her for next summer.

## Tiandra Is Getting Hot Inside and Needs Some Options

As the weather warms up outside, Tiandra many need to come up with some temporary alternatives. First, she needs to review the building regulations in her state. There may be guidelines for an appropriate temperature both indoors and outdoors. When days become too hot outside, children need an alternative place to go inside to cool off. Similarly, as the temperature inside the building climbs to 78, 80, then 82 degrees Fahrenheit, the conditions can become unsafe for children. If that's the case, Tiandra may need to work with the site owner (in this case, the church board) to add some air-conditioning window units immediately or find an alternate space within the building and arrange for permanent air conditioning as a long-term plan.

One program received permission to move their afternoon activities into the air-conditioned narthex of the church to watch some movies during the warmest days one August. Another program took their children on informal field trips to the library across the street for some time to cool off. Ultimately the decision depends on the temperature both indoors and outdoors.

In terms of programming, water bottles should always be available with plenty of ice, and many simple recipes will help keep the children cool, such as chilled watermelon, snow cones, ice cream, frozen grapes, and fruit smoothies. Tiandra can reserve active games for early morning or late afternoon or find shady alternatives, such as yoga under a tree, rather than kickball out in the hot sun.

In cases where it's just uncomfortable but not dangerous, changing up the routine with more water activities could be a fun change of pace. As discussed previously, pools—even those small inflatable ones available at drug stores in the summer—are typically not allowed, per regulations. However, sprinklers, water games, squirt bottles, or water-balloon tosses can offer a fun distraction. There are many sample ideas for activities available online.

# THINK. ACT. REFLECT.

## Think.

During the school year, parents typically have limited options for their children because they need a school-age program that is convenient and close to their work, home, or school district. During the summer, there are many different options for summer camp, and parents frequently have more flexibility as their options increase and work schedules shift. Think about your experiences during the summer as a school-ager. Where did you spend your time? What did you like to do?

## Act.

Look online for summer-camp programs in your community. Compile a resource list of all the programs you can locate. Be sure to look for camps such as 4-H, YMCA, Scouts, as well as weekly camps such as those at a zoo, botanical garden, or art studio. How many are there? How do they differ? What are the pros and cons of each program for families?

## Reflect.

If your school-age program runs a summer camp, reflect on how your program compares. How is your program similar to or different from other programs in the community? If your school-age program is closed during the summer, what options do the families use? Do their children attend some of the programs you located, or do they find in-home care such as a family member or babysitter? How do these varied programs meet the needs of working families?

# Conclusion

Throughout this book, we have laid the foundation of quality programs for children and youth. In the first section, we defined high-quality school-age care, including the role of the administrators. We explored how to develop safe, high-quality school-age programming and curriculum based on the interests, skills, and needs of the individual children. In the second section, we reviewed the developmental characteristics of children, including physical development, social and emotional learning, and cognitive development, and how these characteristics affect the program. The final section highlighted the needs of a comprehensive program by including important topics such as positive guidance, working with families, and the extension of summer camp. In each chapter we offered some challenges with a number of possible solutions, with the understanding that school-age programs by nature are all very different.

As you continue to develop your program, link into professional networks and find local support from people you trust. We all have challenges, and the people who know you and your program the best are likely to offer the best solutions.

Now that you have the knowledge and tools to set up a high-quality program for school-age children, it's time to get to work!

# Appendix A: Online Resources

- **Child and Youth Care Certification Board (CYCCB):** The CYCCB provides an assessment process and certification to child- and youth-care practitioners who demonstrate their commitment to high standards of care and commitment to ongoing competence development. Periodic informational webinars are available. https://www.cyccb.org/
- **Council on Accreditation:** The COA accredits a full continuum of social and human services, including child, youth, and family services. They provide training and resources to support programs as they strive for continuous improvement. https://coanet.org/
- **ExtendEd Notes:** They develop and provide information and resources concerning children and youth in out-of-school settings before and after school and during vacations. https://www.extendednotes.com/
- **Generation Genius:** Next Generation Science has videos and lessons made in partnership with the National Science Teaching Association that engage, educate, and inspire children. https://www.generationgenius.com/
- **National Association for the Education of Young Children:** NAEYC is a professional membership organization that works to promote high-quality early learning for all young children, from birth through age eight. They work to connect early childhood practice, policy, and research. Visit their website for a wide variety of topics, including teaching young children, professional development, and position statements. https://www.naeyc.org/
- **National AfterSchool Association (NAA):** NAA is the membership association for professionals who work with children and youth in diverse school- and community-based settings to provide a wide variety of extended-learning opportunities and care during out-of-school hours. https://naaweb.org/
- **National Institute on Out-of-School Time (NIOST):** NIOST supports the healthy development of children, families, and communities and advances the out-of-school-time field through research, training, advocacy, and tools. They help before-school, after-school, expanded-learning, and summer programs improve what they do. https://www.niost.org/
- **PBS Learning Media:** Free, standards-aligned videos, interactives, lesson plans, and more for educators. https://pbslearningmedia.org/
- **Science Kids:** Science Kids offers science experiments, cool facts, online games, free activities, ideas, lesson plans, photos, quizzes, videos, and science-fair projects. http://www.sciencekids.co.nz/
- **Steve Spangler Science:** Offers a wide variety of science experiments, including step-by-step instructions and videos. This is a great place to find challenging science-fair ideas. https://www.stevespanglerscience.com/
- **Ultimate Camp Resource:** Offers instructions on a wide variety of games for school-age children, including cooperative games for indoors and outdoors. https://www.ultimatecampresource.com/
- **You for Youth (Y4Y):** The Summer Learning Initiative offers research, tools, and planners to help leaders build knowledge, skills, and the capacity to effectively lead their program development. https://y4y.ed.gov/summerlearning

# Appendix B: Recommended Children's Books by Age

## Five to Seven Years Old

Adler, David A. 1993. *Cam Jansen and the Chocolate Fudge Mystery*. New York: Penguin.

Adler, David A. 1999. *Young Cam Jansen and the Lost Tooth*. New York: Penguin.

Arnold, Tedd. 2003. *Parts and More Parts*. New York: Puffin.

Cannon, Janell. 1993. *Stellaluna*. New York: Houghton Mifflin.

Cleary, Beverly. 2010. *Beezus and Ramona*. New York: HarperCollins.

DePrince, Michela, and Elaine DePrince. 2014. *Ballerina Dreams*. New York: Penguin.

English, Karen. 2009. *Nikki and Deja: Book One*. New York: Houghton Mifflin Harcourt.

Gannett, Ruth Stiles. 2014. *My Father's Dragon*. Mineola, NY: Dover.

Kline, Suzy. 1997. *Horrible Harry in Room 2B*. New York: Puffin.

Lobel, Arnold. 1979. *Frog and Toad Together*. New York: HarperCollins.

Murphy, Jill. 2018. *First Prize for the Worst Witch*. New York: Puffin.

Park, Barbara. 1992. *Junie B. Jones and the Stupid Smelly Bus*. New York: Random House.

The Amelia Bedelia series by Peggy Parrish

Rylant, Cynthia. 1996. *Henry and Mudge: The First Book*. New York: Simon and Schuster.

Ueegacki, Chieri. 2014. *Hana Hashimoto, Sixth Violin*. Toronto: Kids Can Press.

Willems, Mo. 2014. *Waiting is Not Easy!* New York: HarperCollins.


## Eight to Ten Years Old

Dahl, Roald. 2018. *Roald Dahl's Whoppsy-Whiffling Joke Book*. New York: Puffin.

DiCamillo, Kate. 2015. *The Tale of Despereaux*. Boston, MA: Candlewick.

Gaiman, Neil. 2008. *The Graveyard Book*. London, UK: Bloomsbury.

Gandhi, Arun, and Bethany Hegedus. 2014. *Grandfather Gandhi*. New York: Atheneum Books for Young Readers.

Jamieson, Victoria. 2015. *Roller Girl*. New York: Random House.

The Diary of a Wimpy Kid series by Jeff Kinney

Lo, Ginnie. 2012. *Auntie Yang's Great Soybean Picnic*. New York: Lee and Low.

The Magic Treehouse series by Mary Pope Osborne

The Dog Man series by Dav Pilkey

Ringgold, Faith. 1991. *Tar Beach*. New York: Random House.

Smith, Cynthia Leitich. 2002. *Indian Shoes*. New York: Harper Collins.

Smith, Jim. 2013. *I Am So Over Being a Loser*. London, UK: Egmont.

Telgemeier, Raina. 2010. *Smile*. New York: Graphix Scholastic.

White, E. B. 1952/1980. *Charlotte's Web*. New York: Harper Trophy.

Joke and riddle books

## Ten to Twelve Years Old

Alexander, Kwame. 2014. *Crossover*. New York: Houghton Mifflin Harcourt.

Baron, Chris. 2019. *All of Me*. New York: Macmillan.

Farmer, Nancy. 2004. *House of Scorpion*. New York: Atheneum Books for Young Readers.

Grimes, Nikki. 2011. *Planet Middle School*. NY: Scholastic.

Hiranandani, Veera. 2018. *The Night Diary*. New York: Dial Books for Young Readers.

Lowry, Lois. 1993. *The Giver*. New York: Houghton Mifflin Harcourt.

Paulsen, Gary. 1986. *Hatchet*. New York: Macmillan.

Rhodes, Jewell Parker. 2010. *Ninth Ward*. New York: Little Brown.

The Percy Jackson and the Olympians series by Rick Riordan

Sumner, Jamie. 2019. *Roll With It*. New York: Atheneum Books for Young Readers.

The Goosebumps series by R.L. Stein

Stroud, Jonathan. 2013. *The Screaming Staircase*. New York: Little, Brown.

Tingle, Tim. 2013. *How I Became A Ghost: A Choctaw Trail of Tears Story*. Oklahoma City, OK: Roadrunner.

Yang, Kelly. 2018. *Front Desk*. New York: Arthur A. Levine.

Zusak, Markus. 2007. *The Book Thief*. New York: Alfred A. Knopf.

## Twelve to Fourteen Years Old

Cisneros, Sandra. 1984. *The House on Mango Street*. New York: Penguin Random House.

Danforth, Emily. 2012. *The Miseducation of Cameron Post*. New York: Balzer + Bray.

Defoe, Daniel. 1719. *Robinson Crusoe*. [various publishers]

Forbes, Esther. 1943. *Johnny Tremain*. New York: Houghton Mifflin.

Harwell, Andrew. 2015. *The Spider Ring*. New York: Scholastic.

The Chronicles of Narnia series by C. S. Lewis

Lowry, Lois. 1989. *Number the Stars*. New York: Houghton Mifflin Harcourt.

Marino, Andy. 2011. *Unison Spark*. Henry Holt and Co.

Nielsen, Jennifer A. 2012. *The False Prince*. New York: Scholastic.

Ramée, Lisa Moore. 2019. *A Good Kind of Trouble*. New York: Balzer + Bray.

The Harry Potter series by J. K. Rowling

Sachar, Louis. 2015. *Fuzzy Mud*. New York: Delacorte.

Spinelli, Jerry. 2002. *Stargirl*. New York: Scholastic.

Stevenson, Robert Louis. 1883. *Treasure Island*. London: Cassell & Co.

Sugiura, Misa. 2017. *It's Not Like It's A Secret*. New York: Harperteen.

The Lord of the Rings series by J. R. R. Tolkien

Wyss, Johann David. 1812. *The Swiss Family Robinson, or Adventures on a Desert Island*. [various publishers]

Magazines: *Shine Brightly*, *Trains*, and *New York Times Upfront*.

# References and Recommended Reading

Allen, K. Eileen, and Lynn R. Marotz. 2000. *By the Ages: Behavior and Development of Children Pre-Birth through Eight.* Albany, NY: Delmar Thomson Learning.

American Academy of Child and Adolescent Psychiatry. 2017. "Anxiety and Children." Facts for Families. https://www.aacap.org/AACAP/Families_and_Youth/Facts_for_Families/FFF-Guide/The-Anxious-Child-047.aspx

American Academy of Child and Adolescent Psychiatry. 2017. "Home Alone Children." Facts for Families. https://www.aacap.org/App_Themes/AACAP/docs/facts_for_families/46_home_alone_children.pdf

American Academy of Pediatrics. 2019. "Which Kids Are at Highest Risk for Suicide?" HealthyChildren.org. https://www.healthychildren.org/English/health-issues/conditions/emotional-problems/Pages/Which-Kids-are-at-Highest-Risk-for-Suicide.aspx

American Academy of Pediatrics, American Public Health Association, and National Resource Center for Health and Safety in Child Care and Early Education. 2019. *Caring for Our Children: National Health and Safety Performance Standards Guidelines for Early Care and Education Programs.* 4th edition. Itasca, IL: American Academy of Pediatrics. https://nrckids.org/CFOC

American Institutes for Research. 2008. "Afterschool Programs Make a Difference: Findings from the Harvard Family Research Project." SEDL Letter XX(2): *Afterschool, Family, and Community.* http://www.sedl.org/pubs/sedl-letter/v20n02/afterschool_findings.html

American Museum of Natural History. 2019. OLogy. https://www.amnh.org/explore/ology

Asthma and Allergy Foundation of America. 2019. Asthma Facts and Figures. https://www.aafa.org/asthma-facts

Beaty, Janice J. 2008. *Skills for Preschool Teachers.* 8th edition. Upper Saddle River, NJ: Pearson/Merrill/Prentice Hall.

Borba, Michele. 2018. *End Peer Cruelty, Build Empathy: The Proven 6Rs of Bullying Prevention That Create Inclusive, Safe, and Caring Schools.* Minneapolis, MN: Free Spirit.

Building Quality in Afterschool. 2017. *50 State Afterschool Network: Scan of Quality Systems.* Washington, DC: American Institutes for Research. https://www.air.org/sites/default/files/SAN%20Scan%20of%20Quality_OCTOBER%202017%20Update.pdf

Bumgarner, Marlene Anne. 2017. *Working with School-Age Children.* Boston, MA: Pearson.

Centers for Disease Control and Prevention. n.d. Injury Prevention and Control. National Center for Injury Prevention and Control. https://www.cdc.gov/injury/index.html

Centers for Disease Control and Prevention. n.d. "Physical Activity Guidelines for School-Aged Children and Adolescents." CDC Healthy Schools. https://www.cdc.gov/healthyschools/physicalactivity/guidelines.htm

Centers for Disease Control and Prevention. 2014. *The Relationship Between Bullying and Suicide: What We Know and What It Means for Schools.* Chamblee, GA: National Center for Injury Prevention and Control, Division of Violence Prevention. https://www.cdc.gov/violenceprevention/pdf/bullying-suicide-translation-final-a.pdf

Centers for Disease Control and Prevention. 2016. "Coughing and Sneezing." Water, Sanitation, and Environmentally Related Hygiene. https://www.cdc.gov/healthywater/hygiene/etiquette/coughing_sneezing.html

Centers for Disease Control and Prevention. 2018. Obesity. CDC Healthy Schools. https://www.cdc.gov/healthyschools/obesity/facts.htm

Childcare Extension. 2019. "Food Safety Guidelines for Child Care Programs." Childcare Extension. https://childcare.extension.org/food-safety-guidelines-for-child-care-programs/

Child Trends Databank. 2006. "After-School Activities." https://www.childtrends.org/wp-content/uploads/2016/03/indicator_1459167657.538.html

Child Welfare Information Gateway. 2019. *Mandatory Reporters of Child Abuse and Neglect.* Washington, DC: US Department of Health and Human Services, Children's Bureau. https://www.childwelfare.gov/pubPDFs/manda.pdf

Collaborative for Academic, Social, and Emotional Learning. 2019. "What Is SEL?" CASEL. https://casel.org/what-is-sel

Council on Accreditation. 2018. "What Is Accreditation?" Council on Accreditation. https://coanet.org/accreditation/

Cowie, Helen. 2000. "Bystanding or Standing By: Gender Issues in Coping with Bullying in English Schools." *Aggressive Behavior* 26(1): 85–97.

Demircan, H. Özlen, and Ayhan Demir. 2014. "Children's Sense of Loneliness and Social Dissatisfaction, After-School Care." *Psychological Reports* 114(1): 169–175.

Donald, Mark. 1985. "Latchkey Kids." *D Magazine.* https://www.dmagazine.com/publications/d-magazine/1985/july/latchkey-kids/

Dooley, Julian J., Jacek Pyzalski, and Donna Cross. 2009. "Cyberbullying versus Face-to-Face Bullying: A Theoretical and Conceptual Review." *Zeitschrift für Psychologie/Journal of Psychology* 217(4): 182–188.

Fortson, Beverly L., et al. 2016. *Preventing Child Abuse and Neglect: A Technical Package for Policy, Norm, and Programmatic Activities.* Atlanta, GA: Division of Violence Prevention, Centers for Disease Control. https://www.cdc.gov/violenceprevention/pdf/can-prevention-technical-package.pdf

Galuski, Tracy, and Arlene Rider. 2017. "It's All About the Learning." *Exchange* 39(238): 16–22.

Gonzalez-Mena, Janet. 2008. *Diversity in Early Care and Education: Honoring Differences.* 5th Ed. Washington, DC: NAEYC.

Gosso, Yumi, and Ana Maria Almeida Carvalho. 2013. "Play and Cultural Context." Encyclopedia on Early Childhood Development. http://www.child-encyclopedia.com/sites/default/files/textes-experts/en/774/play-and-cultural-context.pdf

Guerra, Nancy, Kirk R. Williams, and Shelly Sadek. 2011. "Understanding Bullying and Victimization during Childhood and Adolescence: A Mixed Methods Study." *Child Development* 82(1): 295–310.

Harms, Thelma, Ellen V. Jacobs, and Donna R. White. 1995. *School-Age Care Environment Rating Scale.* New York, NY: Teachers College Press.

Harms, Thelma, Ellen V. Jacobs, and Donna R. White. 2014. *School-Age Care Environment Rating Scale.* Updated ed. New York, NY: Teachers College Press.

Institute of Medicine. 2013. *Educating the Student Body: Taking Physical Activity and Physical Education to School.* Washington, DC: National Academies Press.

Jason Foundation, The. 2019. "Youth Suicide Warning Signs." Jason Foundation. http://jasonfoundation.com/youth-suicide/warning-signs

Kail, Robert V. 2014. *Children and Their Development.* 7th ed. Upper Saddle River, NJ: Pearson/Prentice Hall.

Koralek, Derry, and Debra Foulks. 1995. *Caring for Children in School-Age Programs: Trainer's Guide.* Washington, DC: Teaching Strategies.

Li, Qing. 2006. "Cyberbullying in Schools: A Research of Gender Differences." *School Psychology International* 27(2): 157–170.

Mangione, Peter L., ed. 2013. *Infant/Toddler Caregiving: A Guide to Culturally Sensitive Care.* 2nd edition. Sacramento, CA: California Department of Education.

McCormick Center for Early Childhood Leadership. 2019. National Director Credential. McCormick Center for Early Childhood Leadership. https://mccormickcenter.nl.edu/services/national-director-credential

McDevitt, Teresa, and Jeanne Ormrod. 2020. *Child Development and Education.* 7th ed. Upper Saddle River, NJ: Pearson Merrill Prentice Hall.

Megan Meier Foundation. 2019. "Bullying, Cyberbullying, and Suicide Statistics." Edutopia. https://meganmeierfoundation.org/statistics

Miller, Andrew. 2011. "Seven Ideas for Revitalizing Multicultural Education." Edutopia. https://www.edutopia.org/blog/multicultural-education-strategy-tips-andrew-miller

Nansel, Tonja R., et al. 2001. "Bullying Behaviors among U.S. Youth: Prevalence and Association with Psychosocial Adjustment." *Journal of the American Medical Association* 285(16): 2094–2100.

National AfterSchool Association. 2009. *National AfterSchool Association Code of Ethics.* NAA. http://naaweb.org/images/NAA-Code-of-Ethics-for-AferSchool-Professionals.pdf

National Center for Children in Poverty. 2019. "Child Poverty." National Center for Children in Poverty. http://nccp.org/topics/childpoverty.html

National Resource Center for Health and Safety in Child Care and Early Education. 2020. "Handwashing Procedure." Caring for Our Children Online Database. https://nrckids.org/CFOC/Database/3.2.2.2

New York State Association for the Education of Young Children. 2018. "Children's Program Administrator Credential." New York State Association for the Education of Young Children. http://nysaeyc.org/childrens-program-administrator-credential

New York State Department of Health. 2002. *New York State Confidentiality Law and HIV: Public Health Law, Article 27-F.* https://www.health.ny.gov/publications/9192.pdf

New York State Early Childhood Advisory Council. 2012. *Core Body of Knowledge: New York State's Core Competencies for Early Childhood Educators.* 3rd ed. Brooklyn, NY: NYC Early Childhood Professional Development Institute.

New York State Network for Youth Success. 2017. "Quality Self-Assessment (QSA) Tool." New York State Network for Youth Success. http://networkforyouthsuccess.org/qsa

New York State Network for Youth Success. 2018. "Afterschool Program Accreditation." New York State Network for Youth Success. http://networkforyouthsuccess.org/accreditation/

New York State Network for Youth Success. 2018. *New York State School-Age Care Credential Manual.* http://networkforyouthsuccess.org/wp-content/uploads/2018/02/2017–18-SAC-Manual-1.pdf

New York State Office of Children and Family Services. 2017. "Child Care Regulations and Policies." New York State Office of Children and Family Services, Division of Child Care Services. https://ocfs.ny.gov/main/childcare/daycare_regulations.asp

Popova, Maria. 2013. "Happy Birthday, Brain Pickings: 7 Things I Learned in 7 Years of Reading, Writing, and Living." Brain Pickings. https://www.brainpickings.org/2013/10/23/7-lessons-from-7-years/

Rafferty, Jason. 2018. "Gender Identity Development in Children." HealthyChildren.org. https://www.healthychildren.org/English/ages-stages/gradeschool/Pages/Gender-Identity-and-Gender-Confusion-In-Children.aspx

Rafferty, Jason, et al. 2018. "Ensuring Comprehensive Care and Support for Transgender and Gender-Diverse Children and Adolescents." *Pediatrics* 142(4). https://pediatrics.aappublications.org/content/142/4/e20182162

Scholastic. 2019. "Count 'Em Up: 5 Skill-Building Math Activities." Scholastic. https://www.scholastic.com/parents/kids-activities-and-printables/printables/math-worksheets/count-em-5-skill-building-math-activities.html

Science Kids. 2018. "Science Experiments for Kids." Science Kids. http://www.sciencekids.co.nz/experiments.html

Siegel, Jane, et al. 2007. *2007 Guideline for Isolation Precautions: Preventing Transmission of Infectious Agents in Healthcare Settings*. Atlanta, GA: Centers for Disease Control and Prevention.

Simoncini, Kym, Jennifer Cartmel, and Amy Young. 2015. "Children's Voices in Australian School Age Care: What Do They Think about Afterschool Care?" *International Journal for Research on Extended Education* 3(1): 114–131.

Steve Spangler Science. 2019. Experiment Library. Steve Spangler Science. https://www.stevespanglerscience.com/lab/experiments

Sutherland, Charmain. 2005. *No Gym? No Problem! Physical Activities for Tight Spaces.*

Champaign, IL: Human Kinetics.

Talan, Terri. N., and Bloom, Paula Jorde. 2011. *Program Administration Scale: Measuring Early Childhood Leadership and Management*. 2nd ed. New York, NY: Teachers College Press.

US Census Bureau. 2020. "America's Families and Living Arrangements." https://www.census.gov/topics/families.html

US Department of Agriculture. n.d. "Child Meal Pattern." https://fns-prod.azureedge.net/sites/default/files/cacfp/CACFP_childmealpattern.pdf

US Department of Agriculture. 2019. "Child and Adult Care Food Program." https://www.fns.usda.gov/cacfp/child-and-adult-care-food-program

US Department of Education. 1999. "Parent Involvement in After-School Programs." https://www2.ed.gov/pubs/After_School_Programs/Parent_Programs.html

US Department of Health and Human Services, Administration for Children and Families, Administration on Children, Youth and Families, Children's Bureau. 2019. *Mandatory Reporters of Child Abuse and Neglect.* Child Welfare Information Gateway. https://www.childwelfare.gov/pubPDFs/manda.pdf

US Department of Health and Human Services and US Department of Agriculture. 2015. *2015–2020 Dietary Guidelines for Americans*. 8th edition. Washington, DC: USDA. https://health.gov/sites/default/files/2019-09/2015-2020_Dietary_Guidelines.pdf

US National Library of Medicine. 2017. "Stress in Childhood." MedlinePlus.gov. https://medlineplus.gov/ency/article/002059.htm

Warner, Gina, and Roger Neugebauer. 2016. "Five Things You Need to Know About Afterschool Care in the United States." *Exchange* 5(231): 66–68.

Woolfolk, Anita. 2010. *Educational Psychology: Modular Active Learning Edition*. 11th ed. Upper Saddle River, NJ: Pearson Prentice Hall.

Woolfolk, Anita. 2019. *Educational Psychology: Active Learning Edition*. 14th ed. Boston, MA: Pearson.

Yogman, Michael, et al. 2018. "The Power of Play: A Pediatric Role in Enhancing Development in Young Children." *Pediatrics* 142(3). https://pediatrics.aappublications.org/content/pediatrics/142/3/e20182058.full.pdf

# Index

## A

## B

before-school care, 1, 6, 38

behavior skills, 131, 159–169, 170–177

belonging and resilience, 127

Bloom's Taxonomy, 83–85

body image

    children (8-10 years old) and, 99

    children (10-12 years old) and, 100

    stress and, 128

books

    acceptance and tolerance, strategies for, 182

    for children (5-7 years old), 145–146, 211

    for children (8-10 years old), 146, 211–212

    for children (10-12 years old), 147, 212–213

    for children (12-14 years old), 148, 213

    language development and communication and, 141

boys

    aggression and bullying and, 130–131

    cognitive, language, and creative development and, 149

    physical development of, 99, 100

    sexual development, gender identification, and attraction and, 101, 102

budgets, 27–28

buildings. *See also* program space

    needs assessments and, 28

    negotiating for space and, 168–169

    safety and, 38

bullying

    child suicide and, 132–133

    cyberbullying, 130, 133

    prevention and intervention, 130–132

    stress and, 128

## C

calm-down bottles, 123

cell phones, 130, 160

Centers for Disease Control and Prevention (CDC), 38, 98, 106, 132

challenging behaviors

    active supervision and, 165

    alerting parents to, 172

    choices, allowing children's, 167

    conflict-resolution skills and, 168

    eye contact and, 166

    feelings and, 165

    meetings and, 167–168

    peer mediation and, 168–169

    planned ignoring and, 166

    positive reinforcements and, 167

    redirection and, 167

    responding thoughtfully and, 166

    signaling and nonverbal cues and, 166–167

check-in/check-out policies, 42–43

child-friendly spaces

    challenges of, 55, 57, 67

    creating special spaces, 66–68

    daily schedules and, 56

    diversity and, 69–72

    environment, examining the, 57–58

    program space, defining, 59–66

    solutions for, 72–74

    space, negotiating for, 68–69